Children of Bethnal Green

Doris with big sister Eva.

Children of
BETHNAL GREEN

DORIS M. BAILEY

SUTTON PUBLISHING

Part of this text was first published in 1981 under the title *Children of the Green* by Stepney Books Publications

This revised and expanded edition
first published in 2005 by
Sutton Publishing Limited · Phoenix Mill
Thrupp · Stroud · Gloucestershire · GL5 2BU

Copyright © Doris M. Bailey, 1981, 2005

All rights reserved. No part of this publication may be reproduced, stored in a retrieval system, or transmitted, in any form, or by any means, electronic, mechanical, photocopying, recording or otherwise, without the prior permission of the publisher and copyright holder.

Doris M. Bailey has asserted the moral right to be identified as the author of this work.

British Library cataloguing in Publication Data
A catalogue record for this book is available from the British Library

ISBN 0-7509-3815-3

The book is dedicated to my dear E.B.

Life's Journey

Together the road we've travelled,
   Holding my hand, you've led
I stand in the valley of shadows
   Because you have gone ahead.

We met at the foot of life's mountain
   Young then, with courage we went
And all the path glowed then with sunlight
   And stumbling blocks seemed heaven sent.

Hand in hand then we travelled together
   Through sunshine, or vale of despair
And nothing could daunt us, or harm us
   As each knew the other was there.

Sometimes we would pause in the valley,
   Or happily tread on life's way
And each night we'd rest with the sure hope –
   Tomorrow, a new climbing day.

And then, we grew older and slower
   But still journeyed on, hand in hand
Looking back, life was greyer and dimmer
   Than the glow of the bright Promised Land.

And now – you have gone on without me,
   Just a few steps alone you've trod
But I'm coming, and know you'll be waiting
   As we walk on together – to God.

Typeset in 10.5/13pt Galliard.
Typesetting and origination by
Sutton Publishing Limited.
Printed and bound in England by
J.H. Haynes & Co. Ltd, Sparkford.

Contents

1. Tilly Goat — 1
2. Dad — 6
3. Day to Day — 17
4. Street Callers — 43
5. Victoria Park — 52
6. Rosie — 59
7. Where Do Babies Come From? — 69
8. School — 77
9. Father Christmas and Mr Thorn — 88
10. The Sanitary Man — 106
11. Making Knickers All Day — 112
12. War — 117
13. Engaged At Last — 121
14. The Big Day — 126
15. Miss Green — 134
16. Ups and Downs — 141
17. My Daughter is Born — 151
18. Flying Bombs — 160
19. VE Day and Peace — 165

Mum.

1

Tilly Goat

Defiantly, I put my arm around Tilly Goat's thin shoulders as we walked home from Olga Street school together that bright day, catching as I did so the queer smell that always seemed to hang about her, even when, as sometimes happened, she wore a clean dress.

It was a smell that used to pour out of some of the open front doors in our street, and always seemed tied up with children I was not supposed to play with. But today was different. Today, I had got a three. Now I could sit next to Tilly Goat, play with her and walk home with her. She was quite nice too, as long as you didn't get too near her. None of my other friends could play with me. I was now a three, and although inwardly I was dreadfully upset I could pretend I didn't care, and I watched Renee and Maudie and May walk past me on the opposite side of the road, put out my tongue at them and shrieked with laughter at something Tilly Goat had said.

Every few weeks, in the early 1920s, Nitty Norah would come into our Bethnal Green school classroom. She was a thin and angular woman, hair scragged tightly into a bun, with a large, round, navy hat firmly pulled on to her head and a starched white nurse's uniform. Her lips were set in a continuous snarl and her nose twitched as though assailed by a permanent nasty smell. Come to think of it, she had a lousy job anyway. I never tried then to visualise her in her off-duty time, but it couldn't have been all that pleasant for her. When other women talked about their jobs, she could hardly boast about being a 'Nitty Norah'. Even school nurse wasn't exactly glamorous in those days, festering sores and impetigo were too commonly their lot anyway; but the nit nurse, on an everlasting hunt for head lice, had the least enviable job of all. No wonder she was a sour creature. I wonder now whether she was glad or sorry if she didn't find anything all day. She must have been a forerunner of today's traffic warden!

We would file out in silence and stand before her while the teacher sat beside her with a book. In one hand, Norah held a metal comb which she dipped into a dish of carbolic. She would lift our hair, peer at our scalps and then utter, one, two or three in a sepulchral tone and the teacher would write it in her book. One, we were clean, two, she suspected nits, and three, dreaded three, we had livestock on our heads!

After she had left the room, the names of the threes were called out, and these luckless ones had to sit alone in a separate block of desks. I had always felt a little pity for these unhappy girls. Some of them, in the dirty block for the first time, would sit and cry, especially as the teacher would warn the class not to play with them again, until they were dealt with. This meant that the nurse would come again shortly and, if they were still unclean, they would be sent to the cleansing station. They would come back from their afternoon trip with clean and shining hair, cut short if it had been long, and the dirty block would be abolished until next time around. Then we would all sit in blocks according to the monthly tests in the good old three 'R's, and I would sit smugly in the top place, month after month.

I could not believe my ears that morning, when the teacher called my name with the threes, after tight-lipped Nitty Norah had gone. I knew I had one, I heard her say it; and I looked frantically round the classroom with swimming eyes. Yes, there she sat, another girl with the same surname as mine. She, who was always dirty, was sitting among the clean lambs, while I was to be cast out! I fought back my tears and tried to remonstrate, but the teacher only tutted. After all, in those days no pupil could possibly accuse her teacher of making a mistake. So I sat in the dirty block and shrank from everyone, trying hard not to cry. I was only 7 at the time, but the memory of that morning has stayed with me all my life; for I learnt at that early age the impossibility of trying to reason with authority.

I crossed Grove Road and left Tilly Goat at the top of Hamilton Road. Later, the name was changed to Haverfield Road – the nearest we ever got to moving in my childhood! I took a deep breath, exchanging the smell of poverty for the lovely smell of new bread. On our street corner was a baker's, with the bakehouse running alongside. The wall was always warm, and stray dogs often sat there warming their thin bodies against it. Gangs of youths sat there too, playing cards, shuffling the greasy packs on the pavement. They had left school, but they were out of work and there was nothing much to do, so they played cards, or football. Our street, being a cul-de-sac, was a favourite place for games, and there were often fights when our own gangs turned on those from neighbouring streets and told them to get back where they belonged. An Englishman's home may be his castle, but the cockney fellow's street was his kingdom, and not lightly trampled on by outsiders. Even we small girls felt this bristling pride of belonging. I lived in the 'court', a narrow slip of a turning at the bottom of the street, and I can well remember shouting 'Get out of our court' whenever children from the main street came down there to play. This was hardly fair on them, and a good job they didn't return the compliment, since we had to traverse their domain to get out of the street at all.

Past the baker's, the smell changed again, for next to the baker's was a dairy. No modern supermarket place this, for it was a real dairy with live cows, poor cockney cows that never saw a field. Often, when we went in with a jug for a penn'orth of milk, we would stand up on the stool by the open window where they served, and see the flanks of the cows and hear them softly mooing and stamping their feet. In the summer there were big sticky flypapers hanging up over the window, and sometimes they were so covered with flies that you couldn't see the flypaper at all. It was possible to buy new-laid eggs there too, since they kept hens in the back, and when my mother sent me for a large brown egg for Dad's tea I would carry it home carefully in my hand. We usually bought things as we wanted them, but I suppose eggs would have been difficult by the dozen, without egg boxes. Anyway, the brown new-laid egg cost threeha'pence each then.

Every few mornings the cows were let loose in the street as soon as it got light, while their stalls were scrubbed out. If they made a mess, it didn't matter in the slightest, because the women would come out of their houses with buckets and take the steaming dung in for their gardens. We didn't often get cow dung, living in the court at the bottom, but we had the advantage on funeral days, because the lovely black funeral horses always came down to the court to turn round, lifting their feet high into the air and snorting and foaming at the mouth. They were awesome creatures, in their black or purple velvet palls, with feathered plumes on their heads and their coats all shiny. Often, while they were waiting, they would lift their tails and drop horse roses. Mum always had a pail at the ready just inside the door on funeral days, and she, or one of us, would grab the pail and a shovel and scoop up the precious stuff before anyone else could get it. Old Mrs Kay who lived right on the corner had the advantage, but she was a fat woman, and slow with it, whereas my mum was on the skinny side and much quicker. Besides, Mum had an added incentive, because a good load of horse roses would put Dad in a sweet temper for once, and that was always worth while. He would whistle softly as he shovelled it gently around our one and only rose bush, reserving a little for his lilies and carnations.

Dad was a real greenfingers, and this little plot of ours was his pride and joy. The place could not have been more than 25 feet long, and he only had a 4-foot strip of soil along one side, but he grew a profusion of flowers all summer long and knew not only every bud, but every petal he possessed. Every fish head was carefully buried near the rose bush, and when we had no manure he would sometimes send us to walk all the way to Hackney Marshes, about 3½ miles away, armed with a small case and a couple of big hairpins. There we had to fill the case with sheep droppings, picking them up with the hairpins. We didn't like the job, but we liked the penny we got for the work. No royal garden was cared for so lovingly as ours.

On the day of the 'three' episode, I wandered slowly home, carrying my dread news and scratching my head because I had seen Tilly doing it. The front door was open and I yelled into the doorway:

'Mum, Nitty Norah came this morning and I've got a three!'

A sudden crash from the kitchen as Mum dropped what she was doing. 'Three!' she shrieked, dashing up the passage and slamming the door. 'Shut up, all the court'll hear you!' Not that they wouldn't know by now, with three of the girls in my class living in the court.

'You can't have a three, you can't,' she cried in distress. 'Your dad'll kill me.' Wiping her red hands on her coarse apron, she began searching anxiously in the copper-coloured silk of my short bob. In spite of her negative search, she was taking no chances. The big black kettle was steaming on the hob as always, and she got out the Lysol bottle. Dinner could wait. Soon my head was tingling and my scalp smarting with the fervent wash in piping hot Lysol.

I sat watching her cook the dinner while my hair dried. She was a very good-looking woman, my mum. Not that I realised it then, but I often heard my aunties say so. Bertha was standing right in the front row when the looks were given out. She had aristocratic features, big brown eyes and black curling hair that escaped from the tight bun at the back in little wispy tendrils. Perhaps her nose looked a big large, but that was because she was thin. Her skin was pink and white, a very good flawless skin, apart from her work-roughened red hands. She was very energetic and moved like lightning, dashing through the chores and working with a will. She was lavish too, lavish with everything, so that our hand-knitted dresses were always on the big side, our dinner plates were piled high and even our toothbrushes well endowed with the camphorated chalk with which we cleaned our teeth. Love and punishment were meted out on the same lavish scale, especially the wallopings! But they were quick hard smacks which she gave, and soon over, whereas Dad would prolong the agony, taking off his trouser belt, or taking the thin hooked cane from the wall and feeling it almost lovingly before giving us a mighty swipe across the legs or the backside. That went on hurting for hours and I went on snivelling for as long as it hurt. My younger sister Gwen was made of sterner stuff: on one occasion, when the thin cane snapped across her bottom, she picked up the broken piece and handed it to Dad with the words, 'Go on then, hit with two halves at once, you bugger.' He was so surprised by the retaliation that he threw the broken cane into the fire and walked outside without a word.

I didn't go back to school that afternoon, one of the very rare occasions when I can recall staying off. Shortly before my father came home from work I got another Lysol wash, just to be on the safe side, and this was repeated daily all week. Even now, the smell of carbolic makes my scalp tingle and the memory of that never-to-be-forgotten episode is as scratch-provoking now as ever.

Next day, Mum came up the school and demanded a recount. Clutching her leather shopping bag in one hand and her worn purse in the other, she bristled at the teacher and cast a few scathing remarks about those dirty old Clarks who spoilt our good name, looking across at Kitty Clark. The teacher looked uncomfortable; it was the first brush she had had with Mum and she had probably realised by this time that it was unusual, to say the least, to see Kitty among the clean children.

Fortunately, Nitty Norah was still on the premises and I was marched into the boys' school by my angry protesting mum. Norah grudgingly admitted I was clean – now. 'No nits at all,' she announced, after a thorough scratchy hunt. I wondered that there was any skin either!

Back in the classroom, I was reinstated in my top place, and next time around saw the hapless Kitty back among the threes where she belonged. My sudden burst of friendship with Tilly Goat ended, but I always had a soft spot for her.

My main friendships were with the girls who lived in our court, Renee, Maud and May. Renee knew everything, except her tables maybe. She was nothing much to look at, being extremely cross-eyed, but she wore steel-rimmed glasses to counteract this, and every few minutes she twitched her nose to push the glasses back where they belonged. She hated helping with the household chores, and once out in the street she would do anything to avoid going back indoors. Out of sight was out of mind, as far as she was concerned. So when she wanted to spend a penny, she would jig and jig and cross her legs and dance about holding herself, rather than go indoors. There was a stale smell about her all the time; unlike Tilly Goat's poverty smell, but very unpleasant, and probably due to wet knickers most of the time. But she knew all the reasons for the street fights around. She could tell us why Mrs Thatcher had a black eye every week, and why Mr Green threw Maudie's handbag out of the bedroom window.

Maudie was a little devil. That was my mother's description. She'd come to no good, that was for sure. I wondered what coming to no good meant, but I shivered at the prospect. She was a beautiful child with bright red hair and when the sun glinted through the court and shone on her, it looked at though her head was afire. She made the most outrageous demands on her poor mum; you could hear her screams throughout the court when she wanted a ha'penny and didn't get it. Poor Mrs Green would come along and borrow a penny for the gas sometimes, and we all knew it was to give to Maudie, because the screaming would stop as soon as she went back.

After her little brother was born, she was even worse. Then she stood watching the baby feed and would yell, 'Give us a drop.' Her foolish mother would take the baby from the breast and hand over to Maudie, who would suck greedily for a few minutes and then spit on the floor. Her father was exactly the opposite. He was always threatening to kill her, and when she grew older, there were the most terrible rows, night after night, as Maud stayed out with the boys and her dad waited for her to come home. He'd throw her bag out of the window, take off his belt and give her a good walloping, but her soft mother would creep downstairs and recover her possessions and next evening give her a sixpence to go out with.

May was quiet and docile, always the peacemaker among us. It was May who would take the end of the skipping rope and turn it, May who was always last in a ball game, and she who would go and ask for our ball back if it bounced down the basement area of the houses at the end of the street. She was a thin, plain girl with straight, lank hair, and it's strange to me that I can remember her, seeing that there was nothing about her to remember. But perhaps she had lasting solid qualities that I sensed rather than saw, because I liked May, and was never happier than when playing shops or schools with her.

2
Dad

How vividly I remember those Bethnal Green days! There were four children in our family. My sister Eva was six years older than me. Gwen came along just two years after me, and Rosie was three years younger than Gwen.

My mother's sister Lizzie lived next door, and she and Uncle Will had three children. Will, the eldest, was the same age as our Eva, Steve slightly older than I was and Jean a bit younger than Gwen. There was a gate between our two gardens and we did everything together, so that I looked upon the boys next door more as brothers than cousins.

My sister Eva said we lived in Bow. Indeed, our address was Bow, E3, and it sounded a bit more posh, but whether she liked it or not, we came under Bethnal Green borough council, voted as residents there and had their dustmen and suchlike. But Eva would always strive to be posh. She was a pretty girl, very self-assured and argumentative, a fact which was always landing her in trouble. By the time I was in the main girls' school at 7, she had left to go to a central school, a sort of half-way house between the elementary and the secondary grammar school. Children went there at eleven plus if they were reckoned to be really bright, but not brilliant enough to get the Junior County, which was the only means of getting to a grammar school without paying.

Eva had been in hospital with scarlet fever at the time of the scholarship, otherwise I expect she'd have made it, but anyway, the central school was something and she learnt French and did algebra and chemistry. This last she really enjoyed and came home full of the experiments she performed. They sounded pretty gruesome to me, but everyone to their taste.

Eva, Gwen and me, 1922.

I suppose she was a bit vain, but she was a nice-looking girl, with slightly curly brown hair, lovely hazel eyes and petite features. She had nice hands too, and I well remember when she bought herself a bottle of nail varnish. It was colourless of course, but I couldn't keep my eyes off her shining, wet-look nails. I'd never seen anything like them before. When she was safely out one afternoon, I crept up and took the bottle from the box under her bed and painted my own nails. They looked so nice, but my joy was short-lived. You can't hide your hands at mealtimes, and Eva suddenly spotted my shining finger ends.

'Thief,' she mouthed at me, 'thief.' Even though she was mad at me she didn't give me away in front of Dad, which shows what a nice nature she really had at heart.

I shot upstairs after tea and scraped and scraped at my nice nails with scissors, finding it harder to take off the polish than to put it on. But scrape and scrape I did, though not without a pause between, while she punched me for stealing.

'Next time you pinch my stuff, I'll tell Dad, you bet your life I will, you fat lump of pud.'

So I kept away from her goods after that, except for an occasional shake of her Yardley's talcum powder down my front, when she grew up a bit and started using such luxuries.

Sometimes, when she wanted to look extra nice, she would put her hair in rag curlers. The long strips of rag were wound round and round the damp hair and firmly knotted. How she slept in them I don't know, but the end result was a load of frizz to my mind, end being the operative word. I remember she once tried it out on me, but she might just as easily have spent her efforts on steel strands. I can still remember the pulling and tugging of those rags!

I've always had a good memory – in fact, I'm sure I can remember being born! The psychiatrists would scoff at that idea, but I suffered badly from nightmares as a child. Whenever I had a cold, or childish upset, tall thin men in white would stand in the corners of the bedroom, and advance on me, swearing loudly and stretching out bony hands to grab me. I would run from them, run and run until I fell head-first down a tiny, tight tunnel. This tunnel was slippery and slimy on all sides, and the slithery walls would press upon me until I felt I should be crushed. Then, just when I could stand no more, I would shoot out from the tunnel of horror into a huge, light open space, cold and echoing. I would start screaming then, loud piercing screams that brought my mother running to me. She would light the candle, give me a drink and sit on the bed awhile, showing me the familiar outlines of the room. But no sooner did she go back to bed than the whole thing would start up again. This nightmare troubled me on and off for years. Every flu episode or bad cold brought the same sensations, until my own first baby was born. In a flash, it came to me that this was what my own nightmare was all about. It was just birth; and it has never once troubled me since. All very far-fetched I suppose, but it's a thought.

I can even recall sitting on my mother's lap during an air raid in the First World War, listening to pinging noises interspersed with bangs. Eva was crouched by her side, trembling and hiding her face in Mum's skirt. 'It's all right, it's only shrapnel on the tin roof opposite,' comforted Mum, but I sensed her fear and cried bitterly. As I was only 2 when the war ended, my mother was amazed when I told her about this episode, and remembered the occasion clearly.

I was supposed to be the brainy one of the family, but I have long since come to realise that cleverness in those days was merely having a good memory. I could look at a row of dates and know them, I learnt my tables in the same effortless fashion, and it was easy to come out top in every exam when it was only a question of remembering which river flowed into which sea and how many half-crowns there were in a pound.

I learnt poetry in the same parrot fashion, my favourite party piece being 'Young Lochinvar'. The family would stand me up on the table and I would begin, very soon finding them all convulsed with laughter. It was not a funny poem, but I ploughed my way through, never realising that it was my hopeless lisp which caused the amusement. 'Through all the wide borders, his steed was the best' was the line that really got them. My lisp was never so apparent as when I had the misfortune to be in the class of Miss Griffiths: I defy anyone to say that quickly and often, and as all my sentences began 'Please Mith Griffithth,' I was always being laughed at.

No one ever suggested speech therapy in those days, and I suppose my lisp was completely ignored because my school reports for those years show 90 per cent or more for 'Reading'. Yet my present family get all steamed up and suggest sending my three-year-old granddaughter to speech therapy classes, because she says she would like a 'tup of toffee' and cannot manage her 'c' sound.

When I compare school today with those far-off 1920s, I shudder to think how the bright young lads and lasses of the present generation would fare. Sitting in serried rows of double desks, we never moved out of them except for the fifteen minutes play between 10.30 and 10.45. Then we would queue up in silence and walk sedately to the playground, with a monitor on each landing of the stone staircase to make sure we did no more than breathe on the way down. We ate our sandwich or whatever we had brought, and went mad for about ten minutes in the small concrete yard. Then a quick trip to the outside lavs and into a silent line again for the return journey up the stairs. There was a big timetable on the wall, and we knew exactly what we would do each day. Every morning started with the singing out of the inevitable tables, but we knew them, they were seared for life on the grey matter of all but the most dim. We had never heard of a 'project' and in today's primary school, when I have asked a group of boisterous children milling around the practical area of their school what they are doing, it's always the same. 'We are working on a project.' If they are standing on the upturned tables, or throwing water and paint at each other, then they are 'doing a play'. No words to learn, nothing to plan and think out, no cues to look for, just 'doing a play'. Heaven help some of these misguided children when they set foot in the hard competitive world around them, when all they seem to know is projects and plays.

I started out left-handed, but continuous raps on the knuckles soon cured me of that. Or did it? Even now, I'm cack'anded, to use my mother's expression. If I wind wool, I tend to put the ball round the wool instead of the wool round the ball, and drying dishes, I rub the dish across the cloth instead of the usual way round. But no one in our school was allowed to be left-handed and that was that.

One day, I tried being funny. I put my mill board on my head and pulled a face. (The mill board was a stiff piece of compressed cardboard about one foot square, on which we rested our drawing paper during art lessons). The teacher rounded on me. 'Do that again,' she said in a threatening voice. So I did, and how she walloped me! I went home sadder and wiser, having had my first lesson in the duplicity of adults.

Our headmistress was a strange woman. She wore thick stockings with a draught-board pattern on them in an age when everyone wore lisle for weekdays and silk on Sundays. Her tweed skirts were thick too, and her woollen jumpers tight across a buxom figure. Her hair was a mousy brown and scragged rather than pulled back and her glasses looked as though they had grown into her nose.

She would sweep into morning prayers and say, 'Good morning girls,' with a terrific rolling of the 'r', to the four hundred or so tightly packed girls assembled before her. 'Good morning Missawkins,' we would chant in unison. Without a moment's hesitation, she would repeat the greeting. And we would reply as before. Sometimes, the whole performance would be repeated time and again, until we got the message and she was satisfied with our reply. 'Good morning girrrls.' 'Good morning Miss . . . Hawkins.'

I wonder now if she was a communist, or whether she belonged to some cranky way-out sect, for even now I remember the words of some of the hymns, of which we sang two every morning.

> Hush, the loud cannons roar, the frantic warriors call,
> Why should the earth be drenched with gore, are we not brothers all?

This was the one I hated most, it sent shivers down my back. One line, 'sweet mercy melt the oppressor's heart, are we not brothers all?' used to really get me and it was as much as I could do not to howl. Freedom was the keynote in her choice of hymn.

> Men whose boast it is that ye come of fathers brave and free,
> If there breathe on earth a slave, are ye truly free and brave?

In lighter vein was:

> Life is a leaf of paper white, whereon each one of us may write,
> His word or two, and then comes night.

She was terribly fond of the brother theme, because we also sang:

> Oh brother man, fold to thy heart thy brother.

I wasn't keen on all these brothers anyway. I didn't have any and, by jingo, I didn't want any either. If we had brothers and they grew up to be men, it would be like having more than one father in the house, and we didn't want that. One was plenty!

My father was a good dad, as dads go. He was a rather short, stocky man, with a little moustache and bushy eyebrows. His hair was thin, carefully brushed to one side to cover a balding patch, but what he missed out on his head grew well enough in other places. His arms were thickly covered and the black hair extended across the backs of his hands, and the thick hair on his chest sprouted even through his vest buttonholes. His fingers were long and sensitive, and he had a hatred of getting sticky. Funny this, because being a french polisher, they were always sticky. But he would never jam his own bread, or peel his own oranges, but hand them to Mum to do. He was powerfully built, and hardly ever used nutcrackers, breaking the nuts in his hands. He cut his finger- and toenails with a big pair of pincers, the same ones that he used to pull 4-inch nails out of wood!

Dad loved his work and many's the time I've watched him doing jobs at home. Spending hour after hour lovingly going over and over the same piece of wood, with little pads of wadding wrapped in linen and soaked in linseed oil. We had some nice pieces of furniture in our house, some of it acquired on a community type basis. My uncle next door was a cabinet maker. His boss would sometimes give him enough wood for three of an article, maybe a sideboard or a cabinet, and he would make up all three in his spare time. Dad would go and polish all three. The boss kept one and Uncle and Dad had one each and all were satisfied with their bargain. A pity folk don't do this kind of thing more often.

Every bank holiday weekend, particularly at Easter, Dad would go out early to find extra work. Bank jobs were his speciality. What he meant then and what young men mean these days by 'doing a bank job' are two very different things. When the banks in the city were closed, there was an opportunity for the long counters to be repolished. Rich mahogany, lovingly tended, not wiped over with a brushful of polyurethane as they are

Dad in his youth.

now. Dad took terrific pride in his work, and I still recall the names of some of the big London banks which he 'did' at Easter time.

All through the holiday he would work, including the Sunday, and then, when he got paid, he would take us out and buy us good new shoes. He had a mania for good shoes. Both he and Mum had bad feet, with corns and bunions and revolting callouses, and he was determined that we shouldn't suffer in the same way. So he would take us all up to Dolcis near Liverpool Street, and pay about 12s 11d a pair for our shoes in a day when there were plenty of shoes to be had for 7s 6d.

He had this same spend-and-be-blowed attitude towards food. Sometimes he would stop in the Bethnal Green Road on the way home from work on Saturday afternoons, and buy smoked haddocks, or juicy kippers, or big rump steaks. No matter if Mum had already got the weekend food in. 'Never a penny is wasted if it goes on your back in the way of good clothes, or into your stomach as good food.' This was his motto, and we did eat well. A cooked midday dinner, something for tea, and when we were old enough to stay up for supper, there was a rabbit stew, or tripe and onions, or stewed eels. Everything had to be of the best.

It had to be cooked well too and no fault was ever overlooked. If a potato dared to look black after cooking, and they sometimes did towards the end of the winter, then it was Mum's fault for buying cheap muck. A tomato had to be English and to skin easily, to be neither too firm nor too soft, and if the bloater for his tea happened to look dark inside when he slit it open, then it was entirely Mum's fault and ought to be rammed down her throat. If he was not in a good mood, I'd watch with bated breath while he ran his knife along the backbone of the bloater and opened it. If mum had been given to prayer, then I think she would have prayed over every steak she cooked him, particularly on Saturday, when he had loitered at the pubs on the way home from work. If it was not tender enough for the knife to slip through like butter, then it might go straight across the room, or into the fire, or at my poor long-suffering mum. I remember her once spending the whole afternoon preparing a crab and making a delicious salad, because we were in the midst of a terrific heat wave and it was too hot to eat. When our lord and master came home, he asked in a very quiet voice what it was supposed to be.

'Why, your meal,' answered Mum, equally quiet.

Then he let fly. 'But where the bloody hell is my dinner?' he roared. The whole plateful went flying across the room, and the next half hour was given over to a tremendous outburst about a man slaving his guts out to provide money for grub, not bloody rabbit food.

Rows in our house were the most one-sided affairs. I often used to think that if only Mum had answered back and stood up to him occasionally, life might have been a bit different, for he was a real bully. But we didn't . . . we just let him roar. Many a night, my young sister and I lay in bed petrified, listening to the almighty din downstairs when someone or something had crossed his path and made him angry. Sometimes, Mum came running up the stairs and came in and sat quietly crying, on the end of our bed. We would pretend to be asleep and he would come belting up after her. He would open the bedroom door and point down the stairs.

'Come down and take your medicine,' he would say in a queer and level voice, and she would go sobbing down the stairs and the thumping began again.

'It's all right, Gwen,' I would whisper, trying to comfort my sister, 'it's only because Mummy has to take some nasty medicine and doesn't want it.' But I didn't believe it, and neither did Gwen.

'The old man was in a bloody temper last night, wasn't he?' Auntie Liz would say over the garden wall, next morning. 'I wonder you're so daft as to stay with him. I'll be damned if I would.'

'T'aint as easy as all that,' muttered Mum to her sister, and then they would see me and shoo me away and they'd whisper together.

Of course, it was only the drink that got him like that. I often heard my uncle Will say that it was a pity that Joe didn't drink a bit more. Something would upset him at work, and instead of coming straight home as he usually did, he would call in at the pub and have a few drinks and brood on everything that had upset him. Then he'd come home and take it out on us, or my mother, if we were already in bed, and if he was late, then she'd make sure we were.

Normally, he came home every evening as the six o'clock hooter went at the nearby factory. He'd whistle a greeting as he came in the door, and we'd know, with absolute certainty, that things were all right. If he didn't whistle as he came in, you could bet your bottom dollar that there was trouble ahead for someone, and we children learnt to make ourselves scarce if that particular barometer reading was not set fair.

Strange, how our timing was all governed by hooters before the days of radio. Everyone knew the time. There was the five to eight, the eight o'clock, two different sounds, and the same at one o'clock and six. Then there was the school bell. Early bell at twenty to, and late bell at ten to the hour.

Uncle was right about Dad though. Because at Christmas time, when he got really drunk, then he was very funny and he and Uncle would sing all the latest ditties, and put their own words to them too.

You never knew how to take Dad, and it used to puzzle me. When Uncle Will staggered home drunk on a Saturday, my auntie could get anything out of him. If we were around, and we'd always contrive to be, he'd pat us on the head, call us his little cock sparrer and give us pennies for sweets. If he was really drunk, he'd give us a whole sixpence, as like as not. We loved Uncle Will. A kind and generous man, he was so easy-going that he was the easiest man in the world to con. He would buy things for his two sons, things they couldn't really afford, and his little daughter could wheedle anything out of him. Although I appreciated that drink mellowed my uncle, I grew up nevertheless with a deep-rooted hatred of drunkenness, and vowed that I'd never marry a man who drank, although at that time I honestly didn't know any man who didn't. All my friends' fathers did, and so did my uncles. Drinking and pubs went with manhood and I knew no different.

Between times, my dad was a good father to us, spending hours trying to help with our education, as he put it. This was my particular spot. He set me essays, and while the others were running about and playing games, I'd be sitting writing or looking up long words in the dictionary. He was proud of me and of my glowing school reports, and his aim was to see me 'go further' than he had had a chance to do. 'I left school at eleven,' he'd say, 'but I'll be blowed if you are going to cut short your learning. I never had a chance, but you are going to get the Junior County and have a decent education.' He taught us all to play draughts, offering us a penny if we beat him. I never realised how good he was at the game then, but since I have hardly ever found anyone to beat me at it, my tuition must have been excellent. Gwen was taught to box and fight. 'Fists up,' he would say, and they'd have a lovely scuffle. I sometimes think that she took the opportunity to give him a real hard one. Once she blacked his eye and he thought it was really funny.

It was one of his deepest sorrows that we were all girls. He was upset when Eva was born, annoyed when I turned up, furious that Mum dared do such a thing when Gwen arrived, and when little Rosie came along the aunties had to toss up as to who should tell him. He went out and got drunk and didn't set eyes on the baby for days. Had he been a duke or King Henry himself, he couldn't have been madder at these daughters.

I was the plain one among the children. The only one inclined to fat, with straight hair and round red cheeks, big teeth and the hated lisp, I was nothing much to write home about. Dad loved me because I was bright and Mum because I was such a good-tempered baby. She had had a hell of a life with Eva and I wonder if that was why there were six years between us. Eva, although a beauty, had been a real crosspatch of a baby, and poor Mum, trying to undress the screaming bundle, would fumble and fumble until Dad came in. He'd take the baby, cut the clothes off it with a pair of scissors and bump it in the cot, shutting poor Mum outside the room. There were endless rows about it, and I can just imagine how much Mum dreaded my arrival. But I turned up, fat and placid and smiling, sitting happily sucking my toes or fingers and troubling no one.

Gwennie, born just two years after me, was different again. She was a little five-pounder, always small for her age, with a tiny heart-shaped face, black tightly curling hair, and mischievous eyes that went into slits when she laughed. She was a little monkey, always ready for a joke or a dare and up to all sorts of tricks. She took after Mum and moved like quicksilver, and many's the time I've seen poor Mum chase her through the house and up the nearest lamppost. Gwen would shin up and sit cussing away on the crossbar, and no amount of threatening would get her down. She'd bargain with Mum though, and come down if she could miss the punishment she was being chased for in the first place.

Rosie was the baby of the whole family. Everyone loved her, a chubby little golden-haired darling, too good for this world. I can remember her birth but always think of her as a smiler, never hearing the baby yell.

I wonder how today's mums would cope with the washing and ironing of a baby in the early 1920s. First and foremost of course, was the binder, a tight flannel stitched firmly around the baby's middle. Then the vests. Flannel one first and a pretty cambric one on top. Then the long undergown, flannel again, coming a good 18 inches below the baby's feet. This was folded over and pinned up to make a big bag over baby's feet. Then came the petticoat, gown and coat, followed of course by the big wrapping shawl and head shawl. Taking baby out meant a bigger, more ornate woollen shawl on top of this lot, a bonnet and a veil. When I think that there were no such things as plastic pants either! The whole bundle could and very often did get sopping wet through. This lasted for about three months, until the baby was shortened. This was quite a ceremonial occasion when the long clothes were discarded and short, ankle-length dresses were worn. What a relief this must have been for the poor little flannel-wrapped parcel. Only then could the little dear show a leg to the world. But, boy or girl, it was dressed in petticoats and dresses and not 'breeched' until about 2 years, or even 3, if male. Indeed, 2 years was being modern and I have photographs of my uncles standing dressed in dainty dresses at about 4 years old. Boys never wore long trousers until they were nearly 14 and the first pair of 'long-uns' was always a great occasion. We were called to the fence to see cousin Will in his first long trousers, and felt him so grown up as to be shy of him.

But none of the delights of fathering sons fell to Dad, and what a blessing that probably was. I can just imagine a grown-up brother dealing with Dad when he started losing his temper, so I reckon the good Lord knew what He was doing when He made us all female.

Dad's one consolation, apart from his rose bush and lilies, was his pigeon loft. A tall, clean, well-painted structure at the bottom of the little garden, it housed about twenty pigeons. They kept him poor but happy, and kept me with permanently aching arms, since it was my job to get the 7 pounds of pigeon food every week, as soon as I was old enough to go to the shops alone. No pigeon mixture this, as most men bought, but a pound of this and a pound of that, all mixed up in proportion by my father.

Every evening, when he came in from work, he would let the pigeons out for a fly round while he had his tea. Then he would sit on a little box in the garden and watch them, whistling them home when he thought they'd had enough. They were very tame and would perch on his hand or head and take food from him. Sometimes we got mad at them. Perhaps, on a Saturday, we had planned to go out somewhere, and Dad would let those wretched birds out for their fly first. This was all very well, but sometimes there were young birds out for the very first time, and they would be nervous, perch on the roof and refuse to come back to the loft. So Dad would whistle and encourage them, but it might take a couple of hours, while we stood and waited patiently dressed in our best, until all the birds were safely in. Only then would he rise from his box and get ready. Perhaps though, he would say it was too late to go out after all; and even if we were going to tea with relations and were expected, he would refuse to go. He never went out visiting in the rain either, if he could possibly avoid it. On many occasions, with us all dressed up and the aunts expecting us, he'd take off his collar and tie at the slightest hint of rain and refuse to go out. 'No one will expect us in such weather,' he'd say. Knowing him, no one ever expected us until they saw us anyway, for such was his contrary nature. I often wonder why my mother didn't just say, 'All right, blow you. Stay at home if you want to, but we're going.' But she didn't. She meekly took off her best skirt, put on the everlasting overall and got us out of our best clothes. No wonder we didn't receive many invitations!

He kept a few fowls too, in our little back. No one called them chickens then, unless they were. But these nice fowls laid eggs, and scratched around in their little bit of dirt and enjoyed themselves. On one occasion though, Dad found that one of them had developed a taste for eggs, and was eating them as fast as they were laid. It didn't take the others long to realise that they were on to a good thing, and soon we were keeping hens and getting nothing from them. Dad kept watch, found the culprit, and gave her a good walloping with his leather belt. But she was too bird-brained to understand what the hiding was for, and apart from making me cry, it did not a scrap of good. Next, he made up a special egg. He filled a shell with mustard, pepper, pickling spice and peppermint. It made your eyes water to go near that egg. He put it in the nest and after one peck, all the hens were squawking around the run and shoving their beaks in the earth. But next day, they calmly went back to eating their good eggs. So Dad took the main culprit out and sold her, made a nesting box with a sloping false bottom, and all was peace once more.

The cockerels were a different matter. Each year, we fattened two for Christmas. These hapless birds, usually Rhode Island Reds, were plied with food until they would eat no more. Then, Gwen and I took them into the kitchen, made numerous pellets of middlings and stuffed them with more food. I held the beak open and Gwen pushed the food down, until Dad came and felt them, and was satisfied that they could hold no more. Towards Christmas, they were kept in the house all night, lest they got stolen. Uncle Will came in to perform the killing (Dad couldn't bear to kill any animal). He would down a couple of pints first and then take the birds out and slit their throats over the dustbin. One year, we came unstuck. Uncle was unwell and unable to kill the birds, so a neighbour offered to do it for us. Dad was very grateful, until Mr Kay came along with the birds. 'Thought I'd do you a favour, Joe,' he said. 'Got the missus to pluck and draw them while she was doing ours, so give me half a dollar and call it quits.' He put the birds on the kitchen table and cleared off, and for once Dad was dumbstruck. The birds on the table were a couple of wizened skinny old things, not, by the greatest stretch of imagination, anything like our lovely fat cockerels. Dad was mad, but even he couldn't insist that they were not his birds. He went out and bought a turkey that year.

When today's children get bored watching the TV, I recall vividly all our jobs. We had no time to get bored. There were a couple of rabbits in the back, and I kept white mice for good measure. Heaven help us if we let the rabbit hutch or mouse house get dirty. Why, we even used to polish our tortoise's shell with margarine, to keep him looking nice. We all loved animals and we had two cats and a dog besides. One day, one of the pigeons was ill. It couldn't eat, and Dad took it from the loft and felt it anxiously. There was something stuck in its crop which it couldn't pass. So he stunned it, held it firmly in his strong hands while my mother cut open the crop, removed the offending object and sewed the bird up with thread. Within a short time it was better and soon flying again.

To cull his flock was simple. A pigeon pie was Saturday dinner, courtesy of Uncle Will's killing instincts, and what a luscious meal it was. A whole bird apiece, the breast covered with fat bacon under the crisp pastry, roast potatoes and green veg, lashings of gravy and an apple tart to finish with.

Sometimes, if Dad was hard up, he would take some of the birds down Club Row and sell them on a Sunday morning. This was a glorious East End market at the top of Bethnal Green Road. No licences were needed, no permits, nothing at all. You just stood around with what you had to sell until you found a buyer. Once or twice, with my cousin Steve for moral support and a share of the spoils, I went there myself to sell a few mice for fourpence each. But I didn't like doing it much, because I was told that the man who bought them was going to sell them to a hospital for experiments. Dad had no qualms about selling the pigeons though. He had one favourite red bird, and every time he sold pigeons, he sold this particular one, as it could always be relied upon to come home within a few days! When we went out for the day on a Sunday school excursion or similar treat, we took the pigeon with us in a shopping bag and set it free as soon as we reached our destination. 'Well,' Dad would say with an air of satisfaction, 'at least we know that they got there safely!'

3

Day to Day

The bakery and dairy were not the only places of industry in our street. Just past the dairy, there were houses on either side: one row with doors opening directly on to the pavement, and the others with a tiny forecourt. The latter were reckoned to be the posher ones, but the other side made up for their lack by whitening the paving stone immediately in front of the door. And woe betide any luckless kid who accidentally trod on a newly whitened doorstep. Halfway down the street was a little shop. It was only a collection of sweets and small groceries kept in the front room of one of the houses, but we sometimes went there, more for the novelty than anything else. The woman was a sad-faced creature who never seemed to smile, or even speak. She would slap down the toffee bar, or whatever we bought, and take our ha'penny with a big sniff. Mum always referred to her as the 'poor thing' but never spent anything there herself.

At the bottom of the street, where it met our court, was a fairly large factory complex, let to a gum maker's and a feather factory. This was a strange mixture. The 'gummies' were a greasy-looking lot, mostly men and very smelly when they passed us in the street. It was a smell like fish and soap together and I used to wonder how their families put up with it when they got home. But they were shadowy beings who just moved through the street twice a day, and we never got to know any of them at all. The women who worked in the feather place were grey: everything about them, coats, shoes and scarves, all grey, even their hair and eyelashes, when they came out from the factory. Sometimes when they were unloading, a sack of feathers would burst and if it was windy we would all get covered with feathers too, and my father would swear as he tried to brush his overcoat.

They made cushions and pillows there, and one night there was a terrific fire. What with the feathers and the gum, the flames were soon licking at every window. The firemen came into our house and stood leaning out of our bedroom window to see whether they could tackle the blaze better that way. We were so excited when, wrapped in coats, we were taken to a neighbour's house further along the road, all in the middle of the night. We didn't realise it ourselves, but Mum and Dad knew the danger. With an oil wharf opposite and a chemical factory next to the gummies, it could have been a dreadful conflagration.

But all was well, and next morning we clambered over the blackened ruins, together with all the children from the street, and looked for unburnt pieces of wood to take home.

There were three houses in the court before ours, but the house I liked best was the one directly next to us. A clay pipemaker lived there, and in his back garden was the kiln. The front room downstairs was the workshop, and we could look through the window and watch the old woman making pipes. She stamped out the bowls in a little machine and trimmed them by hand. Some were just plain clay pipes, but some had queer faces with weird expressions on them. She never looked up from her work, even when, during the hot weather, the window was open and our faces were only a few feet from her. She breathed heavily as she worked, and only paused to take swigs of beer from a big jug at her elbow.

Mr Hawkey, white-faced, white-haired and with a droopy clay-stuck moustache, would carry out the trays of made pipes to the kiln and stoke up with coke and wood. Sometimes it would smoke badly, belching out thick black smuts; my father would swear like mad because his flowers were getting sooty. If it was a washing day, then my mother and auntie next door would swear too, but old 'Awkey pretended not to hear.

If he was in a good mood he would sometimes hand us a chipped pipe each, and we would race indoors and get soft soap from Mum and spend hours blowing bubbles. If no chips were forthcoming and we wanted to blow bubbles, we would pounce upon his dustbin and give it a good raking over before the dustcart came.

Two doors past the pipemakers lived a little Jew who had a stall in the Roman Road. We could always call there for elastic or buttons or tape, or anything else we ran out of in that line.

On the opposite side of the court were two houses knocked into one, where lived two brothers who were cabinetmakers. Sometimes we sat on their window sill and watched them making chests of drawers, every bit made of solid mahogany and all the dovetailing done by hand. Dad used to say that they were real good workers and their furniture was fit to go anywhere. I often wonder where some of these chests might be even now – probably gracing some home where real quality is still appreciated. They were quite expensive, selling even then for as much as a fiver, but the men never seemed short of work. Sam, the older of the two, used to carry on about the slapdash youngsters of the day. 'Never make good workmen of these good-for-nothing boys. They don't like real work and that's a fact.' What he would have thought of today's lads I shudder to think. To Sam, a youngster had to slog all day and every day apart from Sunday, for six or seven bob a week, while he was learning the trade. But he would be taught real skill, though one wonders whether such skills would long be needed, in a world that was even then becoming machine minded.

When the chests were finished, they were covered with sacking and stood side by side on the narrow pavement until one of the brothers tied them on to a barrow and wheeled them away. When the barrow was not in use they would let us ride up and down on it, although only the boys were strong enough to push it.

I could always rely on those kindly men for a bag of sawdust for the mouse house, although they did not appreciate my taking the mice over in my pocket to say thank you.

Just around the corner was a house with an ever-open door. Most of the women would trot across there sometime before dinner and place a bet. 'Tanner each way,' mostly . . . and how I longed to know what was meant by this. Surely, if the horse had to turn round and come back, and win each way, it would be harder for it than just reaching the winning post first. Mum didn't bet, and had scant sympathy for those who were always short of money and moaned about it, yet could always go over to Harts and put their tanner on a horse.

Dad used to have a flutter, but never locally. He always met a bookie's runner in Shoreditch, and if it was a very big race like the Derby, he would allow us to choose the horse we thought would win. If he took our advice, which he sometimes did, then he'd give us each a sixpence if the horse won. That didn't happen very often. Uncle Will always betted on one trainer's horses. At least I think it must have been a trainer, or a jockey, but in any case, every extra expenditure next door, be it clothing or outing, would be dependent on it. 'Daddy says we'll have to see what Mr Cudby says on Saturday,' Jean would tell us, when talking of a day at the seaside or a new pair of shoes.

Our main interests, however, lay in the back of our house, rather than the happenings in the court. The Regent's Canal ran along the back of our garden, and many an hour we spent standing on the chicken shed watching the barges go past. Most of them were horse drawn, and did those horses get friendly! As soon as they spotted us sitting there, they would stop and wait while we ran indoors for a piece of stale bread or a carrot. They were lovely, big, strong horses, slow plodding and sure-footed, and they seemed to pull the heavy laden barges without any effort at all.

Most of all we enjoyed watching the 'monkey barges', narrow long boats gaily painted, with roses and decorative scrolls on the sides. They mostly went by in twos, powered by a chugging engine instead of a horse, and the slightest sound of their motors would send us dashing to the wall to watch them. They were clean and shining, with all the brass on them gleaming and glinting in the sunshine. Even their buckets, swinging on the sides, were gaily decorated with roses. Only the children on the barges looked dirty: poor, ill-clad, scruffy-haired children mostly, and their dogs were lean and hungry-looking. It seemed to me a most romantic way to live, but when I realised they were water gypsies and never went to school I soon cooled off the idea. I loved school.

On the opposite bank of the canal was a big oil wharf. The heavily laden barges would come crawling in to the side and tie up, and the big crane would start its noisy clanking, picking up the barrels in twos and placing them neatly on the path. Then the men would roll them inside the corrugated red-painted sheds, while the crane came clanking back for more.

Further along the canal, just within our line of vision as we sat on the wall, was a railway bridge and a goods yard. The LNER trains came roaring past and occasionally there was a boat train. We'd wait ages to catch a glimpse of this, with 'Hook of Holland' painted on the side. My mind boggled at the idea of going so far. The goods trains clonked and clanked into the yard at the side of the main line, and the trucks would bang into each other, clink, clonk, clink, clonk, clinkety clinkety-clonk. At night, especially when the weather was wet and wintry, there was a strange comfort in lying in bed, listening to those fascinating sounds. They were friendly noises and the outside darkness far less scaring when I could hear the sounds I knew. I hated the dark and would put off going out to the lav at night, until I could persuade Gwen to come with me. Nothing frightened her, nothing and no one.

My cousins next door were more venturesome than we were. On fine days they would slither over the wall and swim in the murky canal water, although it was too deep to stand in, even at the edge, and swimming was strictly forbidden. We sat on the wall on guard, watching for the water cops. These police patrolled the towpath, looking for trouble; and often the boys would have to shin naked up the wall because we'd spotted a water cop in the distance. When he reached us we'd say 'Hello' politely to him, and Gwen would chatter on, hoping to keep his eye from the tell-tale wet marks on the path and up the wall. As soon as he was out of sight the boys would be back again and in the water. They'd swim across and climb on the barges tied up there, and we'd sit and envy them. We used to worry our mum to let us get down and paddle our feet in the water, but she wisely refused. Besides being dangerous, there was a six-foot drop down the wall on the canal side, so we had to content ourselves with watching the boys.

A school group with my sister Gwen behind the doll's house, 1924.

There was tragedy too, in that canal. Sometimes there was a suicide, and some poor devil, having thrown himself off Green Street bridge, would come floating down. Other things floated down too, besides the flotsam and jetsam of the waterside community. Unwanted cats, newborn kittens and dogs that had to be got rid of in a hurry because there was a licence check. Seven and sixpence took some finding then.

I watched them drown a dog one day. It had bitten a little girl, and having no licence, they had to get rid of it quick. They tied its legs together, poor whimpering mongrel, and put it in a sack with some heavy bricks. Then the sack was securely tied and heaved over the wall. We listened, dumbstruck, to the splash. Then the men who did it lit their cigarettes, went back to the pub 'up the top' and thought no more about it. Only I cried myself to sleep over that poor dead dog.

One morning Mum threw a rat over the wall. It was only a dead one that the cat had brought home, but it came flying back with a string of oaths, having hit a bargee fair and square as he passed by.

Dad had another use for the canal, besides using it as a rubbish tip. If we quarrelled over anything while we were playing, he would take it from us and send it flying into the canal. Ludo, snakes and ladders, dolls, books, you name it, we lost it if we dared raise our voices in argument as we played. Only Dad was allowed to shout.

One day a small boy was drowned there, having squeezed through a gate further along and fallen in, trying to catch tiddlers. We stood in silence as the ambulance backed through the gummies' gate and the men came out carrying a little grey bundle. The women cried and the men doffed their caps, but Dad went straight into the garden and began looking out lengths of wood. He rigged up a narrow platform and laying us across it, he lost no time in teaching us to swim, working our arms and legs until we ached in every joint. At length, he proclaimed that we were now swimmers, and I boasted to all my friends at school that I could now swim. It was not until some considerable time later that I went for the first time to the public baths, and found to my dismay that swimming on dry land was an entirely different kettle of fish to swimming in water. I shivered and trembled and slid slowly in, only to find that I sank as soon as I took my feet from the bottom. I went on sinking for years. Gwen had no such difficulty and was soon happily swimming around, and Dad boasted to everyone that he had taught her. It was some years later that I found out that Dad was no swimmer himself!

Uncle had better ideas about teaching his small fry to swim: he took his two boys over the wall and taught them in the water. But one Saturday afternoon he came home after the pubs shut, and boasted to his brother next door that his dog, as well as his kids, could swim like a fish. He took the dog over the wall, but the poor thing wasn't a bit keen, and as they struggled, kneeling at the water's edge, he lost his balance and fell in. What a struggle they had to get him out! Auntie Liz, though, was more worried over the fact that he still had his wages in his pocket than anything else, and she was through his jacket and had the pound notes pegged out on the line to dry long before they were sure the poor man was still in the land of the living.

Unfortunately the towpath made a good getaway route for thieves, and more than once we had all our hens stolen during the night. It was a strange sensation, to come down in the morning and see the fowl-house door wide open and silence in the hen run. After the second loss Dad gave up keeping hens, but we were always very careful to lock the back door securely. Of course, Dad blamed the water gypsies, but he had to put the blame on someone.

There was a village air about our little court, for we were mostly related one way or another, and most of the lodgers were distantly related too. Of course we had lodgers. I can't remember anyone in the whole street who didn't, but no one ever came round and said anything about overcrowding.

It was not until the big council estate at Dagenham began to take shape that officialdom started snooping around and trying to persuade people to move out. In one house in the main part of the street lived two brothers, each with a wife and a whole horde of children: they had about eight apiece and it was difficult to remember which of the children belonged to which family. One family had fourteen children, and when Gwen went there to tea she told us that they all sat up the stairs with their plate of bread and jam. 'It was lovely,' she mused happily. 'I wish we could have tea on the stairs.'

We didn't reckon we were overcrowded, but in our little six-roomed house lived our family, with four little girls, and Grandma and her three unmarried daughters.

We had the two main downstairs rooms, with a gas cooker installed in the back one, while Grandma and her family had the small end room. We both shared the scullery, with its sink, water and big old copper, but we had to go through their room to get to the scullery, and

Auntie Rosie, 1900.

Auntie Lottie, 1900.

we carried all our water through. Of course, our dirty water had to be taken out in a pail, but we never thought anything of it.

We had the two back bedrooms, and Grandma and the three aunts had the big front room. They washed up there, carrying all the water upstairs and down again, but it wasn't convenient for them to wash downstairs, with us all coming and going through their place.

Auntie Rosie was the eldest of the three. She had golden hair and an exuberant happy nature. She laughed and sang, and enjoyed life to the full. She wore gold-rimmed glasses and used lovely golden-coloured hairpins to keep her bun in position. They were always falling out, and I used to hand them to her with great care, thinking they were made of real gold.

Lottie was only two years younger than Rosie and they were great friends, going about together all the time. Lottie wore glasses too, but there the resemblance to Rosie ended. She had the most gorgeous chestnut hair, so long that, when it was unplaited and brushed out, she could actually sit on it. Her hair was more often made into two buns, one over either ear, but on Sundays it was a big fat bun at the back. She was of a more serious nature than Rosie, but we children loved them both.

If we were ever spoilt at all, it was by these two aunties. I would stand at the corner of the court on summer evenings, watching for them turning the corner, then rush up the street to meet them. Rosie was a court dressmaker, employed by one of the exclusive Knightsbridge shops, and Lottie was a grocery assistant, also in Knightsbridge. They were both ardent Salvationists, and every Sunday saw them in their uniform, walking to Homerton, about 4 miles away.

May was the youngest of the three. She was a 'beader' and sewed thousands of tiny beads on lovely dresses, making intricate patterns on them. Sometimes she did

Auntie May.

home work, and we would sit and watch her. But not for long, because for some reason we used to torment her, and she'd jump up and chase us away. I suppose she was only about ten years older than Eva, and nearer to our generation, but whatever the reason, we used to get her rag out whenever we could. Yet she was very kind to us most of the time, and only threatened to tell Mum when we'd knocked over some beads, or made her lose her needle.

My Gran was adorable. For some unknown reason we called her Janet, although her name was Jane. She was tiny: so small in fact that whereas I started out by measuring how high I came up on Janet, I was soon able to measure how far down Janet went on me! She was placid, perhaps the most placid woman I have ever met. She had left school at 7 and could neither read nor write. Her mother had taken her to work with her in a box factory as soon as she left school, and sometimes the little Jane, standing on a stool because she couldn't reach the factory bench, would topple off, having fallen asleep over her work. She was a wonderful listener, and would sit with folded hands whenever we told her stories. Any story we had heard at school, we would run home and tell to our Janet. She used some real old-fashioned expressions, and it amused us that she called scissors 'sithers'. She would ask us to 'run an arrant' for her, up to the nearby shops.

She had had ten children, five boys and five girls. All the five boys had died and the girls lived. 'Very 'ard to rear, boys,' she would say.

Sometimes, Mum would go shopping and leave Janet in charge. Whatever pranks we got up to, whatever we did, the answer was always the same to Mum's query. 'Have the kids been good?' 'As good as gold,' would come the prompt reply, blindly ignoring the contents of her button box strewn on the floor, the overflowing sink in the scullery, or the splashes of red paint on her white cat!

She was very independent too, and although she came in and had tea with us every weekday, she would carry in a tray with her own sugar, condensed milk and bread and butter. Sometimes she would accept our jam, but not often. We fought to sit next to her at tea. I could always put my crusts, which I was not allowed to leave, in her apron pocket, and afterwards I'd watch her feeding them to the birds.

Her white hair was worn fluffed out in the front after she was washed and dressed, but in two tiny plaits across her forehead in the mornings. The back hair was worn in a bun all the time. It fascinated me to see her doing her hair. She would brush and brush it, then plait and plait until the end was no thicker than a mouse's tail. Selecting a hair from her shoulder, or from the brush, she'd wind it round and round the plait. When she'd put all the back hair into two plaits, she'd twist the two plaits together and pin it into the inevitable bun. Strangely enough, she never washed all her hair on the same day! Front hair washing day was far more frequent than back day, probably because the aunties helped her with this.

Mum had all her sisters nearby, with three of them in our house and Auntie Liz next door. The lodgers in that house were an old aunt and uncle belonging to Uncle Will, but they had only the one front room upstairs. Aunt Kate was an amazing old lady. She was known throughout the street as 'Mrs Dearie', because of her habit of calling everyone 'dearie'. She, like Janet, could not read or write, but she never let on about this. She'd sit holding a newspaper in front of her, listening as hard as she could to the talk around her. Then, 'I see the papers say there's going to be another strike,' she'd say, nodding her head. She also used 'face powder' and when she went out, made up 'to the nines' as Janet said, her face was white as chalk. It was only flour she used, but with a little bit of pink on each cheek and a jaunty hat and feather boa, she looked the lady when she went out.

She tried to play the lady at home too, and she must have been the cleanest woman that ever lived. Although she only had the one room, her home was her pride and joy. The big white bed, covered with a snowy quilt, with white starched drapes around it and stiff white embroidered pillowcases, dominated the room, and draped across it was a beautiful neatly folded white nightgown. The bed always looked exactly the same, with its shiny brass knobs and dazzling whiteness, and could easily have been used for a TV advertisement today. Just a snowy museum piece, was that bed.

When she invited us up to her room, we sat in awe on the very edge of a velvet-covered chair, its white antimacassar tied with pink bows. Like a throne it was. Her cooking stove and washing basin lived outside on the landing, and she took her meals by the window, taking off the heavy red velvet tablecover to replace it with a hand-crocheted tablecloth and dainty china. She used to sing as she worked, in a very powerful voice that could be heard throughout the house. On Tuesdays, when she did her washing, she came downstairs and used her niece's kitchen, and then we'd hear her too. 'Mona, I love you, Mona, Mona,' she'd sing. On and on, so that if Dad was home he'd laugh and say, 'Bloody old Mona's at it again.'

Alas though, she had one dirty acquisition: an exceedingly filthy and scruffy little husband called George, who talked to himself and was always drunk. We used to stand outside the lav and listen to him, going on and on.

'That's it,' he'd say. 'Be a man. Nothing to it. Go up and demand. Demand. That's it. Demand. Don't go on being a silly bugger. Stand up.'

We'd shake with laughter and mouth the words to each other. 'Demand, be a man.' I strongly suspect that he took these opportunities, sitting out there on the throne, to decide to assert his authority over his Kate, but it never came to anything.

On Saturday nights George usually fell down on the pavement, and Aunt Kate would get Uncle Will to help her haul him unceremoniously up the stairs. Not to bed, however. 'You don't think I'll have that dirty bugger in my bed, do you?' she'd shout indignantly. He had a little bed-chair in the corner of the room, covered with a serviceable brown hessian. I don't know how they managed, but according to my cousins, Aunt Kate didn't sleep in the bed either.

I know she didn't use it for her afternoon nap, and the boys used to get mad at her because she slept in their room. 'Aunt Kate's on our Willie's bed again,' Steve would say, and we tried to think up ways to dislodge her. It was maddening not to be able to get the Meccano set out from under the bed, or get the chessmen, just because of Aunt Kate. So we formed a terrific plan. When Steve came and told us she had gone in for her nap, we trooped quickly to the garden. Mustering all the tin cans and old baths we could find, we stood quietly below the window. Steve had a watering can, and removing the rose, he put the spout to his lips. We waited a while, until we thought the old lady had dropped off, then we suddenly let rip with everything. Steve particularly made a gorgeous noise with the watering can. Today's plastic ones can't hold a candle to the galvanised variety.

Aunt Kate threw up the window and bellowed at us. She didn't call us dearies then, but all the names she could lay her tongue to. When she paused for breath, my small sister spoke up, loud and clear.

'You shouldn't sleep on our Willie's bed, you old grey mare.' It's a wonder the poor old dear didn't have a fit and fall from the window! We scattered and made ourselves scarce, while Aunt Kate went to find our respective mothers.

Dad used to get annoyed with old George too. Perhaps he had spent hours trying to coax his young pigeons back into the loft when they had been out for the first time, and as soon as he managed to get them down as far as the roof, old George would come out into the garden and throw up his hands, making loud squealing noises. The birds would take off in a fright and George would wave his smelly old pipe at Dad.

'There you are, Joe,' he'd call out with great satisfaction, 'that's got them flying for you again.'

'Silly old sod,' Dad would growl, spitting in George's direction.

It was the aunties and their not riding on the sabbath that first made me realise that prayers do get answered. I was about 5 years old, and they took me with them to the 'Hall' on Sunday. Attired in a new white dress made by Auntie Rose and carefully embroidered with rows of pink and blue featherstitching and french knots, new ankle strap patent shoes and short white socks. I was justly thrilled with my appearance and trotted along through Victoria Park and out into Hackney happily enough. But gradually my fat little legs grew weary and the new shoes started to rub a blister on my heel. And we were not even there!

'Don't you ever get a tram home?' I asked, trying to keep up the pace.

'Only if it rains,' answered Rosie, 'because the rain spoils our bonnets and they are very expensive.'

So when we arrived at last I sat gratefully on the long hard seat in the Hall, and while they all sang and shook their tambourines and clapped and made a joyful noise unto the Lord, I screwed up my eyes and prayed for rain. Rain, on a bright sunny morning, when the beams of dappled sunshine streamed in at the windows, making golden patterns on the floor and turning the captain's plain face to a golden glow.

'Only pray, believing,' sang the captain, her voice wobbling with emotion. 'Amen, Amen,' came a deep booming voice behind me, so I covered my face and sat with bowed head as I saw the others doing.

'Just let it rain, dear God,' I whispered, 'Let it pour hard.'

The service went on and on, and suddenly I saw that the sun was no longer shining. Within a few minutes there was an almighty clap of thunder, and when at last the service ended, the rain was coming down in torrents! No walk home through the park for us – in fact one of the officers carried me to the tram stop and we rode home in style! So God, that God they always went on about in the Hall, did listen, and did bother, even with kids with blisters on their heels.

What tremendous possibilities were now within my reach! That event was one of the biggest milestones in my life, and from then on I began to petition the Lord with all sorts.

Auntie Rosie used to bring home pieces of material, little scraps of velvet and silk, and try and teach us to sew. She would tell us whose dresses they were from. Lady So-and-So is having this for her daughter's coming-out party. Lady This-or-That was being presented at Court in this silk. I took the pieces in my hand, and wondered hard about the Court. There must be lots of different courts. There was our court, but that was a poor narrow street, there was the police court and I'd heard that often enough, especially in rows in the street.

'I'll take you to court, so help me,' the women would yell at each other when they had a fight. But for Lady So-and-So to wear a lovely silken gown to go to court didn't seem right somehow.

So I brooded on this while Gwen and I held our needles in sticky hot hands and did our best to make neat stitches. Gwen took to sewing like a duck to water, but as for me, 'dog's teeth', they called my neatest stitchery. I dressed my dolls by the simple method of cutting a hole in the centre of the material, pushing the doll's head through and tying a sash around the middle. Some of today's young things look as though their dresses are made by the same instant dress method. I must have been years before my time!

We had an absolutely foolproof method of sharing the bundle of pieces, when Auntie Rosie brought them home. We'd spread them out on the table, and toss a coin. The winner would choose one piece, and the loser make second choice. But in case there should be an odd number of special pieces, second choice would also have third choice and number one would have the fourth piece. We always felt this was fairer than taking turn about. We had the same 'fair' method for sharing an apple, an orange or a bar of chocolate. One of us would cut the thing in half and the other would choose which piece she'd have. Never were apples or oranges cut more exactly in halves!

On the whole I was far more interested in the *Daily Mirror* which Auntie brought home from work, than all the bits of silk and velvet. While I was only supposed to read the 'Pip Squeak and Wilfred' bit, I often managed quite a bit more before they took the paper away from me.

My grandma and grandad, Jane and Joe Ware, c. 1880.

'No, Dods,' they'd say gently, 'nice little girls don't read things like that.'

I could never understand why I couldn't read whatever I wanted to. I used to take books that people had loaned to Mum, and read them in the lav, a favourite haunt of mine. I still recall reading *Beyond Pardon*, *A Woman's Temptation* and any Bertha M. Clay books I could lay my hands on, seated on that scrubbed wooden throne in the back yard. I used to take *The Red Letter* and *Family Journal* out there too, tucked inside my petticoat.

Sometimes, I got so carried away that I stayed too long, and when I eventually came out there would be a dose of liquorice powder waiting for me, sure cure for constipation in our house.

When I see today's children picking up their mothers' magazines and reading them, I sometimes shudder, for so much information is outspoken these days, when it was only vaguely hinted at then. 'How to Reach a Climax' I saw in one well-known magazine, lying in a classroom of 7-year-olds. It taught me a thing or two!

None of today's mums seem to turn a hair when their small fry take up and read adult articles. Maybe in these days when so many children can't master the art, the parents are only too glad to see their offspring reading anything more than comic strips.

Sometimes, when Dad came home in a bad mood, I would steal away and sit by Janet's fire and get her to talk about the 'old days'. We never tired of hearing these fascinating tales, although my mum was scathingly unromantic about them. Janet would tell how Joe, her six-foot-two Irish lover, would sit her upon the window sill to say goodnight, and how they would wander off into Epping Forest and dream up plans for a wonderful future. After they were married, Joe would go out and spend whole days dreaming beautiful designs for furniture, which were going to make their fortune when someone took them up. But she never told how he failed to provide his family with food, and how my mum had screaming hysterics when faced with a cod's head for dinner for the fourth day running. 'It was the eyes I couldn't stand,' Mum would say. 'It sat there on the plate glowering at us all, steaming and smelling.'

When the money ran out, the family used to run out too. 'Doing a moonlight flit,' they called it; stealing away at night without paying the rent. Rooms were easy to find and sometimes it would be my mum, Bertha, who found a new place for the family. You just had to take a vase, or something like that, and stand it on the mantelpiece, and that was the accepted deposit.

On one occasion, the family was in dire straits and moved into two small rooms. 'Only room for two children,' said the landlady. So Janet nodded and took the place, taking the two under school-age children with her. The other three were let in after dark, with whispered admonitions to creep quietly. It was a hard life, but Janet never complained.

'Your father did his best,' she would remonstrate mildly, when my mum was leading off about him. 'He couldn't help being off work for weeks at a time with asthma.'

'No,' replied Mum, 'but what about the time when he did a full week, after being away for weeks. How did the money go then?'

This was a story that Mum never tired of telling. Janet had sat for hours on the Saturday afternoon, awaiting the return of her loving spouse. Shawl round her thin shoulders and shopping bag at the ready, she was only too anxious to get out and buy some decent food.

At length he staggered home, smiling and beaming upon them all. 'Janey,' he slurred, 'you're a good little wife to me. Never complain when things are hard, always ready to put up with the hard life.' So saying, he kissed his tiny wife and handed her a little box. 'I've bought you a present to celebrate. Good little wife you are.'

The little box contained the most exquisite pocket watch, a lovely little timepiece with roses adorning its face.

'Oh, Joe, I've never had anything so lovely,' breathed his wife. She wrapped it up reverently, after showing her daughters, and put it in her old brown bag. 'And now Joe,' she murmured, wrapping the old black shawl tightly round her, 'can you let me have some money to get a bit for tomorrow? I thought maybe a nice bit of beef . . .'

'Money? Money?' interrupted the old man, sorrowfully. 'Oh Janey, haven't I just given you a lovely present? I've spent my all on you, and now you ask for more! Janey, have you any idea of the value of that little watch?'

So Janet took the little watch straight to the pawnshop, and it was my mother, who had just started work at three and six a week, who finally redeemed it. It keeps good time even now, though my mother was 87 when she died. My sister has it still.

'There was no RO in those days,' said Mum darkly. 'When you didn't have any money, you went without. And we went without frequently.'

I don't think Mum approved of the RO man, although he was a frequent visitor in our street. It was years before I realised his real title was the Relieving Officer, but I knew him just as a man who called on the scruffy families and the out-of-work ones. The little shops along Grove Road all had a notice bearing the same legend: 'RO tickets taken here.' I saw these bits of paper handed over for bread and potatoes and meat, but we never had them. We paid with real money. Neither did we ever say 'on the book', magic words that meant that the customer handed over neither money nor ticket.

Some of our shops had notices up though. 'Please do not ask for credit.' I wasn't sure what credit meant, but it seemed to me that lots of shops didn't sell it, because I often saw people come in and ask for something in a whisper, and the shopkeeper would shake his head and point to the notice, and the customer walked sadly away.

There was one pie shop in Green Street which had a framed verse hanging up.

> Some people came and I did trust them,
> I lost my money and their custom,
> I'll not give credit any more,
> So do not ask me, I implore.

There was a whole row of shops at the top of our street, starting with the baker's on the corner. I always enjoyed going for the bread. Every loaf was weighed before it was wrapped, on a shiny brass swinging scale, and very often, if it was just under the two pounds, a make-weight was added. Sometimes this was a lovely piece of plaited crust, and I would hurry home and spread it thickly with margarine and yellow sugar. I'd sit on the doorstep and crunch it slowly, licking my fingers and enjoying every crumb. Only Dad had butter every day; we only had butter on Sundays or when we had visitors to tea. Occasionally, the make-weight was a bun, yesterday's bake perhaps, but very acceptable. Sometimes we would get a bun even if the weight was not short. At threepence-halfpenny a loaf, bread was good value.

Next door to the baker's was a greengrocer's. We didn't like them much, so we'd jump up and try to touch the blinds as we passed, just to make them mad. But we could always get bruised apples there, and a couple would only cost us a ha'penny. Sometimes I'd get one for nothing, when I went to get a 'penn'orth o' poterbs!' – the cockney name for a couple of carrots, onions and turnips for a stew.

The butcher was next, and time and again I went there for two separate halves of sausages. Never a single pound, although they were for our dinner. Two halves meant that the scale had to go down twice over, and often gave one more sausage than the pound would have given. My mum was up to all the money-saving tricks. On Saturday mornings we sometimes went there for a shoulder of lamb. 'A nice lean one for about two and nine.' If Mum wanted belly of pork then she'd go herself, because I didn't like to ask for belly, and besides, I might get one that was too fat. My cousin, faced with this awful problem, once asked for a piece of stomach of pork and got laughed at. But Mum didn't mind. 'Want it scored?' the butcher would ask, and when Mum nodded, then he'd yell to the boy in the shop, 'Score this lady's belly, Jim.' Mum would laugh and take it all in good part, but I used to blush if I was with her.

After the butcher, the fishmonger, where I often stood patiently waiting for a soft roe bloater for Dad's tea. Squeeze, squeeze, squeeze, the poor man would pick up all his bloaters one by one until he found a soft one. And all for threeha'pence.

On the corner of the next street was a small grocer's, quaint even by our standards. Two spinsters ran it, thin grey women with sniffy noses. The shop was as clean as a new pin, and the scales which hung from ceiling height were polished so brightly that you could see your face in them. The butter sat on a white marble slab, and when you went in for a quarter, the lady would whack a small piece into shape with big wooden beaters.

It was an expensive shop and we didn't use it regularly, but it was useful for odd buys, or when the weather was really hot, when we would take a glass dish for the butter in case it melted by the time we got home. I'd never heard of a fridge, and the only icebox I knew belonged to the Italian man who stood on the corner of the street in summer, selling lovely lemon ice wafers for a ha'penny. Sometimes ice was delivered in big carts to the butcher and fishmonger, and the boys would try and steal pieces off the cart. We'd pick up a piece if it fell to the ground, but that wasn't often.

Across the next street was the inevitable pawnshop on the corner, and every Monday morning there was a little bunch of women with a bundle each, patiently waiting for the shop to open. They mostly laughed too. 'Just waiting for me wardrobe to open,' they'd call, for they would redeem their husband's suit every Saturday and take it back again on the Monday. There were some people, though, who slipped into the pawnshop quickly and shamefacedly: these were the ones who were getting pretty desperate and needed money quickly. I used to look in the window at the pretty rings and watches, but never set foot inside. Mum was scathing about women who always went to the pawn.

Next door to the pawn was a sweet shop and tobacconist. I was more often in there for a twopenny packet of Woodbines or a sixpenny packet of Gold Flake for Dad than for anything else, because I knew a shop in Green Street where sweets could be had for a penny a quarter, and it was well worth the long walk to save money like that. Gwen and I would share a whole quarter sometimes. Another grocer, where the old man would take about five minutes to slice 2 ounces of 'corned beef' and another five minutes to wrap it, and then a clock and watch shop and an estate agent's completed the next row of shops.

Further along still were other shops, including the post office, the chemist and the oil shop. The last name I dreaded, for rumour had it that the woman there was a witch, and I was dead scared. She always wore a shapeless bowl-like hat pulled well down over her eyes, and she had to peer up under the brim to look at you. Her hands were grimy and smelt of the paraffin and her nose dripped continually. Her coarse apron was always grubby and I loathed going in, though of course we had to have a new mantle sometimes for the gas.

'Dad says will you please make sure it isn't broken,' I would whisper, wishing with all my heart that I hadn't to stay while she took the fragile mantle out of its box and put it back again before wrapping it. 'And don't break it on the way home,' she'd snap, handing it to me with a sniff.

I hated buying paraffin, or a pint of vinegar, but it wasn't quite so bad when I went there with a basin for three penn'orth of jam, or two penn'orth of black treacle. Then I could walk back slowly, sticking my finger in the basin and having a few licks as I walked. These errands were mostly for neighbours though, because Mum bought our jam and treacle in tins or jars. Dad wouldn't eat oil shop jam, anyway, because he said he could taste the paraffin in it.

The chemist was a delight. It was no ordinary shop, being owned by a manufacturing chemist who had his factory next door to the feather factory. Most of his stuff was sold under quaint names, or formula numbers. There was a lovely one for children's coughs and it was worth getting a cough to have a bottle. Another one was very good for colds; Dad swore by this one and was never without it. When the bottle was empty, he would use it for polish, as he did all the empties.

One day he was sent by his firm on an outdoor job – that is, to repolish a surface in a private house; and he came into the room to find the lady of the house delving into his little black case of bottles. She looked up guiltily and said, 'Well, polisher, you've made such a good job of my table that I'm taking down the name and address and formula number of the magic liquid you've used. I shall get myself a bottle and do my own repolishing in future.'

Dad came home in a high good humour that night. 'Silly old cow,' he chortled, 'I'd like to see the mess that cold mixture will make of her furniture.'

He disliked intensely the 'jumped up newly rich' he visited. They never offered him a cuppa, and he might have walked two or three miles from the nearest station. There were no cafés around these new housing estates and he might have to go all day without a drink. But if they were decent and offered him a drink, or a bite to eat at mealtimes, then he'd do little extra jobs, or give them a drop of linseed oil and polish.

There was another shop I hated almost as much as the oil shop. This was the 'orf licence' and I was often asked to go there by the pipemakers, who must have drunk an awful lot. Almost every day, Mrs 'Awkey would come to the street door and stand swaying in the passage until she could catch an unwary child to send up the 'orf licence'. The reasons we hated going were threefold. First, it was a fair distance away and across the main road, secondly, the jug was a heavy old thing and hard to carry home without spilling, and thirdly, she was a rotten payer. Rarely more than a ha'penny, even if we had both a jug and a bottle to carry, and sometimes it was just a

Our once-yearly trip to Southend with Sunday school.

'see you later on' and nothing more. So when we saw that big, fat, swaying tummy appear round the doorway, even before we saw the head, we made ourselves scarce. She had a habit of nodding too, nod nod nod, with her arms folded in her apron and her bag at her feet, waiting to catch someone, while we huddled quietly in a doorway and waited for the danger to pass.

Her own two daughters worked hard. They were always doing something about the house, singing as they worked. They were both very musical. It amazes me that they never had a piano lesson, yet they could both play all the latest tunes, singing in lovely tuneful strong voices. Those two could have made a fortune with a pop group in these days. One was called Hilda, but I never knew that until I met her in school. With Hawkey as a surname, it was a poor choice. 'Ildrawkey' was her name, as far as we were concerned. Her mother called her Illy.

On the opposite side of the main road was a big pub, and I never knew it by any other name than the 'Vic'. 'Up the Vic' was the usual answer of the children when asked where their mother was. Most of these 'Vic' women wore their husband's old cloth cap by day, with an old coat or jacket slung round their shoulders, or a black shawl if they were old. They would leave off work, even on washing day, as soon as the pub opened in the morning, and pop up the 'top' for a quick drink. Sometimes they were still sitting there yarning when the children came home from school at dinnertime. Then they'd rush home and give the kids broken biscuits or an egg for their dinner because there wasn't time to cook anything decent.

Mum never went alone to a pub and was sharp tongued about those who did, but we always went up to the Vic to see them all set out on their yearly outing. They were already laughing and shouting rude things even before the charabanc set off for Southend, but they didn't wear cloth caps and coarse aprons then. 'Done up to the nines,' Mum would say. As they set off they would throw ha'pennies out to the gathered children, and everyone would scramble for them, but this practice was stopped after several children were injured diving for the money under horses' hooves and bikes.

Gwen and I had other means of making a penny too. My choice was baby minding and I'd take anyone's baby out, up and down the street for hours and, when I got a bit older, to Victoria Park for a whole morning. I used to love doing this, especially if it was a nice, clean baby in a posh pram. I'd pretend I was a nursemaid, and I'd walk sedately behind a couple of real nursemaids in the park, until at last they began to talk to me. I really fancied myself then, for they wore uniforms and talked of their employers as madam. I thought how wonderful it would be to be a nursemaid, and always have a posh pram with silk covers and sun canopies. What bliss to spend a whole morning in such company. And then, when I got home I'd get a penny, or even a silver threepenny bit, for having enjoyed myself!

Gwen wasn't so keen on the babies. She took in mangling! We had a big heavy wringer in the scullery, and Gwen would call and collect washing, ready folded, from several of the neighbours, and put it all through our mangle. Once for thin things and twice for the thick ones. A hefty task for a little shrimp of about 8, but she'd earn two or three pennies in this way, and it would save the women hours of ironing.

Mum and Dad on a day trip to Southend, 1928.

    Occasionally, we'd collect up all the empty jam jars and take them up to the grocer's in Green Street. About half an hour's walk this, but you could only take jars back to the shop where they came from. A farthing on each pound jar, and a ha'penny on a two-pound one. It was a heavy struggle to take a bob's worth of jars back, but well worth the trouble, especially before excursion days.

    There were two excursion days in our young lives. One was the Sunday school excursion, either to Southend or Loughton, and the other the Band of Hope, always to Southend. These two days, and perhaps an occasional one day a year with our parents, made up the whole of our summer holiday by the sea.

    The Band of Hope was held at the Lycett Methodist Church in the Mile End Road, nearly 2 miles from our home. But we went to the Lycett every week, and signed the pledge every week, too!

    At seven o'clock on one Saturday morning a year, we were marched to Stepney station, five or six hundred of us, and taken to Southend for the day. I was always so relieved to get on to the train. There was a notice just inside the station which read: 'Loiterers will be treated as trespassers', and it was this which scared me stiff. For even the Lord's Prayer knew about this awful notice, and every week at Sunday school, and every morning in day school, we all prayed 'Lead us not into Stepney station,' right in the middle of the Lord's Prayer. So it was very important not to stop there a minute longer than was necessary. What might not happen, if you were unfortunate enough to have to wait there for a train and get accused of loitering!

I loved Southend! When we went on the excursion, we prayed and prayed for a fine day, and usually got it too. With a whole shilling to spend we were millionaires for the day: we could buy a plate of cockles and have an ice cream and a 'go on the mat' (a big helter-skelter outside the Kursaal) and even a threepenny boat ride. We paddled and built sandcastles and crammed all our bliss into one day.

Once, watching a poor bloke playing an accordion and not collecting much for his efforts on the beach, Gwen and Jean started dancing, a pretty little dance they had learnt at school. People stopped to watch them and, not to be outdone, I joined in with my hopeless voice and sang. 'There's a blue ridge round my heart Virginia,' I warbled, all out of tune, but powerful. And soon the pennies started pouring into the hat and the onlookers clapped the dancing.

The bloke was delighted, gave us a penny each and asked us if we'd like to come up the beach a bit further with him. But we had to decline, as we were soon off to tea.

Tea wasn't much. Just the usual jam sandwiches and plain or fruit cake to follow, but as we'd spent all our money and eaten all our dinnertime bread and dripping, we were glad enough to eat up every crumb.

Then home we went on the train, everyone accounted for and nothing worse than a scorched neck or a grazed knee between the whole party. Rock for Mum and Dad and Eva and jelly sweets for Janet. What a day!

In some ways, it was even more exciting on the rare occasions when Mum and Dad took us. This time, we would get up early on a Sunday morning and walk to Bow station, for there was a cheap train from there. The platform was solid with people long before the train steamed in from Fenchurch Street, and I used to pray like mad that we wouldn't be standing by train bumpers or a guard's van when it stopped. We would shove and push our way in, almost as solid a mass as the people waiting for the tube of today in rush hour, and as long as we had one seat for Mum, we'd be glad. There would be children on the racks and all over the floor and on everyone's laps, but for two and ninepence it was worth a bit of discomfort. Once there, we would stream down the High Street, just as we did with the Band of Hope, but once we reached the front, things would be different. We would make straight for one of the big pubs, probably the Ivy House for they had a sort of gallery in the yard, lined with trestles and benches. There we would sit and eat our bread and cheese and tomatoes, and Mum would cut us thick pieces of cucumber, while Dad went down to get a couple of pints. Then we'd enjoy all the excitement down below, where the firms' outings would be gathered in full force, wearing saucy hats and dancing 'Knees up Mother Brown', showing their knickers, and singing 'Bye Bye Blackbird'. They'd be drunk of course, but safely up there in the balcony, we'd be out of harm's way and could laugh at all the fun.

After Dad had downed a couple of pints, we'd leave the excitement of the pub and go to the beach. Until afternoon closing time, Dad would keep on popping back to the pub, while Mum sat leaning against a breakwater, keeping an eye on us while we paddled. All too soon, the wonderful day would end and packed tightly in the train, clutching a straw bag of oysters and a jarful of cockles in vinegar, we would journey happily home and wait patiently for another year.

Mum used to talk hopefully about spending a whole week in this haven of perfection, but Dad had no paid holiday and could never afford to save a whole week's wages. He never felt aggrieved about working fifty-two weeks a year; he was just grateful for having the work. So we made the most of our day and spent the rest of our school holidays in Victoria Park with just a couple of trips to Loughton.

Loughton! What joyous memories we had of Epping Forest. Dad loved it too: he knew all the main footpaths, all the birds and trees, and a walk there with him was an education in itself. Besides, there were no pubs in the forest, which added to its attraction for me, and it was not until we had walked the 3 or 4 miles from Loughton to the Wake Arms that Dad took of liquid refreshment. But he never drank too much there. He was himself, a truly happy man, among the trees and the birds. We even saw deer there sometimes, when we sat quiet and still. Dad would fill all his pockets, and ours too, with the soft brown leaf mould, and carry it home and put it reverently around his rose bush.

If only we had been able to live there, his life, and ours in consequence, would have been so different. He whistled as he walked, he didn't smoke his endless cigarettes and he didn't even swear. He was in heaven and forgot all his troubles and perplexities.

When Loughton first started building semis, Mum had a wild dream of going there to live. She even saved the £10 deposit once, and found a builder who would pay all our moving expenses if we'd buy one of his houses. As an added attraction, we could have a £5 rebate off the cost of the house if we undertook the scrubbing out and cleaning up of the new house. So glad were they of buyers of new houses in those days. But never would Dad sign on the dotted line. 'All that debt,' he would roar. 'Me, buy a house and get into debt for five hundred pounds! Me, who never bought anything at all on the never-never! You must be mad!'

In vain Mum pointed out fearfully that the repayments would not be any more than we paid in rent, but there was no moving my father and we never got to live in Loughton.

The Sunday school took us there once a year, but this outing was a much more select affair than the Lycett treat. There were plenty of teachers to control the children and there were no rough elements such as we met up with at the Band of Hope. We took a big ball and played games together, and although we enjoyed it the whole thing lacked the excitement of the Southend 'do'.

Funnily enough, although I loved day school, I was very loath to join the Sunday school. My older sister started going at about 11, and after a few weeks she took my two younger sisters with her, where they loved being in the infant department.

Mum certainly encouraged this, although Gwen would sometimes stuff the knuckle bone from the shoulder of lamb in her pocket, to eat when she got there.

Thinking back, those lonely Sunday afternoons were among the highlights of my week. No sisters to interfere or quarrel with, and the undivided attention of the aunties or Janet, if they happened to be about. No one chivvied me about staying at home as long as I played quietly, until the sad day when Steve gave me one of his tiddlers after a fishing trip over the canal wall. I was delighted; put the fish in a jam jar and ran with it into the house. No one around – my parents had gone up to bed for their afternoon nap. I dashed up the stairs, barging straight into their bedroom with my tiddler, my face beaming with pleasure.

Dad let out a roar of disapproval as I stood, open-mouthed and wide-eyed, for it seemed to me that he was being cruel to my mum, just about squashing every breath out of her, lying on her side on the bed! Before I could say so though, they

The organ and the pulpit in Victoria Park Church.

both roared at me to get out and stay out! I couldn't believe it. Mum shouting like Dad! I picked up my tiddler and retired, quaking in advance at the row I was going to get. Downstairs, I went into the garden and killed the little fish, swishing it down the lav. Strangely enough, nothing more was said about the affair, and it all blew over, or so I thought.

On the following Sunday, I stood watching my sisters getting ready for Sunday school, when Father, in that dreadfully quiet voice that heralded the storm, told me to get my coat on.

'But I don't go to Sunday school,' I quivered, wondering at my own daring in opposing him.

'Then it's high time you did, you bloody little heathen. You'll go, if I have to kick you up the backside all the way!' So saying, he flung me and my coat out of the door, muttering something about little snoopers. I snivelled all the way there, and Eve told me sharply to stop bawling, giving me a clip round the ear for good measure.

The Sunday school was large, cold and dark, being held in the huge basement hall underneath the Victoria Park Baptist Church. There were about 200 children gathered there, and they were singing lustily when I was ushered in by my sister. There was a tall, thin man standing on a platform, a kindly looking soul with gold-framed glasses and red cheeks. The classes were just groups of forms, three forms around a chair, where the teacher sat. I was placed in a class with girls of my own age, while all the boys sat on the opposite side of the hall. There were several men walking around to keep order, but it all looked quite interesting, and I felt that Sunday school might not be such a bad place after all. Besides, it would be easy to talk to God here and I might have some more prayers to be answered.

But my content was short lived. The girl beside me gave me a shove, so I promptly turned and trod hard on her foot. She was a nicely dressed, brown-haired girl with big brown eyes, but there was no welcome for me in those eyes.

'I'll stand no nonsense from you,' she whispered cuttingly, under cover of her hymn book. 'That happens to be my father up there,' nodding towards the platform, 'and one word from me and you'll be punished.'

'All right, show-off,' I shrugged. 'And my father just happens to be head policeman of Bethnal Green, and one word from me and you'll go to prison.' So we sat and bristled like two tom-cats, and it was nearly nine years before we really spoke to each other.

My father was always the policeman when I was in trouble. When I got pushed off a swing, or some boys tormented me, I was always going to tell the head policeman, my father. This faith in the police is still widespread. I have a friend who, when widowed, asked a policeman neighbour if he would let her have an old police hat. This she keeps in prominent display on a hall table just inside the front door, and she is sure it deters unpleasant callers.

Unlike my imaginary father, this girl's father really was the Sunday school superintendent, and I envied her with all my heart. She really was a somebody in that Sunday school.

Before we came out, we sang a closing verse, called a vesper. It was a nice quiet tune and I enjoyed it. Only one thing puzzled me though. The last line was 'Grace and peace and joy. Bisto.' Why on earth they had to put gravy powder on the end of that verse beat me. It was ages before I knew it was 'bestow'.

After a few weeks, I settled down and stayed the course, so that years later when my dad complained about me being so damned holy, I smiled inwardly and longed to remind him that it was he who kicked me into the Kingdom of God, anyway. Yet he never went to church himself, only on the rare occasions of hatch, match and despatch.

The Band of Hope was entirely different. Held on a Monday evening, it attracted so many children as to need two sittings. We would queue up for about three-quarters of an hour, and the line was so long by the time the doors opened that there would be another 300 or so waiting to get in when we came out. Some of the children came out and tagged on to the end of the queue again, so much did they enjoy it.

Yet it was a very simple meeting, really. We sang cheerful hymns, flashed on a big screen, lovely hymns about drinking pure water and not yielding to temptation. One favourite was

> Give me a draught from the crystal stream,
> When the burning sun is high

Not that any of us had even seen a crystal stream, but it was a nice gooey tune and we could really yell. But the top favourite appealed to me very much, the words had so much meaning for me:

> As on the path of life we tread,
> We come to many a place,
> Where if not careful we may fall,
> And sink into disgrace.

There was a really rousing chorus, which we yelled at the top of our voices.

> Don't step there, don't step there, don't step there,
> For if not careful you may fall, don't step there.
> The drinker's path is one beset with many a hidden snare,
> Oh, shun the drink shop's fatal spell, I warn you,
> Don't step there.

After the hymns the lights were lowered and we had a story, illustrated by magic lantern slides. A deep hush settled over us as we listened to the lovely stories. Nearly always about poor children living in hovels, whose fathers drank away every penny. My dad was a saint compared with these fathers. How we all wept, when father stole the blankets off the children's bed to take to the pawnshop for drink money. And we sobbed audibly when mother walked the streets in the snow to get help for her sick baby, clasped to her breast for warmth, while dad lay in a drunken stupor on the bare-boarded floor. Then the minister or the vicar met up with the family, and when the dog collar went into the hovel, the sin went out. Father broke down and admitted the evil of his ways, all the family were saved, father got a job immediately; and they all lived happily ever after. This was the bit I found hard to swallow. I knew that even good men, when they lost their job, didn't easily get another. But I supposed the minister helped them, because the last picture showed them all well dressed and smiling, sitting in a well-furnished room with flowers in a vase on the table, and even the sick baby had taken a miraculous turn for the better and was now a chubby darling sitting on father's knee.

Then the lights went up and we sang another hymn and made for the door, taking a ticket and signing the pledge, week after week. 'I promise to abstain from all intoxicating drinks as beverages.' I didn't understand the last bit, but this one thing I knew. That ticket was my all-important pass to the Lycett Christmas party.

Every week, the signed ticket was handed in; they must have needed quite a staff to cope, and when the time came for the party, the party tickets were numbered according to the attendances made during the year.

The party was good fun, including a pantomime given by some of the children. One year I was chosen to take the part of one of the ugly sisters in *Cinderella*. I wasn't very excited about this, because Eva kept teasing me and saying how well chosen I was for the part. 'They must have taken one look at you and realised you wouldn't even need any make-up,' she laughed. But I did my best, knowing that I'd been chosen because I would speak up and be heard throughout the hall.

After the pantomime, a sing-song, and then, the highlight of the party – The Present. We sat in rows, according to our ticket numbers, with the highest attendances in front. There, on display, was the most wonderful collection of toys. Dolls by the dozen, dressed in every hue, books and games and cars and wooden horses. We came out in turn, to choose one thing from the array. There was no time for sympathetic pondering though. Your mind had to be made up before you got to the front. If you hesitated, you'd get handed anything the helper thought fit. A money box or jigsaw maybe, or any ordinary thing.

Gwen and I, together with our cousin Jean, always contrived to get in the front row, with a full attendance record. We always wanted a doll, nothing else entered our heads and we'd even prepared our other dolls beforehand. 'We are going to buy you a new sister,' we'd say, as we set off.

We'd count the boys in front of us, knowing they could safely be relied on to choose something else, and then make our choice. 'The doll in the pink dress, or if it's gone, the one in the blue. Then the black-haired one . . .'. We had them all lined up in order of preference. Gwennie would always choose a black-haired doll, probably because it was like her, with her tight black curls. That was apart from her one stringy strand in the front. She had a habit of sucking this curl, and it always hung damp and limp at the side of her face.

After the present we lost interest in the party until the end, when we were given a big paper bag as we made our way out of the church. Into it went the inevitable orange, but what a store of other goodies beside! Nuts and sweets and chocolate, and a whole packet of figs! It was a Christmas feast in itself, and well worth the trotting those 2 miles there and back, rain or shine, every Monday evening.

But what if one of us couldn't make it? Maybe a bad cold or something would keep us away. Did we lose our front seat for full attendance? Not a bit of it! The one who got there would hold out two hands at the doorway in the great push out, one hand to one helper and the other to another and like as not we'd get a pledge ticket thrust into either hand. No one noticed in that crush and we gleefully took home the extra ticket.

4

Street Callers

There was always something going on in our street; you never saw it empty for long. The milkman came twice, even though the dairy was in our street. The first call was very early and he hung the cans of milk on the door-knockers. But he came back at midday and this time he loitered, making half a dozen stops in the street. We took out our empty can, paid him for the morning half pint, and took a clean jug out for another penn'orth. He would dip his long-handled metal measure into the churn of creamy milk and pour it into the jug, giving an extra dash as a bonus. He would stand and kick a ball for a few minutes with the boys, or pause to admire a new baby. At first, he just had a handcart, but after a while he had a horse, a good-tempered beast who'd let us all give him a pat, or take a sugar lump from our hands. We all liked the milkman.

In the summer months, we loved the water cart. A slow, ponderous animal pulled this cart, and the water came out in a spray, the full width of the cart. He'd come down one side, turn in the court, and go back up the other, to be followed after about half an hour by a road sweeper. If it was very hot and the driver wasn't looking, we'd sometimes take off our shoes and socks and walk after the cart, letting the cold water spray on to our legs. Mum got mad at us if we did it, but if she was out shopping we'd join in with the rest and it was good fun.

There was 'Ole moaney gabbert', too. Every morning we heard him coming down the street, calling out, 'Ole moaney gabbert'. He was the greengrocer, and it was years before I knew that his cry was meant to be 'All morning gathered'. Anyway, everyone called him 'Ole Moaney', but he was a very pleasant red-faced man and his stuff was good. His prices were higher than Green Street or Roman Road, but then, you paid to have stuff brought to the door. Mum didn't get much from him, since, as she so often said, it paid to watch every penny. So she went, at least twice a week, either to Green Street or Roman Road. If you walked up Grove Road to the Aberdeen crossroads, there was a market in either direction. Roman was dearer than Green Street, but a little bit posher: not many second-hand stalls or scruffy ones there, and not so many scruffy people either. So Mum mostly went to Roman, unless she wanted eels, because the best eel shop was in Green Street.

She always took two shopping bags, both made from real leather. They were chair seats which Dad had brought home from the upholsterer's. She machined them, sewed on thick handles and cut a scalloped pattern all round the top. She'd buy the potatoes, 4 pounds in each, because, like the sausages, you'd get one more this way.

Four pounds for tuppence-ha'penny was the usual price, although King Edwards were threepence.

The hearthstone man came twice a week, and sold both green hearthstone and whitening. We all knew that was the way to get a nice doorstep. First scrub it, then dip the green hearthstone in clean water and rub it on, then cover that with whitening. He did a good trade with us, because Mum whitened the copper and the lav floor as well as the front step. He was a thin-faced little man, who always looked hungry. He was very polite and touched his cap when he gave us the change. I expect he was pretty poor; he needed to sell a lot of hearthstone to make much profit.

The shrimp and whelk man came on Saturday afternoon, soon after the pubs shut. Nearly everyone came out to buy shrimps or winkles for Sunday tea, and a pin was quite a usual accompaniment to the plate when we laid the Sunday tea table. First, you'd prise off the winkle's cap, stab it with the pin, twirl it around and bring it forth in triumph from its shell. Then you'd dip it in vinegar, still on the pin, and pop it into your mouth. If the full ones and empty shells got mixed up on your plate, as they often did, then you'd have to blow into each one. They made a dull sound if full, and a whistling noise if the shell was empty.

The muffin man was a regular, too. He carried his tray of muffins on his head, covered with a white cloth, and rang a handbell as he walked. It always intrigued me that he never lost his balance, and that tray sat on his head as though glued there. It was winter when he came, and the sound of a little brass bell still makes me think of big fires and toasted muffins, all dripping with melted margarine.

How we loved Sunday tea! There was sometimes a jelly, or a head of celery, and in the summer a big cos lettuce. Mum would cut it in big chunks and you could fill the chunk with vinegar and crunch it. We never seem to meet with a real crunchy lettuce these days. Most weekends, Dad had his favourite delicacy: Dutch herring. This we had to go and buy on a Sunday morning from the Jewish shop in Green Street. We had to take a plate with us, and fight our way into the overcrowded little shop. Most people seemed to run out of things on Sunday morning, because it was always jam-packed. Dad liked the bread there too, big shiny loaves covered with seeds on the scrumptious crust.

No one ever queued, so you just worked your way in towards the counter and kept on shouting, 'A threeha'penny Dutch herring please.' At length the old shopkeeper, in his greasy coat and cap, would grab the plate, roll up his sleeve and dive his arm into a vinegar-filled barrel near the door, and come up with a slimy, slithery pickled herring, slap it on the plate and cover it with a scrap of plain paper.

One Sunday morning Eva had been sent for the herring, a job we all hated; and when she reached home, the plate was empty! Fortunately, she found out before she knocked at the door, and she went skeltering back the way she had come. In the next street she found Dad's herring lying on the pavement, too salty even to be eaten by a stray dog, though heaven knows how many might have sniffed it. Anyway, she picked it up, put it back on the plate and took it home without telling anyone. Poor Dad. So often things happened and we didn't tell. He did go so barmy if we told.

One day, our black cat pinched his Saturday steak from the frying pan. One minute, it was just beginning to sizzle gently, and the next, the pan was empty and the cat purring under the sink. Mum dived after him with the copper stick and managed to retrieve the meat. She put it under the tap and back into the pan smartly, but knew she didn't have to say 'Don't tell your father' to the onlooking girls. The cat might have gone into the canal in a sack if we told, as we well knew. So Dad ate his steak, germs and all, because, as Mum often said, 'what eye don't see, heart don't grieve over'.

Mum liked that cat, but she had her problems with him. Dad never allowed the cat on the bed, and one evening, going up in the semi-darkness, Mum spotted him asleep on the bed. She grabbed a stinger, the small sharp cane she used on our legs, and whacked hard at the offender, only to find to her horror that it was not the cat on the bed but Dad's best bowler. He never did find out what caused that dent.

The cat was a dreadful thief, but he was a wonderful mouser and ratter. In fact, the feather factory welcomed him with open arms, and an open window too, and night after night he brought home a dead rat. We would hear his plaintive mewing outside in the yard and rush out to see what he had brought home. He never brought in his finds, but left them as offerings on the back doorstep. Occasionally it was not a rat, but a still-wriggling shiny fish which he had caught from the canal. Once it was a half-cooked, still-warm kipper! Not wanting trouble with the neighbours, Mum rushed and took it from him and threw it in the dustbin, but minutes later, old Tim was back with the kipper's mate, and this time he retreated behind the coal bunker to eat his meal in peace.

The only time he made a mistake was when he landed smack in the cold canal, while trying to catch a seagull. He came home a sadder and wiser cat, and Mum dried him and sat him by the fire.

He was not a jealous cat and was most protective towards my cat, a tiny ginger one, which we had trained to do lots of tricks. This cat played high jump with us, and would take his turn over the rope stretched across the garden. In fact, so used did he become to this jumping exercise that he would run and leap over the rope if we left it there when perhaps we went in for tea, never thinking to run straight under. We made him a swing from a shopping basket hung on the clothes line, and this so delighted him that he would climb in and sit and mew plaintively for a push whenever anyone passed by. At mealtimes, if father was not around, we would sit him up to the table, where he would eat daintily from a doll's saucer. I can't recall that he ever caught a mouse, but Tim was there to do that sort of thing.

Janet had a white cat, with one blue and one pink eye, a big fat lazy animal, who felt that his chief role in life was to keep himself clean. All our cats were 'doctored' toms, for Dad would tolerate neither 'shes' having kittens all over the place, nor toms which had not been done, for they were stinking things, wetting up the walls and making the whole yard smell. No, our cats were nice, clean, healthy cats who caused no trouble.

We had a cats' meat man calling every day. He came along the street with a basket on his arm, calling 'meeeeet, meeeeet' as he came. A veritable pied piper was he, with all the cats of the neighbourhood running at his heels. The pieces of meat were threaded neatly on to wooden skewers and he would throw down a skewerful to the customers' cats as he reached their doorway, collecting his penny on the way back. If the door was shut, he would leave the meat under the knockers and I often saw our Tim trying to balance on someone's door handle to reach a knocker full of meat. Today, we shove meat pieces on skewers, dress them up a bit and serve them in la-de-da restaurants, with fancy names like kebabs, but they always remind me of cats' meat.

When my husband was a small boy, he lived over a cats' meat shop. The horseflesh was delivered raw and cooked in the kitchen, so that the smell pervaded the whole house. As for the flies, half a dozen flypapers couldn't cope with them all. They were rowdy roughs, these cats' meat people, and had a bad name in the area. Sometimes on a Saturday night they would fight among themselves, bringing out the big meat knives to threaten each other. The scared little chap upstairs would lie quaking in his bed, hoping that the lock would hold when the drunken meat men went chasing up and down the stairs.

We had other visitors to our street. There were several bakers', for the big combines were gradually beginning to vie with the little local men, and Nevilles and Prices and the Co-op sent their big vans around. They would offer incentives to the women to try their bread, nicely wrapped in printed paper. Sometimes a whole week's bread would be free, and another time there was a half tea service free if one used their bread for six weeks. Of course we did so: Mum was always on the lookout for such offers, but as soon as possible we reverted to the baker with the two-wheeled handcart and the warm crusty loaves he carried. Some of the wrapped bread was steam baked, 'bloody cotton wool', my father called it, and he wouldn't eat it, even when it was free.

The carbolic man called every week, pushing a little handcart and shouting his wares. Mum used a lot of carbolic, and would take out the smelly blue bottle to be filled with the whitish liquid every week. She used it in the lav, on the dustbin, down the drains, and in the water when she scrubbed, over-lavish with it as with most things, and it was no small wonder that her hands were always scarlet and cracked in winter. That was Melrose time. We all used Melrose. It was sold in a little square box and was a yellow, rounded, wax-like lump. We warmed it in front of the fire and rubbed it on our chaps. Not only Mum and Janet had chaps, although theirs were very bad, bleeding in the worst of the winter. We children always had chapped knees, for there were no tights or trews for us, or long trousers for our cousins. No, we all went out and got our knees wet and cold and got chaps and chilblains, and put up with it, accepting such discomfort as a normal part of winter life.

Chilblains were a common complaint every winter, especially on our feet. No fur-lined boots for us. Mum firmly carried out Janet's old-world remedy, old-fashioned even in those days, and today's children would die with horror. I wasn't a bit keen, and I'd keep quiet about my chilblains as long as I possibly could. But the itching eventually gave me away. I had to go and get the big 'Jerry' from under the bed, squat down and produce as much water as I possibly could and then stick my itching feet in it while it was still warm! I can't see that it was a cure, for I seem to remember chilblains every year.

At one time, we had a tape man who called, with his pathetic little supply in an old pram. He was wizened and frail and ancient, and most horribly dirty. 'Tape, tape,' he would cry, stopping the pram every now and again to cough, a dreadful hacking cough. Mum took pity on him once, and bought a couple of yards of tape, so whenever he came along after that, he would stop optimistically at our door. Sometimes Mum would buy linen buttons from him, which she used on workday underwear. Pearl buttons would soon break in our big mangle, but the linen buttons would last and last. One day, the poor old tape man came along later than usual, and as luck would have it, Dad was already home from work, having finished an outdoor job early.

'Tape, tape,' came the quavering voice, when I opened to his knock. 'Not today, thank you,' I replied quickly, knowing that Mum was forbidden to buy at the door.

'Oh me dear, now ask your muvver, ask your muvver, do,' appealed the old man, touching my elbow as he spoke. Poor tape man, he must have wondered what hit him. Dad rushed out of the door and knocked the old man's pram flying.

'Assault my daughter, would you,' he yelled, unfastening his leather belt. The poor old chap gathered his pram, took to his heels and ran, while Dad went in and let rip to Mum about encouraging beggars and tramps. We never saw the tape man again: he gave our street the go-by and I don't blame him.

There were a couple of tally men who came once, trying to get Mum to buy on the never-never. Mum said No, quite firmly, but as she tried to close the door, one of the men put his foot inside, not knowing that Dad was standing there. With a terrific roar, he hurled himself at the young man. 'I'll teach you to step uninvited into my house,' he called, taking off his belt and lashing out. 'An Englishman's home is his castle,' he shouted, giving chase, and the neighbours all came to the doors to watch Joe Clark in his temper. The two men were quicker than Dad and

My dad, 1934.

were soon away, but I knew that Mum was in for a time of it after that. He always blamed her. 'You encourage them,' he would yell, 'looking at them with your soft eyes.'

He always felt bitter towards tramps and buskers and the like, but I suppose he had a point. One bitterly cold Sunday morning, just as we were finishing breakfast, a dirty old tramp called and asked if we would make him a drink of tea. 'Just to warm me guts, guv,' he whimpered to my father who had opened the door. Dad must have had a very good night, because instead of the expected roar, he took the tramp's blue enamelled pot from him and filled it with hot sweet tea. The old fellow took it and shuffled away, muttering his thanks.

'Gone to sit in the park shelter, I expect,' said Mum, half-wishing she had dared give him bread as well. Five minutes later, Mrs Kay, from the corner house called. 'Joe, did you give that old fellow some tea just now? He's just poured it down the drain and now he's knocking on another door. He only wants money.' Dad didn't stop to change his shoes, but put on his cap and chased off up the street. But the wily old devil had seen the red light and was away on a tram before Dad could catch up and bash his brains in, as he had fervently vowed to do.

Occasionally, when there was a glut of anything, the barrow boys would come along, selling peas, or cherries, or ripe strawberries. Ridiculously cheap they were, even for those days, but there was no way to keep soft fruit and it was better to sell it cheap than to waste it all.

Today, modern man has really progressed. Gluts of fruit are ploughed into the ground, good food is chucked into the sea, God's bounty is thrown back in His face, to keep the prices up. We, who were poor folk, could sit on our doorsteps in the summer evening sunshine and eat a whole bag of cherries or Victoria plums, revelling in simple pleasures that today's kids never know.

The old rag-and-bone men who came round were very popular. One pushed a handcart and the other, obviously a more prosperous individual, had a little grey donkey to pull his cart. The handcart man gave money, just a penny or two, for a bundle of rags, but the other, a rosy-faced old chap, gave china. A little plate, for a couple of items, a cup and saucer for a fair bundle, and all three for a big load. How carefully they were chosen, these pieces of china! Possibly, you could match something this week with a piece from the previous week and the old man had all the time in the world. If we had rags, Mum would stand and ponder, trying to decide between a big thick cup for Dad, or a sturdy mug for one of us. She would talk over the decision with the rag man for all the world as though she was paying shillings for the items.

One day, when Rosie was playing with us in the street, the old man gave her a beautiful plate with roses on it. He had stopped and asked her what her name was, and when she smiled and told him 'Rosie', he had patted her head and handed her the lovely plate for her very own, without asking anything for it.

The old iron man who came each week was a stingy old fellow. He would grope around in his pockets in the hope you might say, 'It doesn't matter,' but we knew him, and stood our ground until he handed over something for the leaking iron kettle or old fire irons we gave him. But we accepted the small coins gladly, because as Mum said, it was stuff we'd have thrown in the canal anyway, if he hadn't been coming round.

Sometimes there were street singers, mostly poorly clad men or women, or even both together, who shuffled along in the middle of the road, singing in a croaky voice and looking optimistically up at the windows, or into the open doorways. Sometimes, people would throw down a penny, but often they went the whole length of the street without getting so much as a single coin. Poor things, they made me feel all lumpy in the throat, and if Eva wasn't around, I'd like as not have a good cry over them. Eva always called me a water cart, or a snivelling crybaby, if she caught me crying over nothing. But I wondered what they'd do if they didn't get any money anywhere. Maudie's mum said they only pretended to be poor, and that they went home to big houses on the train, or even owned motor cars, but I found it hard to believe, especially when they wandered up and down the street in the pouring rain, as they often did.

I remember one day when a lavender woman came. She sang in a high-pitched voice, which was surprisingly clear, the old tune we all knew well.

> You buy it once, you buy it twice,
> It makes your clothes smell very nice,
> Scent your pocket handkerchief,
> Put it in your drawers,
> Sixteen full branches, one penny.

She carried her lavender in a big basket on her arm, and she had just reached our court when it started to rain, coming down suddenly and quite hard. The poor woman had no coat, so she folded her apron up over her arms and tried to shelter in the doorway opposite. It was a chilly day and within a few minutes the rain was an absolute downpour. Mum came to the door and stood looking across for a few minutes, and then called to the woman to come and shelter in our passage for a bit, so she wouldn't get so wet.

'Ain't you got a coat?' asked Mum, looking at the thin, wet blouse. The woman shook her head and shrugged her thin shoulders. Mum stood for a few minutes; you could actually see her thinking. Then she went upstairs and came down carrying an old brown coat with a big fur collar. It was not a coat she wore, it was really very old, but was used as an extra blanket on our bed when the weather was very cold. I had often put it on, and played bears with the big fur collar when I was supposed to be asleep in bed.

Diffidently, she held it out and the woman's eyes lit up, and then actually filled with tears.

'You're welcome,' said Mum, 'I never wear it.'

Soon afterwards the rain stopped, and the woman went on her way dressed in the coat, handing me a bunch of her sweet lavender as she went.

'Don't tell your father,' said Mum shortly, but I was so impressed by her kindness, that I saw no harm.

'Mum gave the lavender woman the old brown coat off our bed, and the woman gave me all this lovely lavender,' I told Dad excitedly when he came home that evening.

'I see,' said Dad in his quiet voice, 'I see.' I knew immediately that I should have kept quiet, but it was too late. 'Now I can clothe every old tramp and good-for-nothing devil that comes my way.' His voice began to rise as the storm broke and I fled outside with my lavender, but not before I had seen Mum's tear-filled eyes and the stricken look she gave me as he began his usual tirade. The kids could perish with the cold, she'd be crying and whining for a new coat next winter, and blankets for the bed, but he'd swing first, before he put his hands in his pocket. He was always going to swing first, though I never knew then what he meant.

'Get up the stairs and give them my bloody best suit,' he ranted. 'Plenty more where that came from. I've only got to slave my guts out to dress you all, that's all.'

He stormed out of the house as was usual when he was mad, and I knew that when he came home again he'd be drunk and would start all over again. If only I'd thought before I spoke, I might have known what would happen. 'Big mouth,' snarled Eva at me as I went upstairs, but Mum didn't say anything, she never did – only went quiet and wore her sad face all evening.

Sometimes we had an organ grinder to pay us a visit, and we would run up and crowd around him, joining in if he played the well-known songs. He usually got more pennies than the singers, but the most lucrative buskers were a bunch of men who sometimes came with an organ. They were mostly young fellows, about six or seven of them, all dressed up as women. They wore high-heeled shoes, loads of heavy make-up with big cupid's bow lips, and big balloons down their fronts to make busts. The women, especially the rowdy ones, would join them and have a good laugh, shrieking as the dancing men showed their bloomers, all lace trimmed and hanging down over their knees, and maybe one of the women would go up to give them a penny and stick a hat pin in the huge bosom so that it exploded with a loud bang. What entertainment we enjoyed when they came. They did quite well for pennies, but earned every coin they got.

It was evening time when the tea chest men came. I could never work out why they came, or what they got out of it, but they would occasionally come halfway down the street with a big horse and cart, laden with tea chests, each chest filled to the brim with broken bits of plywood. These they would give away, throwing them down in the roadway and calling to folk to come and get them. They were not much use for firewood, being hard to chop, but we children in particular gathered quite a store. The foil linings could be used for lots of things, and one summer we got two and a half chests at an angle, and there we had the most wonderful dolls' house. We lined it with wallpaper and spent weeks making cardboard and plywood furniture. When it was all finished, we put some of the mice in it and had great fun, watching them run over the chairs and tables we had made. Another time, we peopled it with caterpillars, but Mum drew the line when I tried catching black beetles from the hen run to put in. I was always in trouble for catching creepy-crawlies, for I loved everything that moved, apart from worms. I still hate them, but my hatred probably stems from the day when two big boys in the park put a huge, fat worm down my back. I can still remember how I screamed and screamed, until a passing man stopped and put his hand down my back and brought the pink wriggling thing up. I looked at it and was promptly sick.

The lamplighter was a nice man and we always ran to meet him, trotting with him from lamp to lamp as he lit the gas with a long pole which he carried over his shoulder. If it was winter, we would gather round the lighted corner lamp until our mothers called us in. Occasionally we would persuade Gwen to climb up the lamppost and tie a rope from the crossbar at the top, so that we could swing around the post, heedless of the bruises we gave our shins in the process.

Of all the street callers, though, our favourite was the gas man. Dear gas man, he went on being my favourite for many a year, even after I was married.

He would kneel down in the passage, just by the door, and shake out the big pile of pennies from the meter on to the doormat. Then he'd stack them all up in piles of twelve, and count them into a cloth bag. But it was the next bit we enjoyed. He'd consult the meter, then the little book he carried, write out a receipt and hand it to Mum, with a little pile of pennies back again. The rebate, they called it, but how lovely it was. Mum would always give us one penny each. A whole penny in the middle of the week! Then she'd call over the fence to Auntie Liz and ask her how much she'd got back. Then maybe we'd have a cream doughnut or a cheesecake for tea, or even, if the rebate was good enough, a saveloy or faggot with pease pudding for supper.

This mouth-watering delicacy had to be fetched in a basin from a faggot shop in Roman Road. It was a long way to walk, but it was smashing, especially with lashings of gravy. That's why we always took a big basin, so that they could give lots of gravy. We'd hurry home with the big, hot basin full, and Mum would put it on to hot plates and we'd have it for supper. Never tastes the same nowadays if I make pease pudding and buy faggots, and as for a saveloy, I doubt whether a butcher would know what we meant. It was a big, hot, spicy red-skinned sausage, and you just peeled off the skin and dipped it in the gravy and pudding. Lovely grub.

Some people had things like that for a dinner, but Mum always made it extra, making certain to cook us a good substantial meal every day. It's funny, thinking back, how well we ate. I think she'd have died with fright if she had lived to see the day when a joint of meat could cost several pounds. We were well fed throughout our childhood and if we went short of anything, it was never good food.

5

Victoria Park

Victoria Park was our haven of delight. Even when we were quite young we were allowed to go there alone, and almost every morning of the school holidays we set off, Gwen, Jean from next door and me. Sometimes Eva and the boys would accompany us, but mostly we went by ourselves.

With a ha'penny in our pocket, a couple of slices of bread and dripping and the everlasting doll apiece, we were gone for hours. We had two main roads to cross, but there was always a policeman on point duty at the 'Aberdeen' where there were buses to the city, and we never had any trouble crossing the road. Not possessing a doll's pram didn't worry us in the least: we carried our dolls in a shopping bag and told them everything that was of passing interest.

When we reached the park gate we would spend our ha'penny, usually on a big thick toffee bar which would last, if it was licked carefully and not chewed, until it was time to eat our bread and dripping. What dripping it was too! Usually beef dripping, liberally covered with the gravy which had jelled at the bottom of the basin. Mum would dig it out and cover the dripping, spread on thick crusty bread. Then a dash of salt and it was a sandwich fit for a king. Sometimes it was pork dripping, smooth and creamy, with occasional bits of crackling stuck in it.

We sat on the grass, took the dolls out of the bag, and had a feast. Then we'd wash it down with a drink of water from the nearby fountain, where the old metal cups were chained to the edge, and drink only from the middle of the cup, not letting our lips touch the rim, as we had been taught. This way, we wouldn't get any germs.

There was a boating lake in the park, and we spent ages watching the boats. There were rowing boats for up to four people, but the men who rowed in the single boats skimmed along at a terrific pace. We would watch them round the little island in the centre of the lake, and try to see how many we could count before they came in view again. There was a chugging motor boat too, and it cost a penny to go right round the lake on that. We couldn't afford it often, but we enjoyed watching other people have rides, and very occasionally we had one too. We'd line up, and hope that we'd get a side seat so that we could dangle our hands in the water, but it was all chance, and you couldn't hold back just to get a side seat. If you sat down the middle, that was that.

One of our favourite games was tormenting the parkie. He was not one of the ordinary park keepers, who patrolled the park dressed in a brown uniform with brass

A Sunday outing to Victoria Park, complete with hats and gloves, 1927. I'm behind with my cousin Stephen, and Jean and Gwen are in front.

buttons. The parkie we tormented was in charge of the little island in the centre of the lake. This was approached by two bridges, one on either side, and a big notice stated that unaccompanied children under the age of 14 were not allowed on the island.

We'd creep across the wooden bridge, knees knocking at our own daring, and sneak around the little winding paths with which the island was honeycombed. It was in truth a lovers' paradise, for in every secluded spot was a seat, and right at the centre was a big red pagoda. Old men mostly sat there, warming themselves in the sunshine and yarning about the good old days. Some of them had birds, poor little finches or linnets in tiny cages tied up in a thick, black cloth. We were too used to this spectacle to think of it as cruel, but the poor little birds, deprived of light and freedom, would sing their very heart out as the warm sun shone on the black cloth of their prison. The old men would discuss the merits of their birds, whom they loved in their own way, never thinking of themselves as heartless. I think that some of today's tough youngsters would have mugged these old men, not to steal their pitifully few pennies, but to set free the little birds. But we saw no wrong in it; lots of people had linnets and finches.

Anyway, we'd tiptoe around until we came upon him, the king of the little kingdom, in his plain grey suit and trilby hat.

'Parkie,' we'd yell, taking to our heels. But we'd split up and race off the island in two different directions, using both bridges to make our quick getaway. Poor man! He who hesitates is lost, but he never seemed to learn this, and while he was deciding whom he had best chance of catching, we were off the island and meeting again by the bird aviary, which stood about equidistant from both bridges. There was a white and green cockatoo in this aviary, supposed to be a wonderful talker. Apparently it could swear too, but I never heard it say anything other than 'Pretty Polly'.

Further round the park was another aviary where there were pheasants and Indian geese and, hard by, a rocky enclosure with a few goats. These last were great fun, because they would eat anything we pushed through the bars, and the boys fed them old paper bags and bus tickets as well as the grass.

There were several lots of swings, each in a well-fenced enclosure and presided over by a 'swing lady'. She had a little hut inside the shelter each lot of swings possessed, where she could brew tea, or bandage knees, or chat with her friends, while keeping a watchful eye on the children. She was most vigilant and woe betide any rough who tried to push a small girl off a swing, or who dared to cheek her.

Swing ladies must have been chosen for their toughness; their word was law and no one ever got the better of them. They wore navy hats like the school Nitty Norah, and were equally to be feared. I've seen a swing lady turn everyone out and lock the gates when she saw any misbehaviour. No one ever stood up on her swings and vandalism was a word we'd never heard. Oh, we weren't a saintly lot, far from it, but we were so much more easily satisfied in those days.

But they were very fair women in their dealings with us, and on a busy day they'd line us up and time our swinging so that everyone got a turn. There was a big rounder too, a number of thick ropes hanging from a central pivot. Each rope was looped with a metal end. We stuck our elbow through the loop and tucked it under our armpit, gripped the rope and hung on for grim death, running faster and faster round the post until the rope swung out and our feet left the ground. Some of the bigger girls could get their bodies almost horizontal. But I was a bit scared of that thing and having seen several broken limbs there, I preferred the comparative safety of the swings.

They had a sand pit there but it was a bit grubby and, surrounded by a climbing wall of concrete made to look like a castle, it was always crowded with boys. So there was not much point in playing there, trying to pretend it was the seaside.

One morning I was sitting in the shelter waiting for Gwen to finish swinging, when a woman with two babies in a pram came up and started talking to me. I could never resist babies, and although these were not of the particularly clean variety, I was soon pushing the squeaky pram up and down the shelter. After a little while, the woman, a skinny, poorly clad person with filthy fingernails, asked me to mind the babies while she went to a shop nearby. 'Just outside the gate,' she said, 'I shan't be a few minutes.' I nodded, but pointed out politely that I didn't think there were any shops near the gate.

'Oh, just a little way along,' smiled the woman. 'I'll bring you back a bar of chocolate if you'll look after them.'

For a while I went on pushing the pram, but it was a chilly morning and I was soon anxiously looking for the return of the babies' mother. Gwennie had finished swinging and was getting fidgety.

'Let's go,' she kept saying, but I shook my head. 'I can't leave these poor babies alone. I'm in charge.'

After a time, both babies began to cry, they were getting as fed up as I was. I didn't fancy nursing them, the little one smelt a bit and the bigger one at the bottom end of the pram was more than merely smelly. So I just sat, and sat, and as the morning wore on, Gwen began to grizzle too. She was hungry also; I was in charge of her as well as these rotten babies, and if I didn't soon take her home, she'd run off by herself and go home alone, and then I'd be in trouble. This was too much for me and eventually I burst into tears myself. There we were, all howling together, and at last the swing lady realised that something was wrong.

'What's the trouble?' she asked, in her thin sharp voice. 'Why don't you get along home and take these kids with you?'

I looked at them through my tears. I didn't really think Mum would like them, and besides, I didn't want to go to prison for stealing them.

'They aren't mine,' I blubbered, and out came the whole story.

'But you've been here about four hours,' she exclaimed. 'That woman isn't coming back, you mark my words.' She sent a boy to find a park keeper, and he in turn fetched a policeman. At the sight of his uniformed figure, my tears fell the faster; and when he opened his notebook and asked where I lived, I nearly had hysterics. At last, he took the pram with its squalling occupants and wheeled them away.

'Oh, please, don't take them to prison,' I sobbed, 'they haven't done anything wrong.'

'That's all right, ducks,' said the swing lady, 'they'll go to a nice place where they'll clean them up and give them a good feed.' I'd never seen her with so kindly a face before, and I dried my eyes.

'What about their mum, she'll be so cross with me,' I said fearfully, but the swing lady shook her head. 'She won't be back,' she sniffed, 'and if she does come, I'll give her a piece of my mind.'

At the gate, I hesitated. I hadn't got much out of this morning's work. 'If she comes, and brings me the bar of chocolate she promised, will you tell her I did look after her babies all the morning, and maybe she'll give you the chocolate to mind for me.' The swing lady nodded and we ran all the way home, to where our anxious mum was waiting at the corner of the court.

'That'll teach you not to talk to every bloomin' baby you meet,' said she, but she wasn't really angry, only worried in case we were not home before Dad got in.

Most of our trips were far less eventful, though, and we wandered at will through the big park, where we had names for all the lanes and footpaths. There were peacocks there, and we would stand for ages waiting for them to open their tails, and for a herd of deer who came up and pushed soft noses into our hands. There was a big glasshouse and we would walk quietly through, looking at all the wonderful flowers there, and sniff the hot, humid air. Something has gone wrong with our modern world. I could never imagine my grandchildren being allowed out for hours and hours alone like that. They'd most likely be assaulted, or worse. Yet in all those years, we only once met with trouble, and that we thought was extremely funny.

We had been sitting playing with our dolls on the grass, and a man was standing nearby, watching us thoughtfully. We didn't take much notice and there was no one else around, just us, and the big expanse of grass. Suddenly, he came nearer, much nearer, exposing himself as he did so. We jumped up, packing the dolls quickly into the bag, eyeing him warily. He had a queer look on his face, and somehow, I didn't like it. I tried hard not to look in his direction, but Gwen and Jean started to laugh, commenting on the size of what they saw, comparing it with our cousins. 'Ain't it a whopper,' they shrieked, yelling with glee.

I joined in then, but tried to usher them away. 'I think it's going to rain,' I said firmly. The man just stood there hesitatingly, a glazed expression on his face, then he turned his back on us and wandered away without a backward glance. Our childish laughter was probably the best answer to the situation.

In spite of my warning not to tell Dad, Gwen could hardly wait to get into the house before she came out with it, and Dad fumed and carried on and said we were not to go to the park again. But after a week or so it was all forgotten, though Mum always warned us to run and tell the nearest park keeper if we saw anything like it again.

One day, a kindly looking man gave us a bag of pears, but as soon as he had gone, I threw them in the waste bin, telling the others that they were probably poisoned. We always threw away any sweets given us by strangers, thinking in our innocence that it was the sweets themselves that were harmful and the reason why we were always warned not to accept anything from strangers.

There was one particular avenue of trees, known to all as 'the Prom'. On Sunday mornings, all the courting couples walked up and down and all the sets of young people from the nearby churches, dressed in their Sunday best. It was a real guide to the who's who of the day, and we knew who was going out with whom. When we got a bit older, we would watch to see who was walking with Eva, and if it was the same young man more than twice running, we knew something was going on. Yes, the Prom was the place to show off your new clothes and smart hats and I longed to be old enough to walk up and down with a young man.

Not far away was a little group of trees, with seats around in a circle, and here a mission group would meet every Sunday morning. They had a small harmonium, and a big blue banner proclaiming 'The Out and Out Mission'. They were a devout group of about fifteen people, and they sang rousing hymns with jolly choruses. We would go and sit on the seats and listen, and I'd hope for my favourite.

> Look and live, my brother live, look to Jesus now and live.
> 'Tis recorded in His word, Hallelujah, that you only have to look and live.

I used to sit and wonder where I had to look. I gazed at their shining faces, especially at one badly crippled young fellow whose face absolutely beamed, and thought how happy they looked. People might snigger as they walked past, but they seemed to have something special. They called each other brother and sister just like the Salvation Army, but they didn't have a band, only this little thing where one of them sat and pedalled away like mad.

Years later, I met the people who ran the mission and found out that the badly crippled fellow was the only son of the family. He didn't have much to look so happy about, because he suffered terrible pain from his crippled legs and he couldn't get work either. When there wasn't nearly enough work for the fit, then the weak and helpless had to make do as best they could. There was no welfare state to care, so he didn't really have much to sing about.

Only once can I recall the park being shut for several weeks. This was at the time of the General Strike in 1926. I didn't understand all the whys and wherefores of it, I only knew that there were soldiers camped out in big bell tents in the park and the gates were shut, apart from a small one where a sentry stood guard. We would walk along Grove Road where it ran between two sections of the park, and talk to the soldiers through the bars. I suppose it was all right to talk to strange men when iron spikes separated us. Steve and Will were particularly keen on doing this, and the soldiers would tell them of the foreign countries where they had been stationed. It all sounded very exciting, and I think that Will made up his mind from then on that the army was the life for him.

Everyone kept saying that the strike was terrible, and my poor aunties set out to walk all the way from Bethnal Green to Knightsbridge every day, since there was no transport. One morning our little dog Peggy followed them, and when they got as far as Aldgate, they managed to get a lift on a lorry. Peggy had disappeared in the crowd, and when they came home at night, they were very upset to think that she was lost.

Although Dad was very tired, having walked to work and back, he got out the dog's lead and walked all the way to Aldgate in the hope of finding her. He had no luck, but about a week later she came scratching at the door; thin, muddy and starving, but delighted to be back with her family once more.

On summer evenings, the band would play in the park at weekends, and although it cost twopence to go and sit in the enclosure, you could hear all you wanted from the grass outside. Very occasionally we went there with Mum and Dad for a stroll, instead of going to bed at our usual time of half-past seven. We would listen to the band and Dad would tell us all the names of the trees and flowers, and the history behind the big memorial fountain, and we would really enjoy his company.

On the way home, we'd call at the Crown pub, just outside the park gates, but Dad had a poor opinion of people who left kids outside pubs all evening, so he would only stop for one drink, bringing us out a big arrowroot biscuit to munch while he and Mum had their drink.

He wore his best suit on these occasions, with a gold chain across his waistcoat, and his bowler hat and best boots. My dad looked a real toff when he went out. He was always fussy about dress though, and never went to work as many men did with just a scarf around their neck and no collar or tie.

Every morning he held out his hand for a clean, white, folded hankie, which Mum gave him together with his dinner shilling and two small packets of sandwiches. The sandwiches always had to be in two packs, so that he could slip one into each pocket without showing a big bulge. He would never dream of going to the drawer and getting a hankie for himself, it was part of the ritual to have it handed to him.

Once, when Mum had flu and I had to get up and make the sandwiches, I omitted this and he stood with his hand held out. 'Don't I get a bloody hankie?' he asked, in an injured tone.

Sometimes we would all go out for an evening trip and take a bus to the city and walk all the way up to Oxford Street. Oh, the excitement of looking in the shop windows and seeing the things posh people wore and used. Dad would stand and gaze at the furniture shops, showing Mum the merits of the various things, pointing out what was good and what was just shoddy veneer. I was terribly proud of Dad, and felt that he knew nearly everything about everything.

6

Rosie

On the end of Dad's watch chain was a small gold locket, and inside was a photo of Rosie, my dear little sister, after whose tragic death my mother began to look older, and stopped singing as she worked. Indeed, for ages she never even laughed.

I was 4½ when Rosie was born, and remember creeping into the bedroom to see my new little sister. At least I was glad she was another girl. I was allowed to push the pram up and down the court, though not old enough to take her out on my own. But when Eva was with us, we would all go to the park together. Rosie had golden curls, a complete contrast to Gwen, with her tightly curled black locks. Her cheeks matched her name and she was altogether an adorable child.

When she was 4, she fell sick one day, and that evening Dad took her to the doctor. A very rare occasion in our home, but Dad said he was worried and didn't like the look of her. She wasn't very ill, just sick and pale and headachy, but towards evening she became much more lively and began to look better. She had a fork in her little hand and was helping to spear pickled onions from a jar, laughing with glee whenever she caught one.

Early next morning, we awakened conscious of the unusual noise. A strange voice on the stairs and a sound of sobbing. I crept out on to the landing and saw my mum, her old brown overall tightly wound round over her nightie, her eyes red with weeping. One of the aunties took me by the hand and she too was crying.

'Go back to bed, Dods, there's a good girl. Rosie is very ill.'

We all three sat up in bed and listened. Now we heard the unbelievable, a man crying, deep shaking sobs that frightened us all. As Mum passed by our door, we called out and she put her head in the room, her white face with its red weepy eyes a never-to-be-forgotten sight.

'Get up now,' she said quietly. 'Rosie is dead and there's nothing anyone can do.'

Dead! It just wasn't possible. Not our baby. Other people's babies died, but not ours. We got up and made ready for school. No one queried our lack of breakfast and we went out into the quiet street. When we reached the Infants' Department, I hesitated with my hand on the knob, then shrank back. If I went in, then I might start crying and Eva was always teasing me for this. Yet Rosie had recently started school and I always took her in and helped her with her coat.

I ran up the stairs and sat down at my desk. After a time, the headmistress of the Infants came in and stood talking to the teacher. They both looked in my direction and then called me out.

The only photograph of Rosie.

'Your little sister isn't at school today,' said the head kindly.

'No, she won't be coming any more. She's dead.' I tried hard to speak as though it was of no consequence, looking straight ahead and concentrating on the window pane and a sparrow outside.

'Oh, my God!' The head turned away abruptly and I went and sat down again, without a tear. Somehow I mustn't cry.

I sat there and wondered what Rosie was doing. Was she really there, above the bright blue sky, as we sang in Sunday school? Had they given her a white gown and a golden crown? I couldn't really see why God had to have her. There were so many other children He could have picked on. But then I suppose He was entitled to take the best, just as my Dad was the only one allowed to pick any flower he wanted from our garden.

The next days were nightmarish. We were there and yet not there. We were fed and washed and put to bed, but it all had an unreal quality. Mum didn't come in to kiss us goodnight, the aunties did it instead, and Dad talked in a hoarse kind of whisper and didn't shout once.

We all went up to Green Street to buy new clothes. Black coats and dresses and little black felt hats like pudding basins. Trimmed with black ribbons for Eva and me, and Gwen's white-trimmed because she was the youngest. Our new dresses were black and white check and Mum bought yards of black velvet for our Sunday dresses. Black bordered hankies and black scarves; and Mum of course had black jet beads.

She took us in the front room, where Rosie lay on the big round table, covered with a white blanket. Not that any blanket could warm that little marble figure. She was dressed in a white nightie, with thick lace at the sleeves and neck. Never had I see anything so beautiful as that little statue, in its white lace shroud, surrounded by the golden curls.

'Perhaps she isn't really dead,' I whispered, but Mum burst into tears and I wished I had not said anything.

Then they came and took her away, and I listened while they talked about post-mortems and suchlike; and how the doctor was exonerated from blame. He couldn't have known that night that it was meningitis, and by next morning, when Dad ran for him, it was too late. He must have been a very young doctor at the time, and it was probably his first death, because it was he who had sat crying at Rosie's bedside.

Now the talk of hearse and horses took on a new meaning, for it was real; and this was one funeral when we wouldn't laughingly get the bucket ready at the door to beat old Mrs Kay to it. There was the usual collection among the neighbours and they all gave liberally. Then they gave a huge wreath, the 'Gates of Heaven'. That was what they always gave, if enough money was collected. Golden metal gates stretched across pillars of flowers, with a white dove at the base. 'From the Neighbours' it said, in big purple letters. The wreaths were lined up in the street outside the front door for all the neighbours to see and they all came along and stood in silence. Then they began to gather, crowding either side of our door, as we always did ourselves at other funerals and I peeped through the upstairs window to see the horses arrive.

But just when they were due, Auntie Maisie put on our new black hats and coats and took us out, much to my disappointment. Only Eva was allowed to go to the funeral. Auntie took us for a bus ride to a distant park, but there was little enjoyment in it. She herself was upset, and we were fed up at missing all the excitement. I'd much rather have been sitting in that big, horse-drawn coach than riding on a bus.

By the time we got home again, they were all back at the house and the tightly drawn blinds, shut all through the street, were open again; and the aunts and uncles were eating plates of ham and tongue, all seated around that big round table where the little body had lain. Disconsolately, we wandered out into the back garden and began sorting out Rosie's toy box, sharing her little treasures among us, and even fighting a bit over who should have what. Talk about the scripture, 'They parted my raiment among them'. I have often thought when I've read the Easter story, of us quarrelling over those little possessions.

This funeral was not like most of the street funerals I knew. There was no beer, it didn't turn into a sing-song or a pub crawl as so often happened, and before long they all left, leaving us alone with our grief.

That death had a profound effect upon us all, and changed our life in some ways. There was no radio, no gramophone even, in our house, and nothing broke the quiet stillness of those weeks that followed. Dad sat in his seat, watching the pigeons, and Mum sat with folded hands, not even knitting, just doing nothing, a thing I'd never seen before.

Our slightest headaches were cause for coddling and fussing and a mild bilious attack saw us being rushed to the doctor.

The aunties did their best to help us over the bad patch, and they started taking us out with them quite a bit, so it was only now that I really made the acquaintance of my great-aunt Rose. She was Janet's younger sister, who lived in Hackney. Normally she didn't bother with us very much, as she was far more fond of our cousin Jean who visited her regularly, but we had been occasionally to visit our great-grandmother Piper, Aunt's mother, who lived with her.

Great-grandmother Piper was a domineering old lady in her nineties, and when we visited she would bring out her ludo board and demand that we sat and played with her. She always insisted on being red, and the red corner of the board was absolutely worn away, where Grandma Piper got excited and her thumb kept trembling on the edge of the board.

One day I caught her cheating, flicking the dice over to a six. I had been suspicious of this for some time, and when I caught her red-handed, I jumped up and yelled that I didn't play with cheats. Aunt took me by the shoulders firmly and sat me down again.

'Get on with the game,' she commanded firmly. 'When you are 90, you can cheat too.'

I sat down again, but made faces at her behind her back, which got me a smart rap on the knuckles from the old lady. I wasn't very keen on her, anyway, she was almost too old to be real. Her skin was thin, almost like tissue paper, and it worried me lest she got it torn. Once this happened, she might split all down, and come tumbling out of it and bleed all over. It was a nightmarish thought and I wasn't very happy being left alone with her. She wore black beaded blouses and long black skirts, a black shawl pinned with an enormous diamond brooch, and her snow-white hair was piled in a neat little bundle on top of her head. Her skin showed through, all pink and soft looking, but that was the only soft thing about her. With piercing, deep-sunk eyes and a very long nose, she was altogether forbidding in appearance.

German born, she had been travelling with her family to Australia and they had stopped ashore in England. Janet said they had been shipwrecked, but I never found out whether this was so. Anyway, while they were in England the little Rosalie had

The three sisters, after Rosie died, 1925. I'm sitting, and Eva is at the back.

Great-grandmother Piper.

been taken ill, and was so sick that the family went on to Australia leaving her with relations. It was intended that she follow at some later date, but maybe travel for a child alone was pretty impossible in those days; at any rate, she never joined her own family, and when I knew her she was the matriarchal head of a big family of her own.

Her sons were all businessmen and owned some thriving concerns between them; her youngest daughter Rose married a German, and married well, and only little Janet and her other sister Eva who lived in our court didn't do well in life. They were the poor relations, and as far as our wealthy Piper relatives were concerned, they could stay poor.

Privately, we always referred to Aunt Rose as 'yer aunt' and even Mum, who liked us to be polite, joined us in this nickname. This was because her husband Harry always referred to her as 'yer aunt', when talking to Mum.

These were our posh relations. Their house was a big one of the type which has now sadly degenerated into flatlets and overcrowded dwellings, but in those days Hackney was something, and a cut above Bethnal Green. The hall of the house was a wide, high one, and when I entered it I would gaze in awe at the chairs and table it contained and compare it with our narrow passage where there was barely room to pass.

My aunt had a maid too, though she always called her 'the girl'. My mum referred to her as 'yer aunt's poor Skivvy', and she certainly had to toil and toil in that house. Aunt would sit and read and cook and tidy up, but Skivvy was always on the go, rubbing and scrubbing. When Skivvy, who was a poor, thin angular woman, finally left, yer aunt managed with a daily, and by the time I was visiting her frequently, she made do with a char for a few mornings weekly.

But she had other signs of wealth, to my mind. She had carpets on all her floors and the stairs, a shiny piano in the big parlour, a gramophone with lots of records, and she possessed the very first wireless I had ever heard. How it fascinated me to put on the little black earphones and listen to someone really talking, miles away! If Gwen and I were both there together, we would sit in silent ecstasy with one earphone each, listening to whatever programme was on.

Hardly anyone in our school had a wireless then, and I could boast to my friends about it. Later on, she was the first person I ever knew to have a loudspeaker installed, and even now, the football results given out over the air take my mind back to those far-off days when we sat like little mice while uncle tutted or oh'd about the results.

Uncle Harry adored his wife. Like Janet, she was extremely small, but she was much more sharp featured than my beloved grandma, and her hair was a dull mousy brown. She had a large, firm bosom, but when I leaned my head on her one day, I was surprised to find it hard and bony. I mentioned this to Gwen, who nodded wisely. 'I think she sticks teacups inside her stays,' she said. Whatever the truth, she was well whaleboned all down, though all the stays in the world couldn't stop her looking like a little teddy bear in her brown fur coat.

When Uncle came home from his office, he would bend over his wife, kissing her fondly and with a lingering touch that I found surprising. 'And how has my darling been today?' he would ask. Then he'd put on his slippers and light his smelly old pipe, ignoring whichever of his great-nieces happened to be there, and talk of how he had saved old so-and-so a couple of hundred pounds. I never knew exactly what he did for a living then, but he must have been an accountant, from the way all his talk was about books and money. He owned quite a few houses in Bethnal Green, and a big bungalow near Southend, but according to my father he was a tightfisted landlord who squeezed every penny out of his tenants and did nothing for them.

When Mum was a girl, Uncle and his brothers had owned a large boot and shoe factory, and it was in this factory that Mum had first worked. Poor little Bertha! She often told me about the first week she went there. Uncle had walked through the factory and looked at her feet. 'Can't have you working for me in those shabby old boots,' he told her. 'Get yourself measured for a decent pair at once.' So Mum went home in brand-new boots, thrilled to bits at her uncle's bounty. That was, until pay day came and she found he was stopping her sixpence a week from her three and six, until the boots were paid for.

Dad didn't like the old man one bit. They had had terrific arguments in the past, of which I was too young to get the gist, but they were all about the new National Insurance scheme. Uncle thought he had found a way round paying the employer's share and my hot-headed father had called him a twisting old bugger to his face and forbidden Mum to visit there.

They had big parties there occasionally, when the aunts let their hair down and joined in singing all the latest songs. Lottie used to sing a pathetic solo about a poor blind boy, and they all joined in a riotous chorus which went: 'Don't send my boy to prison, it's the first crime what he's done.' The men played jokes on each other, the prize one being pouring piccalilli down each other's trousers. All these excitements came to us as hearsay, however, for, as I said, we were not on visiting terms. But after Rosie died, 'yer Aunt' started having us to Hackney for the day on Saturdays, taking turns with Jean.

I always enjoyed my trip there, and looked forward to my turn. For one thing, she always left me to my own devices during the morning, when she was busy with the dinner, and I could read whatever I wanted to. She never said I shouldn't read *The Red Letter*, or *East Lynne*, or even the daily paper: as long as I was quiet I could please myself. I would creep up to the big parlour and pick out 'God Save the King' or 'Good King Wenceslas' with one finger on the shiny piano, singing to myself as I played.

It was thrilling to go shopping with yer aunt, and the biggest thrill of all was to go to Woolworths. I used to stand inside the door and take a deep breath. 'Nothing over Sixpence' it proclaimed in the big gold letters, and I used to imagine what I would do if only I had a sixpence. Why, I could buy anything in the whole shop! Saving a sixpence was, from then on, my great ambition.

Once, Aunt Rose bought me a row of beads. She let me choose, but vetoed my choice because it was green.

'I wouldn't let you bring them in the house,' she said, 'if you had the green ones. It's terribly unlucky to have anything green.'

On one occasion, I had walked all the way to Hackney when it was my turn, dressed in my new coat. A lovely green one it was, with a grey fur collar. When I reached the house, she opened the door and held up her hands in horror. 'Oh, Dol, fancy coming here in a green coat!' she exclaimed, 'Your mum should have known better. Can't understand her getting you a green coat in the first place.' My face fell, and the lovely coat assumed sinister proportions. 'It was cheap, Aunt, she got it in a sale. It was only twelve and six.'

'Not surprised,' snorted my aunt. 'You'll break a leg, or get run over in that coat, you mark my words.' All this time, I stood hopefully on her doorstep praying that she wouldn't send me packing to walk the 2 miles home again.

'Tell you what,' she said at last, 'take the coat off and roll it up and put it in the shed. Go the back way, so's you don't bring it through the house. You'll have to stay home if it isn't warm enough to go out without a coat this afternoon, though, because I'm not walking out with you in that thing.'

There were lots of other things that were unlucky too, as well as green. It was unlucky to sit on a table, to turn a thing right side out if you'd put it on inside out in the morning, to pick up a dropped glove (you didn't lose it, you merely got someone else to pick it up for you). If you went out and remembered something you'd left at home and went back for it, you had to sit down and count ten before setting out again. To open an umbrella indoors was unforgivable and to break a mirror was the absolute end, for then there was no way of avoiding seven years of bad luck! All these things, and many more like them, were Aunt's religion, and she never tired of telling me how true she had found them to be.

Besides taking me to Woolworths, she sometimes took me to the pictures, and what a thrill that was. I had only been with the penny rush before that. The penny rush was held on a Saturday afternoon in a cinema just off Roman Road, and it was just what its name implied. My cousins made it a regular Saturday treat, and Eva often went with them, but none of them liked taking me. As we hurried along, clutching our orange or bag of peanuts, they would talk between them of Norma and Richard Talmadge and lots of other stars, but all I did was to pray like mad that no one would kill anyone or fire any guns.

When the doors opened we all rushed in, and for some reason that I could never fathom at the time, they all made for seats near the back and only the latecomers sat in the front rows. As soon as the film started, the piano would start to play, the pianist dressed in a long black skirt and wearing a fancy white waitress-like hat.

As soon as things got going, the piano would play loud banging music and I'd grip my hands on the seat and shut my eyes tight, just in case anyone fell down dead. When a car came towards me on the screen, I was dead scared in case it came right out and ran me over, and when the cowboys and horses galloped in my direction, I would shoot under the seat and stay there.

If, however, the picture was sad I would burst into tears and have to be taken outside in disgrace for making a noise. Mum and Dad took us to see Charlie Chaplin in *The Gold Rush* as a very special treat, but I broke my heart over the poor little man having to stew his boots for food.

'Oh, please, please,' I cried aloud, 'please can't anyone give him some food?' So, all in all, no one was very keen on taking me to the pictures. But when I grew a bit older and learned to control my emotions, nothing delighted me more than being taken to the pictures by Aunt Rose. Even the cinema she frequented was different, as it didn't smell of smoke and oranges and sweat; there was a smartly dressed young lady who walked around spraying something into the air, and it smelt more like the perfume department of a big store.

The pictures we saw were nicer too: we never saw cowboys and Indians there, but there were ladies and gentlemen kissing each other and holding hands and getting married and riding in lovely carriages. Or else they were dying gently in big beautiful beds, even better than Aunt Kate's. 'Kiss me Charles, and be good to baby,' would flash on the screen, and the audience in Aunt's type of cinema would read quietly, and just sob gently, if it was very sad. I would keep putting out my tongue to catch the tears as they rolled down my cheek, lest Aunt should see me crying and not take me again. The piano played soft haunting music that made you want to keep on swallowing hard, and when you eventually came out into the bright sunshine, you could pretend you had something in your eye and keep on wiping it.

But Aunt had developed a sudden cold too, and had to keep on sniffing, so we'd sniff and wipe our way home, where the two dogs would give us a boisterous welcome and Aunt would make tea, talking all the time about what she'd have done, had she been the heroine. 'She was too soft with him, don't you think, Dol?' she would call from the kitchen and, thrilled to be talked to as an equal, I would discuss with her the merits of the film.

At the penny rush, everyone read the captions out loud.

'Oh leave me, sir,' we would all call out, as the maiden struggled with the villain. We had incentives to become fast readers in those days. Perhaps today's children would become better readers if the TV went back to the old, silent days for its stories and children had to use their brain to read, instead of being spoon-fed with all their entertainment.

It was not until the era of the 'talkie' that people like Aunt Kate and Janet went to the pictures, and I'll never forget when Mum and Auntie Liz persuaded Aunt Kate to go to see her very first film, *The Singing Fool*.

Everyone was singing, 'Climb upon my knee, Sonny boy,' and Aunt Kate set off in joyful expectancy. What a scene they had with her when she came home! She cried and cried all night, and half the next day too, standing at the corner and wiping her eyes on her apron, the tears making rivulets down her powdered face.

'Oh my Gawd, it was lovely, I haven't slept all night for thinking about it.' 'When Aunt Kate went to the pictures' became a talking point all through the family for weeks after that.

I had another reason for longing to go to Aunt's, too. Her younger son Herman (known as Bert) owned a typewriter, the very first one I had ever seen, let alone touched. And he, dear Bert, would put a sheet of paper in it and let me sit and type. I was almost speechless in his presence because he had written a book and had it published, and though no one would let me read it, I knew how clever he must be. I read through lots of his other books, though, and he never dreamed of saying I wasn't old enough.

What affluence there was at this house! They even owned their very own deckchairs. (The only time I'd sat in a deckchair was when someone in the park had got up and handed us their tickets because the three hours that they got for their twopence were not up.) When the sun shone, I could sit on the lawn in a deckchair and read grown-up books and pretend that I was very rich. There was a cherry tree and when the fruit was ripe Bert would come out and pick a few cherries to share with me.

Next door was a Salvation Army Mother and Baby Home. If I climbed the wall, I could look down into the cots and prams out in the sunshine, with lovely little babies lying in them. Aunt used to tut and say they were all very sad and the mothers no better than they should be, but I thought the babies were lovely and said so.

One sad day, Aunt was taken suddenly ill and rushed to hospital for an operation. Uncle came to tell us when it was over. 'A lion,' he said, 'a lion, yer aunt is.' He had been drinking to celebrate the news that his darling was going to pull through. His hat, perched on his head at a rakish angle, tilted forward over his eyes every time he leaned his head against the wall. 'A brave little lion,' he repeated, pushing the hat back again. 'A brave little lion.' He ambled off up the street, still muttering, and Janet ran along to tell the good news to her sister Eva.

'Well,' said our Eva, when he had gone, 'so now we'll all be off visiting the lion of Judah.' We giggled at this, because we sang about the lion of Judah in Sunday school.

> For the lion of Judah shall break every chain
> And give us the victory again and again.

Privately, the nickname stuck, and my sister always referred to 'yer Aunt' as the lion of Judah.

7
Where Do Babies Come From?

Eva had just started work about this time, and had entered the grown-up world where we could not hope to follow. She was allowed to stay up long after we went to bed, and sometimes Mum and Dad went to the pictures, telling Eva to send us to bed at eight o'clock. On these occasions, she had her friend in, and we would sit on the top stair and listen to all their talk when we were supposed to be asleep.

She now had her own money to spend as she liked, and was even allowed on the little island in the park. Lucky thing. She saved up carefully for her clothes, for she had wonderful dress sense, and sometimes she would take me with her when she went to Hackney, to the big shops. We would get on a tram together and she would pay my penny fare and I really thought myself somebody. On the rare occasions when I had managed to save a sixpence, she would leave me at the door of Woolworths and I'd spend a blissful hour choosing my purchase. It was excitement enough to dream about all the week.

Eva worked at the manufacturing chemist in the next street, and we began to hear more and more about the wonderful formulas and cure-alls that were made there. She recommended one special indigestion tablet to yer aunt and uncle, and they swore by it. Aunt would take one, sitting as she always did in the big basement kitchen of her house. Then she would burp loudly, again and again, and if Uncle was in, she'd go to the foot of the stairs. 'Can you hear me, Harry?' Burp, burp. 'Wonderful tablets these!' Burp, burp. So Eva's stock really went up, and soon she was able to recommend a corn cure as well.

'Yer Aunt'.

Even the lav became more interesting, because whereas we had always used neat squares of newspaper, cut up and threaded with string, like everyone else, we now had out-of-date health catalogues, which were just the right size and better quality than newspaper. What reading there was now! No more need for *The Red Letter* tucked up my jumper, it took me all my time to read about boils and piles and female pills.

When Christmas came, Eva was invited to the firm's dinner. I'd never met anyone who'd been invited to a dinner dance and the very idea of dinner at night made my eyes pop. I listened eagerly as Eva discussed her dress with Auntie Rosie who, being a court dressmaker, should have had really first-class ideas on the subject. But her ideas, to Eva's mind, were blooming old-fashioned. 'She'd have me dress like a flipping schoolkid,' she commented bitterly. But the choice was very limited anyway, for being only a few months after Rosie's death, we were in mourning anyway. So she wore a black velvet dress with a white lace collar. She bought a pair of waving tongs and did her hair, too. Even now, the smell of singeing hair brings back the memory of that black velvet dress.

Another milestone came at this time. Auntie Lottie was made manageress of the grocer's where she worked. This meant that they had the flat over the shop rent free. There was a kitchen, a big parlour and two big bedrooms. Such a chance was too good to miss, and so they moved away.

Alas, there was no more Pip Squeak and Wilfred, no more big pocket to take my crusts, and no more trips to Homerton to the Army meetings. How we missed them all! But with their going, and Eva now at work and earning twelve and six a week, we were able to climb the social scale of our little community. Mum decided to keep the whole of the downstairs, and only let the one upstairs room which had been the aunties' bedroom. She had a gas cooker put on the landing outside the room, and had no difficulty in letting this apartment for four shillings weekly.

Our new tenants were a nice young couple, recently married. He was a postman, and they were probably the very first people I got to know who were not relations. They were very quiet, and sometimes they would invite me up to their room, though Mum would stress that I was not to make a nuisance of myself. But Mr Reynolds would sit and play draughts with me, and even taught me how to do a weekly competition in the *John Bull*. This was called bullets, and we had to make an apt comment on any phrase on a list. Sometimes we would come up with a really good one, and Mr Reynolds would pay out the sixpence required and send it in, and we'd dream all next week about what we'd do if our entry won the prize. And what prizes were offered! Sometimes as much as ten shillings a week for life. Though I worried a bit, because if they had all that money coming in, they'd move away and I'd miss them.

The cooking smells were a bit powerful nowadays. If we came in from school and smelt onions, they could be ours, or coming from the landing, if Mrs Reynolds was cooking. And if she was cooking onions and we were having fish, it was a really overwhelming aroma!

I had just started going with Eva to chapel on Sunday mornings then, and I'd walk back thinking about my Sunday dinner. It was blessed to be hungry on a

Sunday. It was written in the Bible: 'Blessed are they who hunger and thirst after righteousness, for they shall be filled.' To my mind, I'd qualified on the righteousness bit by going to chapel, and now I was entitled to be hungry and thirsty. To open our front door and smell it all, beef with the fat making splashing noises on the fire oven door and dripping its gravy into the pudding cooking in the tin underneath it, and lamb and mint sauce wafting down the stairs: gosh, it was worth being righteous for!

I don't know what made Eva suddenly take up this morning service lark; I expect she went along because she and her friends had their eyes on a couple of the young fellows who went with their parents, but once I had been with her, nothing could keep me away. I hadn't even realised that anyone could go every week; we at the Sunday school usually went in the church twice a year, on Christmas Sunday and on Anniversary Day.

How we all loved this special day! The whole Sunday school, having practised special hymns over and over again for about ten weeks, would go into the actual church and sit in the gallery, where we filled every seat. Everyone wore a flower in their buttonhole, and it was the day for the wearing of new clothes. New hats and coats for the girls and women, and a new shirt and tie for the men. We always hoped for a fine day, and folk who had moved away would treat the day as one of reunions. Those who had married came back, bringing their babies to show to their friends, and there was a real air of festivity about the place. I loved it all, especially the hymn singing, and when I found I could go and sit downstairs with the grown-ups any Sunday I cared to, I took to going along with Eva. She always pushed me off afterwards, for she and her friends went a-walking on the Prom, but I didn't mind, and sang all the way home.

I knew Mr and Mrs Reynolds were not poor people, because they had a real gramophone, with lots of records, and none of us had one. Only 'yer Aunt', and she didn't play hers. I had a toy one that played real records; it was probably the most expensive toy I ever possessed. The aunties bought it for me the Christmas after Rosie died, and all the family played it. Even Dad bought a new record for it sometimes, because it was our family music. The records were small, about the size of a 45rpm single, but the latest tunes could be bought in Woolworths for sixpence each. Some of these records I still have: 'I don't care what you used to be, I know what you are today,' 'Paddling Madeleine home' and 'I'll take her back if she wants to come back, the girl that was stolen from me'. I still have the tiny gramophone too, with its little horn and the key to wind it. But in those far-off days we played it incessantly, dancing to its jigs and hornpipes.

I used to love sitting by the Reynolds' fire, listening to their real gramophone, for they were such nice people. They didn't drink, or even swear, and sometimes they would sit and hold hands by the fireside. But as they had only one room all their coal and water had to be carried upstairs and all their dirty water carried down and outside. Today, we would hold up our hands in horror and picture them as living in a real slum. Yet they were not: they were clean and tidy and decent and knew what thousands today never do, the bliss of contentment. They were not engaged in an everlasting struggle to live up to the Joneses, but were happy to live together in love.

One morning, I awoke to the sound of strange voices and my tummy lurched. Not more trouble! I padded to the door, to see Mrs Reynolds standing on the landing in her nightie, and old Mrs Horner from round the corner standing talking to her.

'You'll be all right, duck,' she was saying, 'and by the time your Alf gets back, I reckon we'll have good news for him.' Mum came along then, and shooed me inside the bedroom. 'Now you'll be good today and not give me any bother. Mrs Reynolds isn't well and you mustn't make a noise.'

Not well? She didn't look ill to me. Not ill enough for Mrs Horner who always went in houses when people had died. She didn't look ill enough for a doctor either, standing there and laughing, like she was. Grown-ups were funny. I decided against going to the park even though it was bright and sunny and a school holiday. Something mysterious was happening and I didn't want to miss anything. So I went across the court to call for Renee. She always knew everything, anyway. I told her about Mrs Reynolds and she just stared at me.

'I heard my mum saying she was late, last night.'

'Late for what?' I enquired anxiously, and a slow look of incredulity came over Renee's peaky face. She pushed her glasses back on her nose.

'You don't mean you don't know? Where's yer eyes, gal? The baby, of course. Your lodger's having a baby.' Then as she looked at my stunned expression she added, 'My Gawd, don't tell me you really didn't know!'

'I didn't know, how could I?' I asked. 'The doctor isn't there, and he doesn't always bring one when he comes, anyway.' I knew that, to my grief. Several times, when Mum had been ill, I'd pleaded with her to call the doctor. I honestly thought that babies were a sort of consolation prize given occasionally to women who had to stay in bed. As to where they actually came from, I just hadn't a clue. Even the mice had baby mice, appearing overnight by some sort of magic.

I stood open-mouthed, while Renee called to Maud who lived next door. 'She don't know where babies come from, she really don't know.' I stood before them trembling in my ignorance and Renee took a deep long breath. She was going to enjoy this, actually finding a little innocent who thought that babies came in doctors' black bags.

'Look Dol, you can see she's having a baby. She's all big and fat in front, where the baby is lying in her belly. When her time comes, she gives a whopping great scream and it comes out.'

'Splitting her right through,' added Maud with relish.

'Then they have to sew her up,' finished Renee.

I walked to the corner and stared ahead with disbelieving eyes. It couldn't be true. Renee grabbed my arm. 'Look, I'm not lying. Look at Mrs Gibbons, just going up the street. Remember how thin she used to be. Now look at her big fat belly. You'll see, she's only got a week or so to go.' I looked at Mrs Gibbons, remembering her as she had been. Mum had been in the habit of calling her 'that beanpole'.

I went back home and sat on the doorstep, listening anxiously. Only the sound of a bowl clattering on the landing. No doctor, no crying; and thank goodness, no screaming either. Mum was busy in the kitchen; it wasn't likely that Mrs Reynolds was going to split open, otherwise Mum wouldn't have been in the kitchen making meat pie.

After a time, I went back to where Maud and Renee stood giggling together on the corner. There was something else I just had to know. 'How does the baby get into the belly in the first place?'

With much shrieking of laughter, Renee caught me by the ear and whispered. Her breath smelled of onions, and the appalling few words she whispered seared through my being.

'Of course they don't – that can't possibly be true!' I shouted in my distress, but there stood Maud, nearly 14 and knowing everything, just nodding her head.

'Well,' I gathered up the remnants of my dignity, 'your father and mother might do such things, but I'm certain my Mum and Dad don't. They couldn't.'

'They just could,' laughed Renee heartily, 'or you wouldn't be here yourself, you little fool.'

Unbidden, my mind flashed back to that Sunday afternoon when Mum and Dad had shouted to me to get out of their bedroom, when Dad had been squashing Mum.

I had to know everything now. 'How then does the mum know when there is a baby growing?'

Renee sat down on the kerb and shook her head. 'This kid don't know anything! Don't you even know about periods?'

Miserably, I shook my head and they proceeded to enlighten me. 'And if it doesn't happen to you by the time you're 15, you die. So it's no good saying you don't want it.'

At that moment the doctor arrived, and propping his bike up against our window, he went into the house. Renee was quicker than me and much more daring. She darted across the road and lifted the top of the flapping black bag still on the bike. 'No baby in there, is there, Dol,' she taunted.

After a time, the doctor came downstairs, took the bag off his bike and went into the house. I slipped indoors to where Mum stood at the foot of the stairs. 'Get out and play for Christ's sake,' she shouted, and then I knew that things were at crisis point, for she didn't often swear at us like that.

A small knot of women had gathered by the corner lamppost now, standing with their arms folded in their aprons. 'Poor little devil,' sighed Auntie Liz. 'I thought she'd have it rough. Been hanging about a couple of days already. Reckon he'll send her away if it doesn't come soon.'

She flapped her apron at me then and I wandered off, to where Steve was playing cards by himself in the doorway.

'Steve,' I demanded, 'did you know Mrs Reynolds was having a baby?'

'Sure,' he answered. 'Everyone knows.' 'But Steve,' I persisted, 'do you know how babies start?'

My cousins Jean, Steve and Will.

'Course I do.' His tone was non-committal; he was much more interested in his cards. But Steve had taught me so much, I just had to go on. 'Do you believe it, Steve?'

'Oh, of course I do. Look, if you're that keen, come up to our room and take your bloomers down and I'll show you.'

'No, thank you,' I replied indignantly. 'Don't you think it's the most horrible thing you ever heard?'

'No,' he answered, thoughtfully, 'not really. Actually, they say it's very nice. Do you want me to show you or not?'

He shuffled his cards together and packed them up. It seemed to me that he was now quite interested. He stood up, hand on the banister. 'Coming?' 'No,' I answered shortly. Unconsciously female, I drew back now that I had roused him. 'I'd much rather you showed me how to castle in chess, like you promised.'

'All right, get the chessmen out.' Steve was easy-going, like his dad, and we settled down to a game. When I looked out of the door, the doctor's bike had gone, so I ran home, where Mum greeted me with a big smile. She took me up to Mrs Reynolds' room, where she lay smiling with a lovely little baby girl in her arms.

I longed to ask if she was split open, but didn't dare, either then or later, when she was up and about again.

Before long I was able to accept this aspect of the facts of life. After all, I should have known babies came out of mothers. I knew that hens laid eggs, and eggs were only unborn chickens. Once again, it was Sunday school and Bible teaching that came to my aid. 'Once in Royal David's City' explained it all. 'Where a mother laid her baby.' It was the same really, except that a mother hatched the egg before she laid it. Hens laid it while it was still an egg.

Now I began to notice when the mice grew fat, in fact, you could prod them a bit and feel the baby mice inside. It was quite interesting to look for fat women when we went shopping and I watched carefully at the baby-linen shop to see how many of the window gazers were having babies.

But the other fact . . . no. It was out. Why, Mum grumbled when I put my hankie in my bloomers pocket and pulled it out in front of Dad. 'Don't lift your frock up in front of your father. It isn't nice.'

Only once a year did Dad inspect us thoroughly. That was when we had our new combinations in the autumn. How I hated combs! Thick wool and cotton, with legs and sleeves and high necks, buttoned all down the front and with a big vent at the back so that we could manage without taking the things off every time we went to the lav. The combs went over our woollen vests, under our bloomers and petticoats. No wonder 'liberty bodices' were so named, when they became fashionable and took the place of the hated combs. Our under-petticoat was of flannel, then we had a flannelette one, beautifully featherstitched all round, and on top of this, a cambric one, with twice as much featherstitching and a lace edging.

When we went into this winter gear, usually round about bonfire night, Mum would show Dad how well the new combs fitted and we would bend over to let him see that they were not slack, to rub, or too tight, to cut under our legs. Once this yearly inspection was over, Dad steered clear of us and our bodies; he even stayed out while we were bathed in front of the kitchen fire.

When we were older, we had our bath night when Mum and Dad went to the pictures. Mum would carry in the buckets of hot water from the kitchen copper before they went out, and we would have our bath, both using the same water, and then bath the dog too, if she needed it. Then we carried all the water outside and emptied it into the yard.

I used to think it must be awful to have a bathroom and not be able to sit by a big fire to have my bath. The only bathroom I ever saw was the one at 'yer Aunt's', cold and grim and all white paint. I never saw her use it either, she used to take a kettle of hot water into her bedroom to wash at the big marble washstand. It was much more sensible to bath by the fire.

Dad and Mum had theirs after we had gone to bed, and Mum would hang Dad's clean long pants and vest on the armchair by the fire, so that he could get into them all nice and warm.

If the night was very cold, Dad would take the shelf out of the fire oven, all hot and almost glowing red, wrap it in several thicknesses of upholstery velvet, and put it in his bed. Sometimes, if the weather was really bitter, he would take a huge shovel full of glowing coals and go belting up the stairs and put them in the bedroom fireplace, smoke and smuts following him in a great cloud. We had stone hot-water bottles, not much comfort to cuddle, but at least they took the icy chill off the bottom of the bed, though mine invariably fell out of bed in the night with a great thump and woke us all up.

8
School

The new baby upstairs flourished, but before long her parents were looking for a bigger place. I cried when they left us, although when a new couple arrived, the lady had a big belly and it was not long before there was another new baby in the house.

Dad was not so keen on these people, though. The woman called Dad 'old bean', and would even come through our kitchen when we were having a meal, a thing that Mrs Reynolds would never do.

'Just going to get some water,' she'd say gaily. 'Hope you're going to leave some of that dinner, old bean, it smells ever so good to me.' And she'd come up to the table, and sometimes laughingly pick a potato from Dad's plate, while we looked up in frozen horror, wondering at the woman's daring.

For a couple of months she got away with it too, but one day she went too far. If she'd had any sense, she'd have realised that when Dad didn't come in whistling, he was in a bad mood, but it didn't matter to her that he was in one of his very quiet moods, just looking for someone or something to start on. Even the dog kept out of his way on such occasions; you needed to be really thick not to know Dad's moods.

We were all sitting in silence eating our dinner when in she came, bouncing across the room with her water jug. Her 'Hello' was greeted with a glare, but as she returned with her water, she had the nerve to tip Dad's cap forward over his eyes as she passed his chair.

'Cheer up, old bean,' she laughed, and wondered what had hit her. Dad leapt to his feet, called her all the names he could lay his tongue to, and, using all the words we were not allowed to say, he told her to get out and find new lodgings by the end of the week. 'I'll swing first, before I'll let you stay,' he bellowed. Then, of course, he turned on Mum. She'd let the low-down, common bitch take the room, she should have seen what she was.

The little family moved out at the end of the week, and Dad vowed we'd have no more lodgers. He'd manage to give Mum another half a dollar and we'd keep the house. A whole house, with no lodgers! I couldn't wait to get to school and boast about it. Lots of my friends were the lodgers and only had a couple of upstairs rooms, but I knew of no one who had the whole house.

Eva was delighted too, because this meant she had a bedroom to herself. A whole room! Gwen and I shared the big end room, and we talked for hours about what we would do with it. We even bought several pounds of macaroni, painted it all in different colours, broke the long sticks up into little pieces and made a long bead curtain for the window. It looked most artistic too.

Auntie Liz laughed at us. 'I suppose you fancy your bloody selves now,' she teased over the fence. Well, what if we did? We had something to boast about, anyway. Mum went down Roman Road and bought some new curtaining. Heavy cretonne, with big bold flowers all over it. She hesitated a bit, because the pattern was not painted all the way through, and the stall keeper groused. 'What do you expect for a tanner a yard,' he moaned, 'bloody gold thread? You wouldn't get it if I hadn't nicked it.' We laughed at that, because they always said they'd pinched the stuff, even within the hearing of a copper. Anyway, Mum bought it, and it never wore out. She gave me some of it, during the war, and even now, my cat reclines on a cushion made from the stuff.

There was another bonus to our occupying the whole house. We were now able to have gas in our bedroom instead of candles. Before this, we had not been allowed to use upstairs gas, as it came off the lodgers' meter, but now Dad bought gas fittings and we had real mantles and proper lights in the bedrooms. Mum even looked at stair carpet, but Dad would have none of it.

1926 – Our class of 56 girls. I'm centre – wearing a bead necklace.

'Enough's enough,' he growled. 'How would you keep it clean? Tell me that. How would you scrub the stairs?' So we had new lino and made do, but it was lovely anyway.

I was glad of the light in the bedroom, because now the Junior County scholarship loomed ahead. This event, predecessor of the eleven-plus, was held twice yearly. The successful candidates went to grammar school, called secondary school at that time. But not many children were successful, because most of the places were taken up by paying pupils, and only a dozen or so scholarships were available at each school. So competition was fierce, and any school which managed as many as three scholarships at any one time really had a feather in its cap.

The names of the successful ones were painted on a big roll of honour hung in the school hall, and it had been my ambition to see my name there for as long as I could remember.

Dad put the pressure on: it was mental arithmetic with my tea and an essay afterwards. Train sums were his speciality. If a train travelling at 40 miles an hour leaves Liverpool at ten and passes another travelling in the opposite direction at 30 miles an hour and having left London ten minutes earlier . . . so on and so on, until I felt I could work out the train timetables for the whole country. Compound interest, fractions, decimals and percentages, I did them all.

I read recently that a comprehensive school headmaster found one of these Junior County papers and set it to his whole school, the youngest of whom was older than I was when I sat the paper. Only one child out of the thousand would have gained a grammar school place on the results and two hundred could not answer a single question!

I wonder why. I suppose intelligence alters over the years. When I listen to children on radio and TV quizzes I know I was not as bright as these children are. They astound me with their knowledge. Yet when I recently told a group of 9-year-olds that I would give a sweet to the first one who told me what nine eights were, they could not answer. Perhaps mental arithmetic is an out-of-date subject. They have calculators and machines to give change in shops, but how will these children know that they are getting a fair deal in the supermarkets of the future?

I have been bulk-buying recently as a means of saving on grocery bills, but you need to be able to calculate to find out if an article is worth buying in bulk, for some things are not. Maybe money is becoming so valueless that it doesn't matter what you pay, as long as you get what you want. I know that money in a purse just melts, which is why I've bought a big freezer!

Anyway, came the Saturday of the Junior County and away I went with my pen and pencil and rubber and ruler, and came home feeling quite pleased with myself. Dad's train sum had a place in the problem paper, so he was as pleased as punch. 'If you get it, my girl, you'll have your dad to thank,' he purred. And get it I did. He gave me ten bob, the very first time I had owned a piece of paper money. I rushed into the street with it, singing at the top of my voice, 'I've got a money note, I've got a money note.' I bought a leather case with the money, and Dad put my initials on it.

Now there were schools to be considered and places to apply to. Dad and Mum had to go and see the school head, and I was eventually fixed up with a place in Clapton: dear old Laura Place, or the John Howard School for Girls, to give it its rightful name. There was a grant with the scholarship too. Nine pounds a year. Nine whole pounds! I could hardly believe it, and floated on air for a while, until we came down to the brass tacks of buying my brown school uniform. Everything was so dear, and couldn't be bought in Roman Road. It all had to be just so, and even Auntie Rosie couldn't run up something that looked near enough.

Added to this was the cost of my bus fares every day, a penny each way, and three and six per term for the use of plate, glass and cutlery at the school meal table. There was no suggestion of school dinners of course; only the paying pupils could afford them.

Now life took on a new meaning and was entirely different. Not even the holidays were the same as the elementary schools, and we had every Wednesday afternoon free. Mum used to take me out sometimes, and I really loved it, looking forward to getting home and hearing her say, 'Now then, where shall we go today?'

I had to get out each morning soon after eight to catch a bus, and what a business this was. No one then had ever heard of queuing for a bus, so we all just stood where we were and hoped the bus would pull up in just the right spot. The young fellows stood round the corner from the bus stop and jumped on as the bus slowed down to round the corner. Sometimes I would stand there too, and pray hard that the policeman would hold the bus up just as it got there, so that I too could jump on, but this wasn't often the case, and sometimes I would get shoved and pushed about for nearly half an hour before I managed to get on. There was one nice conductor, though, who would let me stand under the stairs, even when the bus was full, and I just loved those mornings. It was easier to get on when it rained hard, because lots of people wouldn't go on top in the rain. But I chanced it, and sat with the canvas cover over my knees and the brim of my hat turned down all round. I think queues were about the best thing to come out of the war!

Going to the school in Clapton gave me one nasty shock. I wasn't so wonderful as I thought I was! There were girls around who could do arithmetic as fast as I, and even faster. Most of these girls were Jewish and learnt Hebrew and somehow found it much easier than I did to grasp German, which was the compulsory other language.

The teachers didn't think I was very wonderful either. I remember the shame of being hauled up in front of the whole form for saying 'we was'. 'Oh, was we,' taunted the girls when we got outside, and one of them looked at me as though I was something the cat had dragged in. 'You come from Bethnal Green, don't you?' she asked and turned to her friends. 'I don't know what this school is coming to!'

I pulled up my long brown stockings and made faces at them, but I didn't do too well on this score either. I wasn't very big for my age, and a couple of girls were real bullies; before the first month was over I was bitterly disillusioned with the whole affair, and didn't like this grand school one bit. Not that I'd admit it at home. I made out that it was all one glorious adventure. I was half-scared of the teachers too, for they wore long black robes over their dresses most of the time, except for the gym mistress who wore a little gymslip and looked like a girl. I thought she was rather wonderful, and used to dream that she would fall as she vaulted over the horse, and that I would rush to save her. Of course, I would get injured in the process, but they would all crowd round and say, 'Oh, Mousie Clark, you saved her life!'

They had soon found a nickname for me. I talked so much about the mice, indeed they were my only claim to fame. I sold some too, for a time, but got such a belting for selling two males as a breeding pair that I got choked off the idea. My customer came up breathing fire at me, having waited in vain for her mice to be lucrative. 'My brother came home from boarding school, this weekend,' she said, 'and he says those mice are both males. Are you scared I'll pinch all your trade?' She gave me such a hammering that I never dared sell any more mice at school, but the name stuck. After all, I couldn't tell which was which, and I had asked Steve. He held the mice up by their tails for ages before he decided, but apparently even he could make a mistake.

Eventually we all settled down and made our own friends, and by the time the term ended I was happy enough. One of my friends was a big girl who had been particularly spiteful to me at the beginning. For some unknown reason she took me under her wing. If anyone tried to hit me, she'd stand there bristling. 'If anyone wants to hit Mousie Clark, they must come to me first,' she'd shout and soon my tormentors would go away, for no one wanted a brush with her. She lived in Stepney, near Chinatown, and told lurid tales about having seen a Chinaman chop another one's head off on the kerb. We never dared say we didn't believe her, either.

My real friend was Gladys, known to us all affectionately as Cutlets. There was something about Cutlets that I loved, right from the start of our schooldays, and now, many years later, things are still the same between us. Life has been kind and generous to me, and hard beyond belief to her, but she is still the same kind and gentle soul I met at that big school. If most of us had had half Cutlets' troubles, we'd have succumbed long ago. Dear blind friend of mine, you made that school for me.

During the long school holidays I forgot all my posh friends, and within a few days I was back in the park, or playing the old games in the street. Children don't seem to play these street games any more, but I suppose the streets are too dangerous.

There were so many skipping games we played, chanting as we turned the rope. Slow skips and bumps, which meant two fast turns of the rope between each jump. We sang out, 'Old mother Mason broke her basin, how much did it cost,' then came the fast jumps, 'penny, tuppence, threepence' and so on. There were long slow skips too. Goodness knows where the words had their origin, but we all knew them.

> All last night and the night before,
> Two tom cats came knocking at the door.
> I went downstairs to let them in
> And they hit me on the head with the rolling pin.

>   The rolling pin was made of glass,
>   They knocked me over and smacked my . . . wheeeeee.

We never said the last word, but just laughed and ran from the rope. There was

>   Handy pandy sugar de candy, french and almond rock.
>   Bread and butter for your supper, that's all your mother's got.

A great favourite was, 'Rosy apple, lemonade tart, tell me the name of your sweetheart,' and then there were innumerable questions. 'What does his name begin with?' And we'd go through the alphabet until we were out. Then, 'Will he marry me? Yes, No, Yes, No.' Next time round, 'What will you wear? Silk, Satin, Cotton, Rags.' Finally, 'How will you get to the wedding? Car, Carriage, Wheelbarrow, Dung cart.' This game took hours to play.

As well as the skipping rhymes, there were the dipping ones, when we had to decide who should take the rope end, or hide first in hide-and-seek. One favourite was 'Tinky pinky, pen and ink, I smell a nasty stink, it must be you.' Unquestionably the law of the Medes and Persians, this one.

Every game had had its season. There were whips and tops. The peg of the top was stuck firmly between the kerbstone and paving stone, and whipped away with a nice piece of cord on a stick. We could keep that top going up and down the smooth asphalted roadway for about twenty minutes.

The boys played marbles in the gutter, with one special glarney stone and a lot of plain ones. The glarney stone was a highly prized transparent glass stone with coloured streaks inside. The greatest prize was a ball bearing, which was worth almost a dozen marbles.

We all played blowsy, even the girls. It was merely a question of putting a cigarette card, picture side down, on the window sill, to be covered by the opponent's card. We then took turns to blow, and every card we blew picture side up, we won. The bigger boys stood half a dozen cards at a time on edge, and competition was fierce among them.

What children these days play fivestones, or gobs-and-bonsters as we called it? Occasionally I have seen children playing a similar game called jacks, but it hasn't the intricate movement of fivestones, with its 'backsie' and 'treble stone', which we played on the pavement.

When we tired of playing, we would sit by the wall and play guessing games, or watch the writing in the sky. So often on summer evenings a high plane would drone overhead and write, usually 'Oxo' or 'Daily Mail', in vapour trails across the evening sky. Even the mums would come out to watch this fascinating performance.

We collected pins too, though what we did with them besides count to see who had the most, I can't recall. Putting a lot of little treasures in a fancy box, we would stand on the corner and call out, 'Pin for a look and a jolly good look.' One girl achieved a wonderful store of pins after an operation on her leg. We all wanted a peep at that shocking scar. Another version of the same game was to put paper squares from chocolates between the leaves of a book. Beautifully smoothed and carefully placed, these small foil squares were greatly prized. 'Pin for a pick and a jolly good pick,' we'd call.

Of course, there were the dare games, but we didn't often take part in these, only watch with bated breath while the boys tied a thin, strong string to a door-knocker, and when it was almost dark, carry it across the road and fasten the other end to the opposite knocker. Then they'd knock, and run away and hide. The opening door would cause the opposite knocker to lift, and when the irate householder closed his door, the other knocker would fall and the whole thing was repeated. Occasionally this went on for several minutes, the mystified occupants getting madder and madder as they crouched behind their door, hoping to catch the tormentor. Why this game was called 'Knocking Down Ginger' I never could find out.

Another dare game was quite simple, but not always plain sailing. We had to go into every shop, from our baker's right up to the chemist's, about fifteen shops in all, and ask for something at every one. All the shops were open until eight and nine on Saturdays, and the poor weary shopkeeper was not very keen on kids coming in and asking for something she didn't sell. My cousin always asked 'How much a dozen are the penny eggs?' or, 'Do you stock tea in ounce packets?' I used to say, 'Please have you any empty boxes, about nine inches square?' which worked, even in the pawn. I stated a size so that I wouldn't get laden with boxes before I was half-way through.

Our favourite indoor game was 'Dead Man's Dark Scenery' and again, I haven't a clue how it got this name. Dividing into two teams, one side would go into another room, and the remaining ones would cover up one, two, or even three of their number with all the coats. How hot it was, lying motionless beneath all the coats! Then, making sure they had left no peepholes, the others would leave the room, yelling as they did so, 'Dead Man's Dark Scenery,' disguising their voices if they could because the first ones would listen hard to the call.

Now it was their turn, to rush into the room and try to guess who was under the coats. No touching was allowed, but it was permissible to try and make the hidden ones laugh, once movement had been discovered. Then there would be a yell for the hidden ones, called by name, to arise, and a correct guess meant a change of sides.

We spent hours playing this game, leaving false clues like a wrong shoe sticking out a little, or a big ball to look like an extra head. It was great fun and any number could join in.

The new school continued to be interesting now that I had settled down, and I used to go out even earlier each morning, because the very first covered buses were now on the roads, and there was one on our route just after eight. I loved to boast that I'd been on a covered-top bus. My other favourite bus was a pirate bus, a bright purple vehicle numbered 525. This did not belong to the General Bus Co., and the driver would madly overtake all the other buses, collecting all the passengers he could. The conductor would stack us in until we could hardly breathe, and never used the hateful words 'Full right up'. I was never late for school when he was around.

Our longest bus rides were to the dentist. Mum had no faith in school clinics and felt that we must have the best as far as she was able. So every three or six months, she took us to the Royal Dental Hospital in Leicester Square; and how I hated it!

Somehow, when people talk today about dental health, I wonder just how much tooth decay is due to too many sweets, or lack of brushing. We all went to the same dentist, had the same food and used the same toothpowder, yet every visit was the same. Nothing wrong with my sisters' teeth, but a load of work to be done on mine. So by the time I was 23, I was well equipped with dentures, while my sisters still have their own teeth.

It was the students who did the work, though my mother fondly saw them all as highly qualified, and I'm afraid they didn't take the work as it came. I would sit there on the long, hard bench with about twenty other folk, watching them all working, and try to guess which one would do my fillings. My name always seemed to be called out by the one I least liked the look of. The kindly looking chaps would sift through the cards and when they pushed one to the back of the pile, I took a guess that that was mine.

Eventually I would be called, sit in the dreaded chair with my mouth open; and the student would start to grind and grind away, his foot working hard on the pedal. When he felt he had done enough, he would call the supervisor, usually the same elderly, thin-faced man with gold-rimmed glasses, a mass of grey hair and a wicked-looking pick in his hand. He would poke and prod and bring tears to my eyes, while I sat and gripped the arms of the chair, not daring to make a fuss, since my sisters were sitting with Mum, waiting to go home. How I longed to join the happy ranks of those who, going to sit in the inspection chair, would hear those magic words, 'Nothing this time, make an appointment for six months' time.' But in all the years I went there, it was never my good fortune. No one ever thought of injections for fillings in those days!

Having a tooth out by gas was even worse. We all sat together in a big waiting room, men separated from women by a big wooden partition, but children with adults. A big notice advised us to loosen all corsets and tight clothing and to go to the WC. I used to sit and wonder whether I ought to unbutton my combs. I went to the lav as advised, but the wait was so long that I was waiting to go again, yet dare not, since my name might get called while I was outside. The children were usually left till last, perhaps because their teeth were easier to pull when the students were tired. I sat watching women go in, all smiles, and come back with blood dripping from their tightly shut mouths. Twenty or more teeth at a time were commonplace extractions, and I lived in mortal dread that they might not remember to stop at one or two when I went in!

Auntie Lottie used to tell me, though, how lucky we were to have a real dentist to go to. At the turn of the century, when she was a girl, there was a monthly clinic held at a church hall in Bethnal Green. Anyone who had bad toothache could go there, line up and have the bad tooth pulled out. No gas, no injections and no painkillers. One day, a neighbour asked Auntie Lottie to line up and mind her place in the queue while she popped indoors for a minute. Lottie stood in the line and got nearer and nearer to the front and the neighbour, who had probably got cold feet by this time, failed to return.

Poor little Lottie reached the front. 'Open wide,' snapped the dentist, and even as she opened her mouth to explain the situation, her head was forced back, a gag inserted and two teeth pulled out! 'I suppose they were bad, anyway,' laughed Auntie, telling us the tale, 'but you ought to be grateful to your mother, looking after you the way she does.'

I suppose I was, but the only enjoyment for me was the trip we made afterwards, if there was time, to the National Gallery to look at the paintings. Perhaps that wasn't a good idea really, because always to associate paintings with toothache is not exactly a child's guide to the pleasures of artistic appreciation. However, Mum liked to get her money's worth, and having paid threepence fare to get up to Leicester Square, she liked to get as much as she could.

After Janet and the aunties moved to Knightsbridge, we had another opportunity to take a long bus ride. How we loved to get on top of a bus and ride all that way!

After I went to the grammar school, Mum used to let us go alone to visit. If I was old enough to go on one bus without an adult, then I was old enough to go on another! Occasionally, we stayed a couple of days with the aunties. We would talk about this holiday for weeks beforehand; Gwen making new clothes for her doll, complete outfits of neat stitchery, while I got by with a new bit of ribbon tied around mine.

We were left very much to our own devices in Knightsbridge, and we'd walk into Harrods, chins in the air and hands tightly clenched, wander across to the lift and ask for the third floor, trying hard to pretend we were somebodies. If we were asked what we wanted, I would come out with the formula I used at home, 'Have you any empty boxes about nine inches square please?' They never had, but would politely suggest that we tried another department, probably laughing up their sleeve at the two little girls with scruffy dolls, walking around their lovely store.

Once, we bumped into a lady being handed in at the door as we left, bows and gracious smiles all round. 'That,' breathed the doorman, 'is the Queen of Spain.'

The museums were a world of wonder too. If it was wet, one of the aunties would hurry us across the road and into the Victoria and Albert Museum at about two o'clock and tell us to stay there until five. Then Auntie Rosie would call for us on her way home from work.

I always thought her shop a funny place. It had about six windows, but with only one dress in each. Silly really, when there was room for about twenty. The prices were mad, for who would pay fifty guineas for one dress!

Most of all, we enjoyed the 'Dead Zoo', which was our name for the Natural History Museum, and it was no hardship to be left there for the afternoon. If Steve was with us, then we went a bit further afield to the Science Museum, where we organised a competition to see who could find the most buttons to press. Not that I ever looked at the models with any intelligence, but I loved to press the buttons and see things moving. After the little shop closed at eight o'clock, we were allowed to play there, and had fun playing shops with real goods and money.

Surprisingly, the people who frequented Auntie's little shop were no better off than the people we knew. They bought little bits and pieces like two ounce packets of tea and a quarter of butter, and there was the same stiff notice about not asking for credit.

There, just behind Harrods, were the little people without decent shoes, who had only oil lamps instead of gas like we had, and who would ask for a rasher of bacon. Indeed, their houses were not a patch on ours, with paint peeling off doors and tatty broken windows.

Nostalgia took me down that street not so long ago. It had the quiet air of a Kensington mews, the houses had wrought-iron gates, electric coach lamps hung in the porchways, and the little row bathed in the glow of having come up in the world. And so it had, for it has become a fashionable place to live. The houses sell for telephone number prices now, yet when Lottie traded there, the place was let at a rental of ten shillings a week.

After they moved away from us, the aunties too came up in the world. With no fares and no rent to pay, they blossomed out and bought themselves fur coats. When they came to see us, it was like having rich relations come to visit and their coats smelt of mothballs, just like 'yer Aunt's' did. They came for Christmas too, and Uncle Will said we'd have to tone things down a bit, if they were staying; and we couldn't treat them like one of the family any more.

I loved Christmas when the family was all together. Uncle would sit looking at a photo of himself in soldier's uniform, which hung in pride of place on the parlour wall, and several times during the evening, he would rise slowly to his feet, glass in hand, and call for silence.

'Stand up straight, Jean, shoulders back, Steve. Put your dolly down, Gwen. Everyone, please be uprising.'

We would all stand up, even Mum and Dad, and Uncle would say solemnly, 'The King, Gawd bless him.' Then we would all sit down again, and Dad and he would go on with the funny songs and ditties that only came out at Christmas. We owned a real gramophone now, and it was not an old-fashioned one with a horn either. Dad had records of the old music hall songs and we joined in them all. 'Daisy Daisy,' and 'Beer beer, glorious beer,' being top favourites. Only Mum refused to sing. Dad once offered her ten bob to sing just one verse solo, but she refused. Something died in her when Rosie died, and she was never quite the same. But all in all, Christmases were hilarious affairs.

Sometimes Gwen and I would go outside for a few minutes, just to hear all the pianos going honky tonk, up and down the street. With 'Knees up Mother Brown' in one house and 'It's a long way to Tipperary' next door, it was a lovely sound, especially as everyone had got sweating hot and all the windows were open. Sometimes a fight would break out and spill out into the street, but someone would throw a jug of water over the participants and that soon cooled things down. Most families had one member at least who could knock out a tune on the old pianos, or, like us, they aspired to a gramophone, and it was music all the way.

On New Year's Eve they had another party in most houses; but even if they didn't all the doors would open as the train whistles blasted and the factory hooters sounded, and the women would come out into the street banging on an old tin tray, yelling 'Happy New Year'.

The noise would wake us, if we were in bed, and we'd rush to the windows and shout out in unison with everyone else. Those who'd been drinking would dance in the street, but everyone was happy, even if they were out of work and hardly knew where the next meal was coming from. Who could tell . . . maybe this New Year would be the one to change their luck. If wishes could help, then things would go well, sure enough.

9

Father Christmas and Mr Thorn

Eva was really growing up now. Gwen and I used to tease her a lot, and looking back, I think she had a lot to put up with. She had the unfortunate knack of rubbing Dad up the wrong way, and now there were more rows than ever. She'd come in at night, after we were in bed, and we'd hear the ominous sounds of things being thrown about and Dad losing his temper. When she had gone up to bed, still tearfully standing up for herself, Dad would, as always, start on Mum, blaming her for the way she had brought us up.

How I wished she would learn to take the line of least resistance as I did, and keep out of his way. I remember once breaking off one of his carnation buds with my ball. I froze in horror as I realised it was his special, a beautiful white flower tipped with rosy pink. Every evening he had gone straight outside to look at it, ever since it had been a newly formed bud. And now, the fat, pink-tinged beauty lay forlornly on the earth! With scarlet face and trembling fingers, I looked guiltily around, picked it up and flushed it quickly down the lav.

The storm was smouldering when I went in, after rushing out to the street to play, but it was nearly bedtime and I didn't wait to be asked if I'd seen the flower. I hurried up to bed with a book.

It's hard to hold a post-mortem without a body, so discounting dogs and cats, who would at least have left the bud, Dad could only blame one of his own pigeons. He stood looking at them all in the loft and I think he felt like slitting all their crops to find the guilty party!

I was not normally a deceitful child, but if deceit would save a row, then I didn't have any qualms. I even saved up a sixpence and bought a packet of Gold Flake cigarettes, the brand Dad always smoked. He would sometimes leave a sixpence on the mantelpiece when he went upstairs for a nap, telling Eva to go and get him some before he woke up. Then, if she forgot, or didn't bother, I'd put the cigarettes on the shelf and take the sixpence ready for the next time. Anything to save a row.

Gwen and I had another excitement now though, because our big sister had a young man. They were not boyfriends in those days, but real 'young men' who came courting. They would walk in the park, up and down the Prom, and we would follow, at a discreet distance. When they came to a road, even a little one, he would take her elbow and steer her across, as though the poor thing couldn't manage the smallest step on her own!

She started attending chapel absolutely regularly now and we, not to be outdone, followed suit. Three times every Sunday, so that Mum and Dad thought they'd got a family of religious maniacs on their hands.

The young man was the chapel organist, and Eva would take her place in the gallery, so that he could come and sit with her during the sermon. His father and mother belonged to the chapel too, and his father was Sunday School Superintendent. His auntie was my Sunday school teacher, and this gave me a real thrill. For in a roundabout way, I was now one of the people I had always envied, a member of a family who really belonged to the place, instead of just one of the kids who came to the Sunday school. After all, if Eva married into this elite family, I'd have relations, in a distant way, at the chapel. It came to me with a shock that I'd always been jealous of the girl I'd fought with on the first day, because she belonged!

I realised suddenly, too, that Sunday school teachers didn't get paid for their work. They just did it, for love of God. It shook me, and I stopped putting toffee papers on the old dear's hat, and saying 'sausage' whenever I came to a word beginning with S in the Bible. I ceased singing 'without a shirt' on the end of every line of some of the hymns, as I had always done for a laugh. My favourite had always been a chorus. 'They shall run and not be weary, they shall walk and not faint.' 'Without a shirt' fitted in marvellously with this hymn.

Mr Brown paddling with some of the Sunday school children.

I envied Eva, and when the family invited us all to tea, Mum and Dad as well, I knew that things were getting serious. The Brown family didn't drink, they said Grace before every meal, and they had a little organ in their parlour. After tea, Mrs Brown played hymns on this, and we all joined in, except Mum and Dad. Sitting there must have been a real ordeal for Dad, poor man.

Duty done, they didn't ask us again as a family, but if ever Gwen or I called there, we were made most welcome. I discovered that there was to be a scripture exam at the Sunday school, and this was right up my street. The lessons were to be held at the Brown house, and every week I went there for lessons, and Eva didn't like it one bit, for Mrs Brown asked me to stay to tea. Eva accused me of going to spy, but it was not so. How could I explain what it was I found there? I didn't really know myself; it was an intangible atmosphere that I could never have described, but I used to think up innumerable excuses to call. Mrs Brown was always laughing, she had an infectious, almost childish laugh that giggled; she called her husband dear, and neither of them ever swore. When Mr Brown said 'Christ' he really meant the Son of God. Theirs was the first Christian home I had ever been in and it made a profound impression on me. They not only attended chapel three times on Sundays, but they went along to a Bible study on Wednesdays and a prayer meeting on Saturdays. I never even knew before that these last named were public meetings, but now I shyly crept in occasionally on a Saturday evening, to listen to Mr Brown praying in his rich Yorkshire brogue. They had only the one son, and it seemed to me that they doted on the little teenager he was all set to marry.

How Eva managed it I shall never know, but Mum and Dad bought a piano. Not a honky-tonk old joanna, but a lovely new piano. Now, when Jim came to our house, he sat and played. Chopin, Wagner, Beethoven, names I had never heard of and didn't even pronounce correctly, Jim sat and played on our lovely new piano; and I longed to have the window open so that the neighbours could hear the real music which came from our house. Eva started having music lessons and Jim and she sat for ages in the front room alone, with only the occasional few bars of music from time to time. But apart from these spells, she was never at home and she never came in next door with us, for she didn't see fit to introduce Jim to them all.

She had started going to Oxford Street now, to buy her clothes, and really thought she was somebody. After all, we had always thought of Selfridges as somewhere to look in the window, not actually to buy from.

My cousin Will was courting too, and often when we went in, his girl was spending the evening there. Nothing highbrow about Phyllis. She stood up one evening singing the latest song, 'Oh, do, do, do, do, something.' She swayed in front of Will as she sang, hands on his shoulders and big eyes tempting him. 'Oh, do, do something.' So he did. He seized a plate of red jelly from the table and put it down the front of her blouse, the red staining the yellow silk. How she shrieked, and how we laughed, as she swore and carried on at him. No, she wasn't in the same class as my sister.

When I looked at Eva walking up the street with her young man, in his neat suit and with a rolled umbrella, I felt a sudden swift compassion for her, and wished we could move away. To live somewhere else, where people didn't know everyone else's business and didn't make rude comments. 'Stuck-up little bitch,' they would call to each other, as Eva and Jim walked arm in arm.

My grammar school uniform didn't help either; and I too was called stuck-up. I was stuck-up maybe, but under it, I was getting desperately anxious, for I still half-heartedly believed what Renee had told me. If I didn't start my periods soon, I was heading for an early grave! I didn't want to die, and snooping around, I found that most of my school friends had started. There were two envelopes in the school gym, and if swimming lessons were missed for this legitimate reason, then our name must be put in the envelope. I watched my friends going to the gym and missing swimming, and I seriously thought about making my will. Not that I had much to leave, but I didn't want them all fighting over my goods. So I divided things out, leaving my Sunday school Bible to Mr Brown, who could make best use of it, and as my fifteenth birthday approached, I waited to die.

The dreaded birthday passed and nothing happened to me and I changed my fear. Renee was wrong maybe, but what if I was so good that I was heading for a virgin birth? Maybe I was having a baby and didn't know it! After all, I bet the Virgin Mary was dead scared when she found out, and no one, absolutely no one, would have believed her tale, especially her mum! My relief when I found I was normal after all surpassed all my wildest hopes! Now I was ordinary like my friends, and the following swimming day sent me on winged feet into the gym envelopes.

Growing older, I was badly in need of more money, for the twopence pocket money from Dad and the twopence from Mum didn't go very far. So I took to baby minding on a bigger scale. The bakers were glad to have me take their baby off their hands for the day on Saturday, and would give me a shilling. 'Sweated labour,' Dad called it, for I'd take the baby, in its posh pram, before nine o'clock on a Saturday morning, bring it back and help get its bottle at lunchtime, rush home and eat my own dinner and take it back to the park from about two until six. Then I'd help get it ready for bed.

That shilling was worth having, and furthermore, the bakers had their very own car, a little red Austin Seven; and they sometimes took me out with them. It was the very first car I had ever been in! I'd have minded the baby for nothing to get that car ride!

Eva started on again about moving, and every few days she'd say something to Mum, and Mum would show Dad the Saturday paper with all the advertisements about houses. All around us, estates were going up in Essex, and we'd dream of a future outside Bethnal Green. On my afternoons off from school, we'd take a train to Buckhurst Hill and actually walk into the new houses, planning where we'd put things, if they were really ours. For £600, we could get a detached three-bedroomed house, with a square hall and a little round window in it. Long gardens . . . side entrances, how many of those houses did we try to own in those early thirties! But Dad was adamant. The pigeons were his latest excuse, for they were not allowed in many of the new areas.

I didn't realise I was getting snobby myself until one of my friends invited me to her house. The furnishings were not so good as ours, and the house itself not much better, but no one sat outside the front door on an old chair in her road, and no one called out rude comments when we walked to her gate. Neither did her front door open directly on to the pavement. Her dad was a policeman and I never saw him sharpen a match to pick his teeth with as my dad did, and he didn't wear his cap in the house all the time, or spit in the fire.

So many things I had always accepted now seemed to me to be wrong, what with the Brown family, where we used table napkins rolled up in silver rings, and the girls at school who lived in Hackney or Dalston.

Mr Brown had a big influence on other girls besides us, for he often found jobs for them, especially school leavers. He had a friend in the City who owned an underwear factory, and like himself, this man was also a Christian. When he needed staff he just asked Mr Brown, and the factory was kept supplied with learners from our Sunday school. Gwen and Jean were now coming up to 14 and both had their eyes on a job in the Holborn factory. I wasn't too happy about this because my father had signed papers for me to stay on at school until 16 at the least and I was now half-heartedly studying for matric. I say half-heartedly, because things were pretty bad in the employment world at this time. Men who had jobs in 1932 hung on to them for grim death and the two million who were out of work were always waiting to step into their shoes. So when short-time work started for Dad and there was less money coming into the house, Mum looked around for ways and means to add a bit. No more lodgers, that was certain, for Dad said he'd swing first, but money was really very tight.

Gwen started work at the Holborn factory and I felt, for the very first time, that she and I were drifting apart. We had always done things together; and when she offered me a threepence pocket money, I felt dreadful. I was afraid she would gang up on me with Eva, who kept making comments about me being kept as a lady, by her. I howled my eyes out and prayed that something might come along. And so it did. Dad's work was cut to half time, and Mum went to the school asking that they be relieved of their obligation to keep me there. So I entered my last term, only nine months away from matric, tore to shreds my dreams of going on to college and becoming a teacher, and began to write stories instead. Having lost heart in work, since I had no goal, I devised a smashing scheme. I'd write a lurid love story, loan it out to my friends in exchange for their prep books, and copy all their work, writing out long equations and theorems which meant absolutely nothing to me whatsoever.

Chapel began to mean more to me than anything else now, because I not only had the Browns, I also had Father Christmas!

I had been helping organise the infants' party when I met him. He was a recent member of the church, whom I had never met before. Somehow, I was amused by the fact that this man had a bowler hat, and when he left his things in a neat pile to dress up as Father Christmas, I took and hid the bowler hat in the pulpit. The church was dark and solemn, and I stood in the silence and listened to God.

It always seemed to me that God was very near in that quiet and deserted chapel building. Then a tram went rattling by and shook me from my reverie. I ran downstairs to where the ladies were washing up after the party tea; and had a good laugh to myself at poor Father Christmas, hunting in all the odd corners for his hat.

Eventually, someone told him that I'd been seen creeping upstairs with it and he chased me for it. We had a good laugh together and he walked with me to the corner of our street. After that, we seemed to meet each other quite a lot, though I knew there'd be hell to pay if Dad found out. Girls at school didn't have young men friends.

Father Christmas called me his little girl in brown, and now all my dreams were centred around him. When I grew up, he would still be waiting for me; and we could get married and he would never ever go to a pub, or swear, or take off his belt to us, his family. We'd have lots of children and take them all to chapel every Sunday and say Grace at mealtimes like they did in the Brown family. Life was going to be wonderful. . . .

Then Eva found out and told Mum and she put her foot down. 'Going around with a man old enough to be your father, I hear,' she stormed at me. 'Your father will kill you if he finds out. So you'd better put a stop to it, and think a bit harder about school. You'll never get a good report this term!'

As though I cared any more about school, since I was leaving anyway. Father Christmas wasn't old enough to be my father, in fact he was only about four years older than me, but a 19-year-old who had been at work for five years certainly seemed a man compared with a 15-year-old schoolgirl. So I cooled off him for a bit, anything to avoid trouble, and I stayed away from the chapel for a time too, never giving any word of explanation and just laughing my way out of it when Father Christmas tried to ask me what was wrong.

All too quickly came the summer. I said goodbye to all my school friends and thought about the big city in which I was to earn a living. There was no question of my going to the underwear factory, for I was hopeless at sewing and I hated it anyway, and I couldn't see myself fitting in at the factory where Eva now held an office job.

For a week or so I moped around at home, but clearly this would not be tolerated. The very air was heavy with reproach when Eva and Gwen put their wages on the table.

'What do you want to do?' asked Mum, perplexed and clearly out of her depth.

'I wanted to go to college and become a teacher, you know that,' I replied, 'but since I can't, I want to write books.'

Mum shook her head, and when our insurance man called she asked him what he thought I ought to do, but he was vague. No office experience, no shorthand or typing, nothing but an unfinished grammar school education. I could recite 'Gray's Elegy' from beginning to end and back again to the first verse, which I had once done for a bet at school. I knew whole scenes from *Julius Caesar*, and I could fathom out most mathematical problems, but that was all. No good at all in the cut-throat world of competition for work.

'What she really needs is a year at a commercial college,' mused the insurance man, but Mum cut in sharply. 'She's left school because we can't afford to keep her there, so it's no use making that sort of suggestion and putting ideas in her head.'

We bought the newspapers for a few mornings, but nothing came of that and after another week or so, Dad got fed up, as I knew he would.

'Plenty of work around, if you look for it,' he said. 'Take a penny bus ride and walk through Shoreditch. Lots of vacancies for girls. No need for you to be out of work. It's only men that are not wanted,' he finished bitterly.

So we set out, Mum and I, past big box-making factories, 'machinists wanted' signs and 'girls to learn upholstery' notices. Everyone wanted girls to use their hands, not their brains, and it never occurred to my poor mum that we were in the wrong area.

At last we came to Featherstone Street, just off Old Street, and there we stood before a sign. 'Girl wanted to make herself useful.' The place was a very small printers and bookbinders, and Mum's eyes lit up. 'Here you are. You said you wanted to write books. You can learn to make them as well here, and you never know, you might get a chance to write for them as well.' I don't think she really believed that herself, but I was fed up by this time and we walked in. It was dark and smelly and I longed to turn and run, but Mum was behind me, pushing me forward towards the seedy-looking individual who was the boss.

So I started in the brave new world of industry for twelve shillings a week. I made cocoa, washed up, ran errands, interleaved pamphlets with newspaper as they came off the printing machine and learnt to use a perforating machine. I also had to answer the phone on occasion, just to lie and say 'I'm sorry, there's no one here but me. Can I take a message?' while the boss stood breathing heavily down my neck, smelling of beer and smoke.

He was a slippery customer, my bald-headed boss, and he was always contriving to get one of the girls alone. After a while, he turned his attentions to me, and he would call me over to the little cubbyhole where I made the cocoa, put his sweaty arms around me and kiss me with wet, slobbery lips. 'Nice?' he would ask, and dumb with misery, I would nod my head and wish I could kill him. Sometimes I would see my father passing by, and longed to rush out and tell him, but I was dead scared of losing my job. I dared not throw it up, and was terrified of getting the sack, so I endured weeks of untold misery. When I felt particularly miserable, I would find myself thinking of Father Christmas with his twinkling eyes and curly hair and his kind and gentle manner. It wouldn't be revolting if he kissed me, but he never did.

One morning, old Mr Thorn sent me to Moorgate, to a big block of offices. I wandered along in the bright sunshine, wishing I was one of those lucky people who worked there, when I stopped to look in the windows of the Methodist Book Room. There was an open hymn book on display, and I thought it would be fun to learn the words of the hymn, two verses on the way there and the other two on the way back. Blow old Thorn and his slobbery kisses; if I kept him waiting for his cocoa, that was his hard luck. So I stopped; and tarried even longer on the return journey, hoping that the cocoa would have been made by someone else. But no such luck, and I had once again to endure his passes.

Next week, going again to Moorgate, I went straight to the bookshop window, glad to see that the hymn book had been changed and another hymn revealed. I began to learn it, and reading it through, stopped dead. Surely . . . this hymn had been put there for me, especially the second verse.

> I thank Thee Lord, that all our joy,
> Is touched with pain.
> That shadows fall on brightest hours,
> That thorns remain,
> So that earth's bliss may be our guide, and not our chain.

Well, my Thorn was certainly my cross to bear, my thorn in the flesh, so to speak, but I thought that I'd put up with it long enough and felt that I wasn't called upon to endure it any longer.

I hurried back to the smelly little printers and into the cubbyhole to make the cocoa, and when the greasy Mr Thorn came up and put his arms around me, I saw red, came to my senses and did what I should have done long ago. No job was worth this, so I caught him a resounding crack on his bald head with the milk saucepan. To my great surprise, he gave me an injured look, turned and walked away, and from then on he left me severely alone. He turned his unwelcome attentions to another poor kid, and started sending me out on errands on every possible occasion. I rejoiced in my new-found freedom, looked in all the shop windows and wandered through the nearby market. I sat in the sunshine in Bunhill Fields, close by the tombstone of John Bunyan and thought how silly I had been not to stand up for myself all this time.

I didn't see much of my friend Father Christmas these days, but I couldn't see much future in it. We'd never got any further than holding hands anyway. He had nice hands, nothing much to look at because they were grimed with stencil ink from his work, but they were nice, firm, dry hands; and if there was one thing I could not stand, it was clammy damp hands. Although I was nearly 17 now, I had no regular young man as Eva had. I found fault with all the boys I went out with, and the most recent one I had parted from just because of his damp hands!

I had set my sights higher than the boys of Bethnal Green anyway. My latest ambition was to be a minister's wife. Not our minister, since he was happily married, but the wife of any vicar, parson or missionary who'd have me. If I'd been a man, I know I'd have been a preacher; I used to spend hours dreaming up sermons, but since I couldn't, the next best thing was to be the preacher's wife. I was deadly jealous of our minister's wife, because of the life she lived. Presiding over the women's meeting, having the deacons and their wives to tea, giving out the Sunday school prizes and making little speeches, oh, she was a lucky woman.

Problem. How to become a parson's wife if you don't know any parsons? Not even half-fledged ones with high hopes. I think I'd have made a beeline for any theological student who swam within my sights, even if he had wet hands and wet kisses, another of my pet hates since my experiences with the dreadful old Thorn. But there it was, all the eligible young men I knew were either shop assistants, printers or postmen, cobblers or carpenters, and though the Lord Himself was a carpenter, I was aiming higher up the social scale, but hadn't a clue about the rules of the game.

One Sunday evening, Mr Brown, who still watched over me with a Christian and fatherly eye, asked to see me for a moment. He took me into the deacon's vestry and began by ticking me off. I had been chairing our youth club meeting on a wet and thundery evening. Our minister, who was due to come and speak, had sent a message saying his wife was not very well, and as she was scared of thunder, he had decided to stay home with her and asked to be excused.

Somehow, this made me spitting mad; and I stood up, gave the young people the message from the minister and then began to read from the Bible, having changed the reading at the last moment. I began, slowly and deliberately, to read the parable of the man who gave a dinner party and when all was ready, the guests began to make excuses. When I reached 'I have married a wife and therefore I cannot come,' I paused significantly and said, 'Excuses, like mankind himself, have not changed over the years.'

This caused a terrific burst of applause from the meeting, but someone told Mr Brown and now he took me to task.

'You are altering, Doris,' he said sadly. 'You are not your usual sunny self. Something is wrong. Is it home, or work? Aren't you happy at work?'

Happy? He had to be joking! I stood looking at him for a moment, then suddenly, out it all tumbled. The horrible old Mr Thorn, the lies on the phone, the aimless wanderings through Whitecross Street and the sheer hopelessness of trying to be anybody, let alone somebody. 'We must get you away,' he said kindly. 'The trouble is, it's hard to find a vacancy, apart from my friend Mr Colston at the factory. But I'll have a think. In the meantime, no more misuse of scripture.'

That night, he called to see Mum and Dad. He was tactful and made no mention of Mr Thorn, but he told them I was doing no good there. Gwen was now earning over a pound a week. She worked an overlock machine on piecework, getting about one and six for overlocking a dozen pairs of knickers. I just couldn't see myself doing this, but there it was. Gwen was getting on and I wasn't.

Happiness didn't enter into it, or satisfaction in work. I knew that even Gwen was not really happy. Admittedly, she loved needlework and was really good at it, but it was designing and the artistry that she loved; and there couldn't be much artistry in overlocking knickers all day long. But the money – there was plenty of artistry in a pound note as far as my family were concerned, and an appointment was made for me to see the great Mr Colston.

In fear and trembling, I went into his office the next day. I wasn't often scared, but I dreaded that he'd see through me, realise that I was hopeless at sewing and didn't want the job anyway. His old father sat in the office with him and smiled at me, such a warm, friendly smile that I felt worse than ever, wondering what questions they'd ask me. I couldn't have lied to them, and dreaded their questions.

'Why do you want to leave your present job?' was a fairly easy one, and although I kept quiet about the trouble with old Thorn, I told them about the lies and the swearing that went on and the sheer waste of time that I endured. 'I just can't work there any longer,' I finished.

'Well, you won't find any troubles like that with us, will she, Father?' smiled Mr Colston. 'And although you'll have to start as a learner, I'm sure you'll soon pick it up and be earning as much as your sister.'

So I arranged to start the next week, and once the excitement of giving in my notice at the printers was over, I had plenty of time to regret the step I had taken. I was sure I'd never even learn to thread the needle of the wretched machine! Gwen was kind and tried to explain all she could about the work, but I couldn't see myself earning one and six a week!

That Sunday night, I prayed for guidance. 'Please God, don't let me do the wrong thing,' I cried. The last hymn of the service should have been a comfort.

> All the way my Saviour leads me,
> What have I to ask beside . . .

finishing with

> For I know whate'er befall me,
> Jesus doeth all things well.

I suppose it was so, but didn't feel very optimistic when we set off together on the Monday morning. We took a bus to Chancery Lane and walked up to Holborn, this inbred saving of a penny still part of our very being. Chancery Lane was the end of the threepenny journey, and not even on a soaking wet morning would we spend that extra penny to ride up to Kingsway.

I reached the factory and took off my coat, feeling very nervous and bitter about setting out to earn my living doing the only thing I really hated and was absolutely no good at.

Some of the girls said hello, but I could feel their thoughts as their eyes lighted upon me. So this is what comes of going to a posh school and learning all that poetry and stuff and all that German? Finishing up as one of us, but all behind. Doing a 14-year-old job at 17! I longed to grab my coat and make a run for it but then, with a sudden clatter, the machine started up. Gwen grabbed a big pile of peach lock-knit knickers and threw herself into the making of them, for time was money and at threeha'pence a pair, you just had to get cracking.

I sat there for a bit and then a tall, very nice-looking girl came out from the little office and told me that Mr Alan wanted to see me. She took me to his door and gave me a friendly smile as she ushered me in. 'Mr Alan' was the Mr Colston I had seen the previous week. 'Doris,' he said, crinkling his face into a smile, 'I've got a feeling that you aren't very keen on learning to be a machinist.' I sat still, wondering whether my face had given me away. Was this kicking-out time? But he was smiling so kindly . . .

'I should think,' he went on, 'that you are fairly intelligent. You've had a good education, even if it has been cut short, but I gather you can learn pretty quickly. How would you like to start in the office? We need a willing helper there.'

Well, now the boot was on the other foot. It was I who felt like kissing, for I could willingly have flung my arms round his neck there and then.

'I didn't say anything the other day,' he went on, 'because I wasn't quite sure. But I like people who are willing to have a go at anything, and I was glad to see that you were willing to start off as a machinist. So we'll start you as our office junior and see how you get on.'

I hardly took in hours or wages – I think I'd have worked for him for nothing, but he cut short my grateful thanks and took me along to the office, where I was delighted to find I'd be under the wing of the girl with the friendly smile.

I took to the work like a duck to water, and my uncanny memory for numbers and figures was a great help. 'Our walking telephone directory' Mr Alan called me, and since every garment made in the factory was known by its number, it wasn't long before I could reel off all the numbers that each of the big Knightsbridge and Oxford Street stores bought. Even the buyers got to depend on my knowing what they wanted, and since the switchboard was my responsibility I was soon on first-name terms with lots of the assistants in the big stores.

I taught myself to type, and although I had no shorthand to begin with I was soon able to write letters for Mr Alan. What a different life it was!

Apart from one short spell during the war, I stayed with Colstons until my first baby was due, thoroughly enjoying myself and never ceasing to be grateful for the chance that had been given me.

Old Mr Colston was a dear. Whenever he had occasion to tick us off, which wasn't often, he would come up to the office with a clean white hankie in his clenched fist. He'd growl a bit and cast withering scorn upon any error, soon reducing his clerk to tears. Then he would put the hankie into her hand, tell her gruffly to dry her tears, and march out of the room. Later, he would come back, contrite and forgiving. 'Doris,' he'd say softly, 'I'm a bad-tempered old man. Put this in your Sunday school box,' and he'd leave a ten shilling note on my desk.

I was very keen on the Sunday school nowadays. I had proved so very often in my young life that there was a God, a loving and forgiving God who bothered about the kids of Bethnal Green. I was so sure of this that I had to make sure that none of the little ones I met would go out in ignorance of this wonderful heavenly care that was theirs for the asking. So I became a Sunday school teacher. It was a far cry from my first ambition to teach, but a very rewarding one.

There was one little girl in my class, who came from what even I called a real slum. She and her three brothers and sisters lived with their parents in a tumbledown house just off Green Street. There were two rooms down and two up, but they let one of the upstairs rooms. The father and the boys slept in the upstairs room and the mother and three little girls slept downstairs. But this division of the sexes didn't prevent new babies from turning up with monotonous regularity, and although I called and duly admired each new baby as it came, I couldn't help wondering why they didn't stop producing.

Perhaps the mother felt this, because on one occasion, she picked up the bundle of wet and whimpering new baby, dropped it into its cot and said, 'Ah well, what's coming to yer, comes.'

Her husband, an out-of-work dockie, was a real Micawber and was always expecting something to turn up. Dock work encouraged this attitude to life, being mostly casual labour, but he did nothing to help himself. 'One day,' he would muse, 'one day, things will be different for us. We'll get out of this hole and start fresh. Maybe I'll get a little job what's regular, with a bit coming in each week, so's we know where we are.' Yet when he did get a week's work and they invited me to tea on the Sunday, there would be gritty cockles and lurid 'Palace Cake' for tea, the baby had a new silk bonnet and the other children bright straw hats and new caps while their feet were still hanging out of their shoes.

Life did change for them in the end in the dual shape of TB, which took four of the children, and one of Hitler's bombs which accounted for the rest and for the wretched slum in which they lived.

They were not the only really poor family in the school and my heart ached for some of the children. I used to invite them to our house to tea and Mum would ply them with home-made cake and jelly. The National Sunday School Union owned a property in Bournemouth, by the lovely name of House Beautiful and when any of the poor children had been really ill, we would manage to get them away for a fortnight. They wrote glowing letters and hated coming home away from the lovely seaside. 'I never knew there was such a big sea,' wrote one, 'it's so much bigger than Southend.' In my heart, I envied these kids I tried so hard to get away, because I had never been any further than Southend myself at that time.

Father Christmas was a Sunday school teacher too, and now I was on first-name terms with him. Out of school uniform I seemed to be catching up with him, and now not even my sister could say that he was too old for me. He walked home with me sometimes after teachers' meetings, but I was always elusive about meeting him any other time. He was poor, desperately poor. His job wasn't much and he had a mother to support. His brother, nearly ten years older than he, was married and lived some way away, so that Eric seemed always to be at his mother's beck and call, doing her shopping because she was out at work, or taking her to the market or doing her housework. I'd heard lots about possessive mothers of sons, so I had a further reason for not wasting too much time and thought in his direction.

It was about this time that I became very friendly with a man I'd never met. Colin Edwards was just a voice, though an influential one, in one of the big manufacturers' offices. Colstons bought rolls of silk from his firm, and it was a standing joke that if our stock-keeper was told that a material was not available, or temporarily out of stock, I could usually manage to get a delivery for us by phoning Colin Edwards personally. I knew he was a fairly important personage in his office and most people phoning got fobbed off with his secretary, but whenever I rang, I had only to say, 'Tell him it's Doris from Colstons,' and I was through. We used to chat for ages about all sorts of things; and then one day, when he rang, he asked me if I'd go with him to his company's Sports Day in Kent.

'Bring one of your friends,' he suggested, 'and I'll bring one of the fellows from the department.'

What excitement this caused at the office! It was easy to find one of the girls to accompany me, and we went up to Oxford Street one lunchtime to buy new dresses. I even had my very first perm for the occasion. Gosh, what agony to endure for a blind date! Sitting for hours with every hair screwed up to a mass of electric wire, getting hotter and hotter as it baked the hair, and then the wrestling match as the frizz was pulled into some sort of order.

Came the Saturday of the Sports Day, and the weather smiled upon us. Colin and his friend Arthur came to call for us at the office, and Mr Colston met them at the door.

'Now, take care of my girls,' he laughed, 'and give them a good time.'

Good time! I'd never had a time like it. To start with, I'd never been to a restaurant for a meal, apart from the odd snack at Lyons, but Colin and Arthur took us to a big grill room. We had chops, and I recall they had little frills around the bone. The chops were not all that tender, to my way of thinking, and I saw the sense in the old saying, mutton dressed up as lamb.

Then came the train journey to Kent and on the way, Colin and I got to know each other quite well. I really liked him now that we'd met, and he was certainly keen.

'You are funny, you fascinate me,' he kept saying. Seems that was his favourite word, because later he said that he'd love his mother to meet me, as she'd be fascinated. I bet she would, I thought, when he showed me a photograph of her. Just a snap in the garden, he said it was, and there was this willowy blonde standing by the net of a tennis court, racquet in hand.

'I suppose the tennis court is in your garden,' I jeered in my most sarcastic voice, and it was Arthur who answered. 'Yes it is.' Just as though there was nothing peculiar in having a whole tennis court in your garden!

Teatime came, and I looked with longing at the lovely cream horns and meringues that were being served; and helped myself to a miserable piece of fruit cake, ordinary as could be. The trouble was, I had spotted the pastry forks and hadn't a clue as to how one ate a cake with a fork. So I left well alone and ate sandwiches instead.

Colin lived in Kent himself, but insisted on getting on the train and coming back to London Bridge with me. We had an empty first-class compartment, and no sooner did the train start than he put his arms around me and began to kiss me as though his life depended on it. It was quite enjoyable too, and I knew I could easily fall for this handsome-looking young fellow, with his Oxford accent and his easy and attractive manner.

We reached London Bridge and I tidied my hair and prepared to say cheerio, but he held tight to my hand. 'I'll see you right home,' he said and I froze in horror.

Imagine Colin Edwards walking down our street, where like as not there'd be a couple of women with babies at the breast standing at the doors, or old men sitting on chairs outside, or small boys watering the gutter. Imagine Colin coming into our house, where Dad would be sitting with his greasy cap on his head, whether inside or out in our garden. Tennis court! We had a pigeon loft and a row of stones, and a tin bath hanging up on the wall.

I shook my head. 'You don't want to come all the way back with me. You know I live in Bethnal Green.' It was common knowledge that Alan Colston got all his staff from the one source.

'Actually, our cook lives in Bethnal Green,' laughed Colin. 'I've been there once when she was ill and I ran her home in the car. Please, let me see you home.'

I shook my head the harder and ran off, to where a bus was waiting. 'I'll phone you on Monday,' I called, giving him a wave.

What a weekend I spent! Goodness knows what attracted him to me, but my real image had not ruined the phone image he had built up. Yet . . . how could he fit in? 'Class is class,' I had once heard my mother say, and I had laughed at this typical Bethnal Green attitude. Yet to go out with Colin would mean cutting myself off from all the friends I had and all I held dear.

He didn't wait for me to phone on Monday, but rang me early, almost as soon as I reached the office. I hedged when he tried to date me, and when I left at five thirty, there he was, waiting outside the office door. He took me to tea; and I settled for fish and chips . . . and couldn't go wrong with them. But I was mistaken again, for instead of an ordinary knife and fork, there were special fish ones, with a curly bit at the end of the knife, though whether you used the curly bit or held it uppermost, I just hadn't a clue. So I toyed with the chips until I got a chance to see what someone else was doing, but it was an uncomfortable few minutes.

We saw each other several times after that and I was sorely tempted. But in my heart I knew that I'd never fit in and besides, he just laughed at me for going to church.

'Well, God,' I prayed, 'you'd better show me what to do, because I really don't know.' And on the following Sunday, when the minister announced his text, my ears pricked up at the words of St Paul: 'For I have learned, in whatsoever state I find myself, therewith to be content.'

There it was, an answer just for me. I told Colin that I didn't want to go on seeing him, and after a few hopeless meetings he got the message. The girls thought I was mad.

'Do you know his dad's a director of the firm?' said our stock-keeper, shaking his head at my foolishness.

But I couldn't help it. Colin's world and mine could never meet, not in those pre-war days.

Eva's courtship was now reaching a successful conclusion. The ring had been purchased and admired and a flat had been found and suitably furnished. My father had come up trumps and got everything in the furniture line at cost price from a little Jewish cabinetmaker in Shoreditch.

'A lovely job,' he told Eva, when she went to see what he had to offer. 'It breaks me heart to have to part with it at such prices, but times are hard, me dear, and I haven't sold a thing this month. Got to pay the rent somehow, and if it wasn't that I wanted to do your father here a favour, I couldn't keep to your prices. I'd get ten times what I'm asking you, from Harrods. Trouble is, they are overstocked at present.' It was true too, he did make for Harrods, though of course he didn't sell to them directly. He made for the big firm that employed my dad, and they sold to Harrods at a much higher price.

So Eva got her solid oak dining suite, her mahogany and walnut bedroom furniture and all her bits and pieces. Gwen made her curtains and I went over to the flat in Hackney to help get it straight, almost envious of her. She did have some nice things.

She was terribly nervous on her wedding eve, and as always, when nervous, she took it out on us. We couldn't do a thing to please her. 'As bridesmaids, you've got to do as I tell you and wait on me,' she kept saying, and did she keep us running around!

Eventually, we were sent to take her 'going away' clothes to the bridegroom's house, as the wedding reception was being held there. I was all for having a row with her, not being nearly so meek and mild as I had been. I was still smarting a bit from the Colin episode, and all Eva's swanking made me mad. I kept imagining the sort of wedding I might have been having in the future, if I hadn't sent him away. But Gwen was the peacemaker and she tried her hardest to cheer me up. When we came to a small church, halfway between our place and the Browns, we stopped and hung Eva's new hat on the railings, dumped her new case on the pavement and sat on a little seat and discussed it all.

'Do you reckon she'll have a baby?' I asked. Babies always followed the wedding in our circles, and we sat there contemplating the unlikely idea of Eva as a mother.

Gwen stood up and took the hat off the railings, knocking out the dent with her fist. 'Well, we'd better get on. At least, after tonight we'll have a bedroom each.'

The highlight of the wedding, to my mind. A bedroom to myself!

The November wedding day was typical: gloomy and inclined to be foggy. The atmosphere at home wasn't much brighter, either. Dad was not in a festive mood. The idea of going to church didn't appeal to him in the first place; and the fact that we were going on to the Browns afterwards was not exactly his idea of a wedding 'do'.

'I don't know how long we'll be expected to stay with those bloody Bible punchers,' he remarked gloomily. He went out with one of the uncles for a quick drink and this put Eva on edge, to say the least. Supposing he didn't come home in time!

But the uncle had been well primed by his wife, and they were not gone for long. When they returned, however, Dad heard our voices raised. We were not exactly quarrelling, but arguing rather, over placing the bridal veil, or the tying of the sashes, or something like that.

'Quarrelling, are you?' he stormed, bursting into the room. 'Don't you think I've got enough to put up with today, without you carrying on? I'll kick the three of you up the bloody aisle, that's what I'll do! And when he says "Who giveth this woman?" do you know what I'm going to say? "Take her, and a bloody good riddance!" You just see if I don't, or I'll swing first!'

We sat in stunned silence. Dad was capable of anything, we knew that. And if he let us all down . . . it cast a black cloud of gloom over the remainder of the getting ready.

When we reached the chapel, I was praying like mad. 'Oh, please God, don't let him do it. Please God.' But I didn't have complete faith in my prayers that day, and although we all walked sedately up the aisle, my heart was pounding like mad when the minister started the service. 'Dearly beloved. . . .'

'Who giveth this woman?' he asked, and Dad gestured slightly. I thought everyone must be able to hear the drumbeat that was my heart. 'I do,' answered Dad, in a meek little voice. So much for his swinging that day!

When we came out of the church, the sun was breaking through and a small knot of onlookers stood outside. Among them, I was amazed to see my Father Christmas, though why he bothered, I couldn't think. Eva certainly didn't invite him to the wedding. As we got into the car and drove away in our pink silk dresses, beautifully made by Gwen, I caught his eye and he gave me a special smile. I knew that he hadn't come to see Eva in all her wedding glory, but just to see me. It was a comforting thought.

There was no honeymoon after the wedding breakfast. November was not exactly seaside weather in England, and the very word 'abroad' was barely in common use at that time. Apart from soldiers and sailors, no one we knew ever went abroad.

So Eva and Jim went off to their flat, and the party, if you could call it that, was soon over. We said our goodbyes to the Browns and I expect the Brown relations were glad to see us go. I know my dad and uncles were like dogs let off the leash, as soon as we got clear of the house. I'd rather have stayed with the Browns, but Dad and the other men made their way to the Vic and the aunts and Mum went home. By the time they all got home, they were ready to sing 'The old Bull and Bush' and fill up their glasses again and again from the bottles the men brought back. But it was not exactly an exciting wedding.

The very next morning, Gwen and I decided to visit Eva and Jim, little wretches that we were. We couldn't wait to see whether marriage had altered our dear sister. Jim was out, playing the organ, and Eva was cooking the Sunday dinner, beating up the Yorkshire pudding and basting the beef, just as Mum did. Then, as we watched, she started to make pastry. Now, Gwen was very good at cookery, it had been one of her top subjects at school, and as she watched Eva's valiant efforts, she observed mildly that the pastry was too wet.

'It'll keep sticking to the rolling pin, like that,' she finished, as Eva scraped and rolled for the umpteenth time.

Eva wiped her hands without speaking, her face livid with temper. 'How dare you, a kid like you, try and teach a married woman how to cook!' She opened her door with a flourish and we ran down the stairs, having a good old giggle as we went.

'I bet Jim won't think that tart is just like mother's,' I laughed, thinking of Mrs Brown's featherlight pastry.

We were doomed to disappointment about the baby, too. No swelling lump marred the bride's figure and all my fond hopes of having a nice little baby to nurse were in vain. It was a shame, to my mind, because Eva would probably have had a nice little baby, all beautifully kept and dainty. Actually, it was ten years before that baby put in an appearance, and by that time I was too busy with my own to bother much about Eva's.

Like most brides of her generation, Eva gave up work immediately upon marriage, for every man expected to support his wife. Not many firms accepted married women anyway, so Mum and Eva went out together, shopping in Roman Road, or going to the pictures.

Nothing was ever said now about moving. Frankly, Eva didn't care, and openly referred to our street as a slum. She was living in Hackney, her flat was in a nice, clean house as big as 'yer Aunt's', and her husband had a nice clean job in the piano world. I felt sometimes that life was a bit hard, because maybe, if we had lived somewhere decent, I might have dared to take Colin home, and who knows what might have followed?

Yet now I know so much more. Colin joined the RAF at the outbreak of war; and he was one of the few whom the many mourned. I'd have been a war widow, and then what would have happened, had I cut myself adrift from my folks? A pretty bleak and lonely outlook, it would have been.

During the following September came an event which changed everything for me, and it was brought about indirectly by Oswald Mosley's Blackshirts. They had been troublesome all summer, holding meetings in Victoria Park and marching through Grove Road. But this particular Sunday, they had a near-riot right outside our chapel, just as the children were leaving Sunday school. Most of them ran through the back streets and some of the parents called to take their offspring home, but we were left, Father Christmas and I, with a handful of little girls. They were too scared to set foot outside, and frankly, so was I. There were police whistles and scuffles, and surging mobs of angry men, throwing stones and jumping off the steps of our building.

Time went on and the white-faced children began to weep.

'Come on,' said Father Christmas finally, 'let's wait our opportunity and make a run for it. If we go through to the back of the church and down the little side steps, we can make it, if we are quick.'

So we took the children's hands and made our way to the back steps. When the crowd thinned momentarily, having boarded a tram they had got off the lines, we made a dash and were soon safe in the small street behind Grove Road. We took the children home, seeing each safely to their door, and breathed a sigh of relief.

'Thank God for that,' I said, turning to him with a smile.

'Now I've got to see you safely home,' he answered, taking my hand.

It was as though a light had suddenly shone through the grey of my day. How right, how very right, it seemed, to be walking along hand in hand with him, and I

An arrest taking place during the Cable Street riots on 4 October 1936. (Tower Hamlets Local History Library and Archives)

knew, at that very moment, that this was the way I wanted to walk, for the rest of my life. All my dreams about meeting the embryo parson went up in smoke, all my vague ideas of being swept away against my better judgement by the glamorous Colin just vanished into thin air; and all my plans about being rich and famous just disappeared. Now I knew exactly what I wanted and my feet were firmly on the path. My Beloved, my Eric, was a real Christian, a man who lived for God and to whom God meant everything, and I wanted nothing more than to share his life, however tough and humble it might be.

That night, as I sank into my bed, my new dream was born. Maybe, some day, I would be a minister's mother. With such a man as mine, our children could not grow up any other way than with a faith.

Some years later, when our first son was born, our minister came into the hospital to see me. He stood looking at the little black-haired, red-faced, day-old baby.

'He'd make a lovely little parson,' he laughed, 'and that pair of lungs would stand him in good stead.' I picked up the screaming little bundle and held him to me.

'Perhaps, some day, he will be,' I replied slowly, 'but I'd never wish him to enter the Church because his mother wanted him to. It would have to be of his very own free will, so I'll never ever suggest it.'

So I kept my secret dream in my heart, and when it was realised and I saw my beloved son ordained, my gratitude to the Almighty was too deep for words.

10

The Sanitary Man

Bethnal Green was beginning to alter now. Some of the worst slums were being pulled down, and the overcrowding was much less severe. People were beginning to accept the new estate at Dagenham, and it was a fairly simple matter to ask for a house there and get allocated one within a few weeks or months.

Steve married and moved out there, and to see him so houseproud with his pretty little wife was almost funny when I thought about the way we used to turn his mum's house upside-down playing games!

Me with some of the Sunday school children, 1936.

Some of the Sunday school children moved out too and Eric and I used to go visiting them. There was a lot of foolish talk about Bethnal Green people keeping coals in the posh new bathrooms, but I never met anyone who ever did, or even knew of anyone who did! As I knew them, removal from the narrow streets broadened their horizons in more than one way, and they tried hard to live up to their clean and decent surroundings. They bought new furniture and new curtains, and even put carpets on the floors. They saved hard and got what they wanted, and you could furnish a little place nicely for a hundred pounds then.

Not everyone went to council estates, though, when they moved from the Green. For they were building hundreds and hundreds of little houses for sale, all around Woodford and Ilford and Barkingside. Eric and I would go out and look at them sometimes on a Saturday afternoon, though any chance we had of saving for the deposit on one was very remote.

Eric's mother was a cantankerous old woman. She hated me with all the proverbial hatred of the mother-in-law and tried her hardest to make sure I didn't get my hands on her son. A mystery surrounded his father, and I was determined to get to the bottom of it, for Eric had never known him and could find no trace of him having died.

'Your brother must remember him, even if you don't,' I said one day, when we were discussing it. After all he was ten years older than Eric. 'Why don't you ask him?'

My easy-going fiancé wasn't very keen on this idea, though.

'Why dig up the past?' he argued.

I nearly exploded at that. 'Why? Because I must know, that's why. Supposing your father is a raving lunatic, or something like that. It might be hereditary, and then where shall we be?'

I could see all my dream children fading into the realm of never-never, and, much as I loved Eric, I wanted that family badly.

So eventually he asked his mother, but, grown man that he was, she clouted him over the head and threatened him with a knife. 'I knew it would mean trouble,' he said, rubbing the bump on his head.

'Think,' I said finally. 'What can you remember? Can you ever remember any man coming to the house or anything?'

'No,' he answered. 'My mother always worked as an office cleaner, for as long as I can remember. She was always at the same big office block in the City. On Saturdays she used to take me with her, and when I was small, I used to sit in the boss's big chair and watch her working. Sometimes, the boss was in the building, and he'd come in, pat me on the head and give me a sixpence. About the only time I ever had any money,' he laughed ruefully.

On schooldays he would come home and go across the street to wait at his gran's until his mother returned from work. 'My gran didn't like me much,' he mused. 'She would never light the gas for me, and I had to sit in the firelight until my uncle came home from work. He wasn't married, and gran and my auntie idolised him. Once he came home, the light was lit, the tea was made and the fire poked up into a blaze. That's why Mum dislikes you so. She thinks I should be like my uncle, and take over our household, now that I'm working. She doesn't think I should marry.'

'Well, that's one blessing,' I said. 'If there was any reason why we shouldn't marry, she'd have been quick enough to tell you.'

At last, we sent for a copy of the birth certificate. The blank spaces where father's name should be told their tale; and in those days, when the stigma of illegitimacy was visited on the children as well as the sinning parents, I knew that there'd be hell to pay if I told my parents. So we let them go on thinking that his mother was a widow. But who was his father? And why the ten-year gap between the sons? Were they two separate follies, or was it a long affair?

Eventually, we went to see Eric's brother, who was not at all keen to have his family secrets hauled out in front of his wife. So he took Eric off for a long walk; and it was not until we were in the bus on the way home that my curiosity was satisfied.

Eric had looked so utterly dumbfounded that I knew he had news. 'Well?' I asked impatiently.

'You know that boss of my mum's? The one I told you about, who used to pat me on the head and give me a sixpence? He was my father!' I was absolutely astounded. 'Him! Your mum must have been stark staring crazy. What did she get out of it? What, I ask you?'

Eric shrugged his shoulders and started to laugh. 'Not even hot water to scrub the floors! She was always moaning about the cold water. I saw his wife and daughter once,' he went on. 'They called in at the office, wearing fur coats, and they drove off in a big car.'

'Where is he now?'

'Dead.' I was sorry about that. I had a crazy idea about forcing him, blackmailing him even, into making the stupid woman an allowance to get her off our back, but it wasn't to be.

'Well,' I said finally, 'at least, you're a gentleman's son. On your father's side you're no cockney. Freedom of the City of London, bigwigs and businessmen, they're your ancestors, wedding ring or no wedding ring.'

* * *

It was early in 1937 that I came home from work to find my mum in a state of deepest gloom.

'I don't know what your father will say,' she said, 'but we've had the sanitary man round today, with a council surveyor.'

'Well, we've had them before, so I suppose we'll get over it,' I answered, but I could understand her gloom.

Whenever the sanitary man had called and decided that repairs were urgent, he would send the landlord a letter, telling him what had to be done. The landlord would keep on putting off the work until faced with a summons. Then he would send an odd-job man, whom Dad invariably referred to as a bloody old bodger, and he would start the work. Then he'd go off and start a similar job elsewhere, just to keep the authorities happy that the work was in hand. We had known them remove a broken gutter and leave us without one for two months, so that the rain poured down the walls and made them damp, and on one occasion they had gone up to repair a leaking roof, spent an hour up there and then gone away. Next time it rained, instead of making a wet patch on the ceiling as it had been doing, the rain poured in. Unfortunately, it always seemed to happen in my parents' bedroom, and many a night I've heard them get up, with Dad swearing like mad, to catch the rain in bowls and buckets. Yet he would not hear of moving. He'd given up keeping pigeons when finances were tight, so he no longer had this excuse.

We had always done our own wallpapering and painting, keeping the place looking nice, but often the best handiwork was ruined by the rain coming in. For years after I was married, even living miles away from Bethnal Green, a heavy rainstorm would send me sneaking upstairs, wherever we lived, just to make sure the house was still watertight.

Anyway, on this occasion, Mum was more gloomy than usual. Not only had the sanitary man found the usual odd jobs, but the surveyor had condemned the whole front wall of the house. It would all have to come out and be rebuilt, right down to the bottom window sill. It was dangerous and would collapse if left, so it needed to be done right away.

It was a couple of days before she dared tell Dad. 'The bloody hell they won't pull down my wall,' he shouted, 'I'll swing first. You let any bloody workman in here to start such larks, and out you go!'

I felt like pointing out that the workman might not need to come in to start pulling down an outside wall, but thought better of it. It was still easier to keep quiet when Dad was having his say.

The weeks went by and nothing happened. It was pretty certain that the landlord, tight-fisted cuss that Dad called him, would not do anything until he had to. He was supposed to pay our rates, but never did. We used to get a summons for not paying them and had to take our rent to the court every week until they were paid, getting our rent book marked at the court. So we guessed the old man wouldn't do anything if he thought he could get away with it.

At last, when the tension at home had died down and we thought the whole matter had been forgotten, I came home one day to see scaffolding outside our house and next door.

Dad came home, went out again and got rip-roaring drunk. He came home late that night, kicked the poor dog and did his nut generally, threatening to stay home from work to stop the men from pulling the wall down. I offered to move into Gwen's room and let them have mine until the front was finished, but surprisingly Mum said no.

Next day, the wall was half down, and a tarpaulin draped across the room, but still Mum left the bed there and said that was where they'd sleep.

'Let the silly old bugger put up with it,' she said bitterly. 'The times I've asked him to move and he's refused. I'm all right, but it won't do his chest much good with all that cold night air and dust. Let him suffer.'

That night, Dad came home in a resigned mood. 'It might only take a few days,' he said optimistically. Apparently he'd been talking to a fellow at work who'd had a similar experience. 'Should be straight by the end of the week.'

Dad should have known better. At least, after all those years, he should have known our landlord. Having shown the work was under way, the workmen didn't turn up the next morning, or the next, and the whole of the following week brought no change.

Thick gloom descended on the household. I hadn't know it so quiet since Rosie died. Yet somehow, Mum was different. There was an undercurrent of excitement about her all the time and she seemed the least upset of us all.

The next Saturday, I came in from work and felt her excitement bubbling over.

'This is your father's last chance,' she said. 'I've found a place this morning. I should have done this years ago.'

When Dad came in, she smacked his dinner down in front of him in a most unusual off-hand manner.

'No workmen, of course,' she said starkly, actually putting the cat among the pigeons.

'What the hell do they care?' moaned my father. 'We can all die with pneumonia.'

'You can. We won't,' replied Mum quickly, then before he had a chance to start roaring at her, she continued, 'I've found a place. Eat up your dinner, Joe, do. Then you can all get your coats on and come with me. We are going to Leytonstone, and once you've seen it, Joe, you'll change your mind.'

We all looked at her in amazement. She hardly ever called him anything but Dad, and this Joe business was in itself unusual.

'I'm not putting my name to any documents,' he roared. 'I'm not signing all my money away for the next twenty years.'

'No one's asking you to. It's a flat,' retorted Mum.

'I'm not living upstairs in anyone's house,' yelled Dad again, but it seemed to me that the roaring was less vehement than usual.

'It's not upstairs anywhere,' said Mum quietly, in the same matter-of-fact tone. 'It's a ground-floor flat, and the people upstairs are not our lodgers. It's a divided house, and the garden is ours.'

Then she delivered her bombshell, that she should have used years before.

'If you don't want to come, Joe, you can stay in this hole by yourself. The girls and I are going, anyway.'

I couldn't believe it, I just couldn't. He put on his coat, paid all our bus fares, and took Mum's arm as we walked through one of the nicest roads in Leytonstone, and Leytonstone, in those pre-war days, was one of the nicest suburbs of East London.

The new landlord was waiting for us at the house. A fine old house, with a long front garden and a big square hall, bigger than 'yer Aunt's'. A huge kitchen, bathroom, hot water system and french doors leading out to a pleasant garden.

'Only snag,' sighed Mum happily, 'you two girls will have to share a bedroom. Will you mind that?'

Would we mind! We just could not believe it.

Dad came in from the garden, whistling happily to himself.

'I'll have to buy a lawnmower, that's for certain. The furniture will look a darn sight better here than it did in the old place.'

'Darn sight?' What had happened to the everlasting 'bloody'? I could hardly believe my ears.

Everything was signed and we arranged to move in the following week. Dad walked about on air, looking at seed boxes, repolishing scratches on the furniture, acting all the time as though the whole thing had been his idea. But we didn't care. We were going and that was all that mattered.

On the following Friday morning, I set out as usual for the bus stop, looking back at the poor old house with its tumbling walls for the last time, and mused all the way to work on what had happened there.

'Gosh, I could write a book about it all!'

I went home that night, home on the train to Leytonstone, to home where Mum, busy and happy all day, had already got everything straight and waiting for us.

Lovely Leytonstone . . . and Goodbye, dear old Bethnal Green.

11

Making Knickers All Day

It was like reaching heaven to think of this lovely old house as being our home. In the front garden was a weigela bush, in full bloom when we arrived in May and the lawn was daisy clad. Somehow, the whole family atmosphere changed. Maybe Mum was not so worried about Dad's temper as he had so much more to keep him happy with a real garden to care for and the opportunity to indulge in his favourite carnations and dahlias, and no problems arose. He was happy and it followed that we were happy too.

Gwen and I went to Leytonstone station and bought season tickets to Liverpool Street. Of course, it would have been cheaper to buy a 'workman's ticket' every morning, but then, I had no intention of giving up chapel, and Eric was very dear to me now, and he still lived in Bethnal Green. So I gladly parted with £2 15*s* and put the precious green ticket in my purse.

That summer of 1938 is one that will live forever in my memory. Eric cycled over most evenings, and we walked together through the forest which encroached on to Wanstead flats and the 'hollow ponds'. To my mind, we were living in the country and we could sit on a log, watch the sunset, and even indulge in a little kissing and petting, which would have been unthinkable in Victoria Park! Yes, they were happy days indeed.

We talked about our future too, though it was all pretty vague. Perhaps we could start buying a house when we married, and sometimes, on Saturday afternoons, we would go to surrounding areas and look at new houses. £500 was about the average price for a small house and the £25 deposit was not outside our reach. Somehow, we completely ignored the rumblings of world politics and my diary of that lovely year makes no mention of the troubled Mr Chamberlain and his 'peace plan'. How devastatingly unworldly and unrealistic we were, with our happy dreams and hopes, and with Eric's mother the only fly in the ointment. But I made a promise, that if she wanted, we would have her to live with us.

'You must be mad' was Peggy's comment, when I told her what I intended, but I couldn't bear to see my dearly beloved worried, and he did worry about his mother so much.

'I think of all she has done for me in the past. How she has sacrificed herself to bring us up,' was Eric's attitude.

Personally, I didn't think much of it; after all, it was Eric who had to bear the stigma of illegitimacy and even now, I had not plucked up the courage to tell my parents the truth. One baby, yes, I knew it could happen, but three! (Eric's brother had told us there had been another, older, brother who died.)

So we drifted happily through 1938, together with our friends at Victoria Park. I didn't go to the prayer meetings so often on Saturday evenings nowadays. Often, we would meet up with our friends and go to the Dominion theatre. There, for one shilling, we could have gallery seats, watch two films and a stage show in between. Eva brought the only bone of discontent into the house. She was happy enough when we lived in the court and her flat was so much better than ours, but once we moved to Leytonstone she began to visit us and refer to her place as a 'slum'. 'Anything is good enough for a poor little thing like me,' she would moan, and she took a particular pleasure in taking the mickey out of me. Always, she referred to me as a 'broody bitch' because she had heard me say on more than one occasion that I hoped to leave work and start a family as soon as I got married.

We were not surprised, then, when she started house-hunting in the same area as our house, and before long she found a ground-floor flat similar to ours. The top floor was to let as well, but she contrived to keep it that way for some time, telling all sorts of yarns to anyone who came looking! But she eventually cooked her goose, and her in-laws, seeing the spacious rooms and pleasant setting, compared it with their own cramped Bethnal Green quarters, and made their own arrangements to rent the upstairs flat! Outwardly, she made the best of it, said it was great to have a handyman gardener living in, but Mr Brown was no gardener, and since their idea of a happy Sunday night was to sit and sing hymns to Mrs Brown's harmonium accompaniment, I don't think she was really all that happy.

I wondered, too, why she didn't start a family. They had been married over three years by then and she just spent her time dressing up and shopping and being, to my mind, as catty as she could. But nothing she said or did could dampen my spirits, and I sailed through the year with my feet on air and my head in the sand.

Christmas that year was a wonderful time. Mum decided to invite Auntie Rose who now had a husband, as well as our dear gran (Janet) and Auntie Lottie. In some ways it was like the old times, with all the family together, but this year we were able to put up lots of decorations without fear of crumbling walls. To add to the fun, Auntie Rose brought her nephew with them, a 6-foot 20-year-old sailor on leave, and he made the most of his opportunity with Gwen. The crowning touch to the festivities was the heavy snowfalls over the Christmas period, and we walked through the forest and played snowballs. Even Eva unbent and joined in the fun and Eric managed to persuade his mother to come to tea. Oh, what a happy carefree time it was! That last year before the war when none of us realised that our way of life was about to end and all the simple innocent pleasures of life as we knew it were about to disappear for ever.

*　*　*

It was early in the new year when I asked my parents if Eric and I could go on holiday together. When I think now of a 22-year-old asking for permission to do anything at all, it makes me smile. But as I expected, both parents refused. 'Not

114 CHILDREN OF BETHNAL GREEN

Great-grandma Piper with her daughters Jane (seated) and Rose, with niece May, Jane's youngest daughter behind.

unless you are going with someone else,' was the verdict, and so we talked it over with our friends, and in the end, six of us decided to go to the Isle of Wight and planned our holiday. We were to stay at a Christian guest house, where Gwen and I had stayed previously, and my dear mum, believing in 'safety in numbers', was not perturbed by the thought of three young couples holidaying together. Poor deluded folk; we planned the holiday for the first week in September!

That was a wonderful summer. My Sunday school children were growing up into young ladies, I coached them for Scripture exams and wrote demonstrations for the children to act. I suppose I was ideally full of the love of God, everything seemed to be going so well, and apart from Eric's mum, there was not a single cloud in my sky. Only Dad seemed more than usually gloomy and moody. He shook his head whenever we spent money, warning us that times would be getting hard. According to Dad, trouble was just around the corner. None of our jobs was safe, nothing was as joyous as we made it out to be, and before long we would all be out of work.

'Cheers,' said Gwen, 'I'm sick and tired of making knickers all day.' I couldn't blame her, she never seemed to get the decent stuff at work. Knickers only paid 1s 6d for overlocking a dozen pairs and Gwen was thoroughly disillusioned. She had always been artistic and had hoped to do designing, but no opportunity had come her way and the knickers brought in 25s a week. I felt sorry for the machinists on piecework. They had no time to 'stand and stare' if they were to earn a decent wage. It was not always plain seams either; some of those knickers had various-shaped gussets. I particularly remember one line which had 'aeroplane gussets' which gave more room in the seat, and how the machinists cursed those wretched things. If they were not exact they'd be thrown back by the examiner, and unpicked. Sheer time-wasters, but the ladies of the smart West End stores liked them and they were one of the best-selling lines. Maybe the ladies who could afford the prices were well fed and had fat bottoms anyway!

On the other side of the factory, away from the overlocking machines, the silk and satin garments were made and at first I was enthralled by the beauty of the nightwear. How on earth could anyone want to go to bed in nightwear like that! But since we dealt only with the top stores in Knightsbridge and Oxford Street and I knew royalty were among our customers, I began to realise, as never before, how the 'other half' lived.

I was a 'special order' clerk, and the only orders that I was concerned with were those that were to be specially made for people with their own peculiar tastes. One lady sent in her own waist petticoat to be copied; she wanted it back the same day and of course we obliged. Apparently, she spent the whole day in the store, mostly in the rest room or restaurant, while we had hoots of laughter at the monstrosity. It was black satin, heavily quilted with an intricate pattern and around the hem were deep pockets. No zip fasteners in those days, there were numerous hooks and eyes and huge press fasteners; and I heard afterwards from the store buyer that she kept all her jewellery in these big pockets.

My greatest delight was in the complaints that were returned to us. People complained about the most amazing things: the lace flowers were not exactly level –

could they have been half a millimetre out? Sometimes we could rectify the error, but very often I was just told to put the article aside, and write the order for a new one. We were allowed to buy these rejects at an amazingly low price, and before long I had acquired a trousseau fit for a princess. My best outerwear might have come from a market stall or C&A, but underneath!

Eva became quite envious of Gwen and me and would even ask me if I had any posh labels which had been cut out from the 'complaints garments' before they were sold on to us. She would actually sew these labels, of the top stores, into her own underwear, as though anyone but herself could see them!

She didn't have as much money nowadays with only her husband's income, but it never occurred to her to go out to work, and all the girls in the factory who got married left when they did so. We always had a collection for them, and on the last afternoon the boss would come up and make a little speech; we would all have a drink of port and lemon, and hand out the presents. The firm always provided the same present for everyone who left to get married, a lovely eiderdown of the very best quality. One of the boss's friends ran a factory nearby, and supplied bedding to the same stores that we dealt with, so we were always provided with the very best for sleeping in and under!

Of all the hundred or so girls in that factory, I can only recall one 'shotgun' wedding. Yet even then, our church came to their aid. One deacon's wife provided a small flat, various folk gave furniture and furnishings and the young couple were wed and housed before the baby was anywhere near due. The disgrace of illegitimacy was such that most of us would never dare to indulge in anything that might lead to a baby, and we were mostly quite ignorant, or innocent and dead scared to take chances. I must admit that nowadays saying goodnight to my beloved was getting harder and harder, I just hated him going, and my parents glowered if I stood too long at the door with him. How I wished we could get married! We had been seriously courting for five years, but the great day seemed as far off as ever. Eric's mum still resented me and since he was her only support, we could not see any way out.

12

War

And so that fateful summer wore on. Still we talked of our holiday, although in July one of our number, who was in the Territorials, broke the news to us that he'd heard that things were looking black and he might not be able to come.

'Oh, it will all blow over, it always does,' I consoled him, and I went ahead with my planning for the great occasion.

On one Saturday afternoon during that July, a crowd of us went on a tour of the 'International Exchange'. How intriguing it all was, and I wrote in my diary that I had actually listened to girls conversing with others in New York. 'It's almost too wonderful to be true,' I wrote. To think that in my lifetime a transatlantic call has become something not worth mentioning.

It amazes me that there is still no mention of forthcoming trouble in my diary. July passed into August and I went out and purchased a new case to take on holiday. Several times during those weeks our boss mentioned that we should do something about ARP, but I'm afraid I just laughed. 'We only need a bit of faith.' My first shock came on 22 August, when I read the headlines in someone's newspaper on the way to work. We never had radio news early; that didn't start until the 'Daily Service' at 10.15. So when I read that Russia and Germany had signed a pact I wondered how it would affect us. But even more worrying to my mind, there was the talk of a threatened rail strike. Surely that was not going to ruin our longed-for holiday!

When I reached the office, we had an air raid drill and a cold shiver ran through me, the whole day was plunged into gloom, and that night I wrote in my diary:

How could I live without my beloved! He is a vital force in my life. If war comes, and God grant that it will not, we will have to get married. I could not let him go, perhaps out of my life for ever, without having really been his. Oh, Lord, how could my mum and little Janet, and all the other mums go through it! They endured the last war, they just could not face it again.

When I reached the office next morning, one of the juniors showed me a lurid cutting from a newspaper. The government have ordered 50,000 papier mâché coffins! I tried to laugh it off, but I half believed it myself. On the next day the King returned to London, met the Prime Minister and Parliament reassembled and passed a 'Crisis Bill'. No more woolly talk of peace in our time. We were advised to start carrying our gas masks, issued a year ago, and to be on the safe side, to keep them handy by our beds.

By the end of August the trains had already darkened the carriages and we found it fun to sit in the gloom on the way home from church. Fun . . . there wasn't much fun around. On the 31st, we saw the stark word 'Evacuation' on the placards, and even I began to believe that war was a possibility. They wouldn't start sending all the children away without good cause.

Nevertheless, Friday 1 September found me starting to pack that nice new case for my holiday the next day! But then . . . we switched on the news. 'There have been grave developments during the night. Germany has attacked Poland.' The news grew worse every hour. England mobilised, blackout was declared and we rushed out and bought blackout materials, got the sewing machine out and began the thankless task of making miserable black curtains. Then, last blow to that never-to-be-forgotten day, a telegram from the Isle of Wight: 'Please. Do not come tomorrow. Evacuees arriving.' So it all ended. It was not just the holiday that was abandoned, but it was the end of an era. More than that, it was the end of life as we knew it. Looking back, it was the end of innocence in teenage years.

Never-the-same-again Saturday was a dreadful day. Eric insisted that his mum could not stay alone and took her to stay with her other son. As his wife and little one had been evacuated we hoped that it might work, but knowing how cantankerous the old lady was, I had my doubts. On Sunday morning we did the same as the whole country, gathered round the radio and listened to the grim words. 'Unless we hear satisfactorily from Germany by eleven o'clock. . . .' And at eleven, the Prime Minister uttered the words, 'We are now at war with Germany.' Almost immediately, the siren sounded. We gazed at each other in shocked amazement. 'The bloody devils must have been on the way already,' yelled Dad. Grabbing the tea cosy, he thrust it into Mum's trembling hand. 'Shove it on your head, Mum, it might keep off a bit of brickwork.'

We rushed to the cellar, having already decided that it was the safest place, although I was not so sure. Why put more wall and building above you? Then the All Clear went.

The rest of the day passed in shocked misery. Then twice during the night we were awakened by the wretched sirens. 'Enough to give you heart failure without anything happening,' sighed Mum.

On Monday, Mum and I went shopping. 'If you're wise, you'll spend your holiday money on sheets and blankets. There won't be much decent stuff on sale much longer,' she sighed. I took her advice and invested in some good saucepans too. Not very enthusiastically, but I lived to be glad I did so. I went to the market with my remaining few shillings, because I had seen a dress I liked the previous week. It was still on sale. 'Eight shillings,' said the stall keeper. 'Eight? It was only six last week.' I was dumbfounded. 'Don't yer know there's a war on?' – a sentence I was to tire of hearing. I threw it back on the stall. 'Come on, Mum, we'll go to Marks & Spencer. At least they won't have put up prices.' Nothing over five shillings from Marks, like nothing over sixpence in Woolworths. So we went to Hackney on the tram and I bought a very nice skirt for 4s 11d. 'We'll stick to Marks in future,' I said. 'Prices won't alter there.' Not in my wildest imaginings could I dream of seeing a coat for sale in Marks & Spencer for £150!

The weather was fantastic during those first war days and as we were both on official holiday, Eric and I wandered through Epping Forest and talked. And talked. We realised that all our plans would have to be altered but we were at a complete loss as to the future. Future? Did we have a future? 'I think we should get married sooner than we had planned,' I said wistfully. 'We need to belong to each other before you get called up.' 'But they are only calling up the 18–20s so far,' said the optimistic Eric. 'It will be ages before they get to 27. The war will be over before then.' He wasn't the only man who thought that. All over by Christmas!

The Home Guard marchpast in Wilmot Street, Bethnal Green, 1939. (Tower Hamlets Local History Library and Archives)

That was the attitude when I went back to work on the following Monday. Just as well because, for the very first time, there were no special orders in the post. Most of the rich clients had evacuated anyway, and if they were still in London they had other things on their minds than new underwear. Things looked very slack, which was just as well, since at least half a dozen girls had failed to turn up, and three announced their forthcoming wedding. I spent a miserable day; we mostly sat and speculated on what would happen. Our junior was definite. 'I'm going to try for the buses,' she enthused. 'If I'm a bus conductress, I won't get called up for military service.' We smiled at that. As if they would want to call up girls! They might want them to go on munitions work, but not military service. How little I knew!

Within a few days, life took on a new aspect. Having no work of my own, I took over the running of the ironing and finishing department. The girls were no longer allowed to call me by my first name, and the 'Miss' sounded dreadfully formal. But I was very glad of the five shilling rise in my pay packet, and before long I had them singing as they worked and enjoying a good laugh. If they made a scorch mark with the iron and it wasn't too bad, we had a swift way of dealing with it. Just rub it with an old half crown. It had to be an old one, because the magic only worked with silver and the newer half crowns were not real silver. There were other little tricks too, which I soon learnt from the old hands. A small bloodstain, made by a pricked finger on the embroidery, was easily removed. Looking up the initials of the worker, we took the garment back to her and she chewed a length of cotton from a reel of white, and rubbed the bloodstain with her spit. It always worked. I've tried it myself at home over the years. Before many weeks passed, the war had become something of a bore. Nothing much happened; the wild talk of the first few days had died away and there were only subtle changes. Not so many glamorous nighties, but thicker, warm pyjamas. Preparing for nights out of bed!

There was one incident which shook me during those first weeks of war. I had sent our errand boy to Oxford Street with a dozen boxes of pyjamas which were urgently required, and an hour later we had a call from the irate buyer of the store, asking me why I had not kept my promise. There was no errand boy around, and his ten-minute trip had taken well over an hour. It was some time later when he returned, full of tearful remorse and minus the pyjamas. Amid his sobs, we heard the story.

A nice man had come up to him and asked him to go into a nearby shop and get him a packet of cigarettes. He couldn't go himself because he had quarrelled with the girl shop assistant. He gave our boy a shilling and told him to get himself a bar of chocolate with the change. He kindly offered to mind the boxes, so innocent little Ron had handed over nearly seventy pounds worth of goods and gone into the shop. 'When I came out, he'd gone,' he sobbed, 'so I didn't even given him his cigarettes.' So began the black market. Throughout the war years, whenever we were offered things that someone had come by I knew how easily the tricksters could get them. So many kids around like our little Ron. I was glad they didn't give him the sack for it.

13

Engaged At Last

Then Christmas came round. Wasn't it all going to be over by Christmas? The children began coming back to London. Nothing was happening, and so many dreadful lurid stories were circulated about the treatment they had received that the most fearful of mums brought their children back. School was a bit haphazard, and the young ones roamed the streets and began to get into mischief. The main pastime seemed to be baiting the wardens; the children were bored with nothing to do, and seemed to take a delight in accidentally kicking over buckets of sand or water.

For me, the greatest excitement was in getting engaged. We went up to an old-fashioned jewellers in Whitechapel and bought a lovely solitaire diamond ring. It cost £7 10*s*, nearly three weeks of Eric's wages, and I wore it with pride for the first time on Christmas Day. It was a very happy Christmas. One or two of our little circle of friends had joined up, but they didn't seem to be in any danger. It was a funny war and not nearly so dreadful as we had imagined. Admittedly, both Eric and Dad were on short time, but with rationing of so much food, we were not buying so much anyway. Eric and his mother seemed to be settling down in the little flat he had found for them, only about ten minutes' walk from where we lived, and life seemed to be going smoothly.

Eva, of course, had been quick to take advantage of the situation. She knew that there would be no question of her husband being called up; he had been crippled by polio as a child and walked with a decided limp. So she started pestering him to change his job. He was a piano tuner for a small shop in Holborn, but Eva wanted more for him. Harrods, no less. So he wrote to them, and to her delight obtained a position straight away. My goodness, she needed a hat two sizes bigger within the week! No more asking me for used labels, she had a discount card and made the most of it. Shopping for Eva took on a new perspective, and soon even the bigger salary he earned was barely enough. This was quickly remedied. She went out and found herself employment, for it was becoming apparent that it was no longer fashionable for women to be ladies of leisure. It was patriotic to work, and as married women didn't seem to be among the likely candidates for call-up, she found a comfortable office job without much trouble.

Gwen, too, was more than restless. It occurred to her that volunteering for one of the services might give her more opportunity than waiting for the call-up, because, if the tales about the men were to be believed, office workers were put into kitchens as cooks, lorry drivers were instrument mechanics and building labourers were put into signal work. Probably all wild rumours, but I agreed with Gwen that it might be a good idea to make enquiries. So she did and very soon she joined the ATS and learned telecommunications. It turned out to be a tough assignment, but it was a complete change from the everlasting lock-knit knickers and petticoats and gave her a career that stood her in good stead for the rest of her working life.

Things were beginning to change now, but in such a subtle way that we were hardly aware of it. All the young girls at the factory, especially those who had been steadily courting before the war, were now planning early marriage, and several of them became pregnant without waiting for the ring! This was almost unheard of, except in shame. The news was getting more and more dismal too. We were fed such tales on the radio . . . it seemed to my mind that it wasn't anything to boast about, that our troops had retreated to a new and strategic position.

Eric and his mother had just about settled down together when he phoned through to the office one day, to say she had been knocked down on a pedestrian crossing and was very badly injured. We hurried to Whipps Cross and found she had several broken bones. The poor soul looked awful and I must admit, I selfishly wondered if she would ever be able to cope alone again. I had visions of her staying in the little flat that Eric had found, after we were married.

As the spring advanced, so did the Germans, and we could no longer pretend that we were just biding our time. No, as they overran country after country, the terrible thought crossed our minds that we might be losing this war! My mind was made up. Like the girls in the factory, I was going to belong to my beloved before he went away, though to have a baby would be asking for trouble. No way would I be able to support a baby on the straightforward private's allowance, and much as I loved my Eric, I didn't think he was officer material. Besides, he was too good-natured to be a sergeant! We fixed our wedding day for 18 May, and daringly enough, I wrote to the people on the Isle of Wight asking if we could honeymoon there. We were thrilled when they wrote back that their evacuees from Portsmouth had returned home, and as far as they could see it would be OK. Nothing was going to stop me from my longed-for visit this time.

We still managed to keep going at the church. Our lovely group of young folk had dwindled sadly, but we held our usual mid-week meeting and, as far as possible, the Sunday services continued. The 'evening service' was now held in the afternoon as no one was keen on being out in the blackout, and the smaller rooms had been turned into a warden's post. Our dear hard-working minister had taken on the post of warden to a rest centre, and though at the moment there was no one in need of such shelter, we all knew that the day was not far off when we would really know what war was about just as our disillusioned soldiers were now doing in France.

Dad was now getting concerned about us. 'Seems a bit daft to buy furniture at this time,' he remarked. 'It will all get blown sky high. But if you insist on furnishing a place, then you'd better let me start looking around.' Both he and Mum were concerned about me living alone, knowing that Eric would be called up long before the year was out, and Mum came up with a brilliant idea. Much as we liked our

My sister Gwen in her ATS uniform.

home, there were plenty of like houses around now, and if we could find one already divided into two flats, that would be ideal. Before long, we found just what we were looking for. Eric and I would have the ground floor, though Dad would have the garden. There would be room for Eric's mother too, if she needed it, although Mum shook her head at the idea.

Dad made arrangements for us to go to the cabinetmaker in Shoreditch where he had taken Eva, but Eric seemed strangely reluctant at the whole idea. It took me a long time to find out what was wrong, but then he told me. 'It's the money,' he said. 'But you told me you had £100 saved,' I cried, 'and we know that's sufficient. It won't be if we wait for long, though,' I added, and he shook his head dismally. 'Mum has hidden my post office book,' he said, and I gazed at him in horror. 'What was she doing with it, anyway?' I asked. It appeared that he had always given her his cash to bank and she usually showed him that she had done so, but what she did with the book in between, he had no idea. Why on earth had he done such a thing? It seemed to me that it was a good thing she was in hospital. 'We'll just have to have a thorough search; and I'll come and help you,' I said, and together we went back to his flat. He seemed reluctant to go through her personal things, but I had no such inhibitions. The old dear wasn't going to stop me marrying her son. He was mine.

It was nearly a week before he found the book, and even then he was apprehensive about drawing out the cash. But my dad, true to his word, had arranged everything for us, as he had done for Eva. The firm he worked for did not actually make the furniture they sold as their own. It was the little Jewish cabinetmakers in Shoreditch who actually made the stuff, and Dad went straight to them, so that we were soon the proud possessors of top quality furniture, polished by Dad in his spare time. All my friends said I was mad, taking a chance like that and spending all the money. 'What happens when the bombs start falling and you lose the lot?' they asked, but I was philosophical. 'I expect I'll go with the furniture,' I shrugged, and I lived to know I had made the right decision, even sixty years later!

We began to dread listening to the news; no one believed that everything was going according to plan, and the rationing was really beginning to bite. The slightest rumour of anything not on ration meant a long and weary queue and people began to get edgy. We were waiting, waiting for something to happen, not knowing what, but convinced that it would be something awful. I felt it when I went to work; the girls were not singing as they ironed. Some of them had boyfriends or new husbands over in France and they felt, as we all did, that they were facing an unknown future.

I was amazed then when one of the juniors, meeting me in the wash room, smilingly told me she'd given in her notice and was giving up work altogether. Supposing she was probably pregnant, I asked what she intended to do. She laughed. 'Earn money the easy way.' She grinned at my blank face. 'Go down to the warden's post every night,' she laughed. 'Money for jam. Gosh, I've got so I like at least three every night and with all their wives away, they don't mind paying for a bit of fun. I get more in a week than I earn in three months here!' I was horrified, but soon realised that she was not the only one. The old values were slipping . . . the old attitudes drifting away. I couldn't resist asking her, a kid years younger than myself.

'Suppose you get pregnant?' and she laughed heartily. 'Oh, don't be daft, girl. There's things you can do. No one has to get pregnant these days, not unless they want.'

I went home that night pondering on what she had told me. It was getting even harder to keep things in control. Maybe we were stupid to bother. Any day might bring death, or separation at least, and we were wasting time that might be spent really together. But there, only a few more weeks, and knowing Eric, he was far too moral to stray and I was too scared to take chances. So, hard as it was, we kept things on an even keel.

I came in one evening to find Eva talking to Mum. 'I've bought a new hat for the wedding,' she said, taking a concoction from a bag. 'I'm not sure about it, though, so I'd like your honest opinion.' She put it carefully on her head and I looked at it from all angles. Goodness knows what had made her buy such a monstrosity. It looked awful and just did not suit her petite good looks. 'No,' I said at length, 'I've seen you in some I liked better.'

'Right.' She jammed the hat back into the bag and stormed out of the door. 'She did ask for an honest opinion,' I laughed. 'But she didn't like the truth. Everyone is bad-tempered lately.'

Next morning there was a letter in the post from her husband. Since I had insulted his wife, they had no wish to attend our wedding, and I would have to find myself another organist! Short notice this, but fortunately one of our friends had not been called up and he was only too happy to oblige.

One week before the wedding, Eric's mum came out of hospital and my mother borrowed a wheelchair and whisked her around the shops, buying all she needed. We moved into the new house and she was soon settled into the room which was to be hers; and I, blind optimist that I was, imagined us all living happily ever after. Gladys, my dear friend from schooldays, shook her head. 'Mousie, you are expecting the impossible. Living with one set of in-laws is bad enough, but two. . . .'

It wasn't all that easy to plan the wedding reception. No one we knew ever had a caterer and Mum and I, with help from the ladies at the church, had worked it all out and bought the food, trying to make it good even with the rationing . . . I had invited eighty people and we spent most of Friday getting everything ready in the big church hall.

14

The Big Day

The great day dawned at last, a cloudless day without even a breath of wind. Dad decided not to put the news on, which showed how thoughtful he could be sometimes. Gwen and Gladys looked lovely in their bridesmaid dresses, painstakingly made by Gwen from taffeta purchased from our factory, and I felt justly pleased with my dress, borrowed from a friend. When everyone except Dad and I had left for the church, he came up and offered me a huge sandwich of bread and cheese. Must have been the week's ration! 'You'll be hungry,' he urged. 'Best have something to eat now.' As though I could!

So, after long years of hoping and waiting, I at last became the wife of the man who was, as I recorded in my diary, the dearest man on earth. In spite of the tight rationing, we managed to produce a really lovely meal, plenty of salad which was fairly easy to come by and other things donated by friends. To me, it was very emotional when one of our friends sang the well-known song, 'Because God made you mine'. To me, this was really true, both at the time and throughout our long married life. I always felt that Eric was God given; and have often wondered what I had done to deserve him.

At four o'clock, we left for Waterloo station, and at long last we were really on our way to the Isle of Wight! I couldn't believe it. Heaven. . . . There were very few people on the ferry going across from Portsmouth, and our host was waiting for us when we got off the train at Newport. A quick supper and we were shown to our room . . . at long, long last, we were alone and no one was going to make us feel guilty. Everything was wonderful at first, then the big question: 'We just dare not start a baby. Have you got the necessary?' No . . . he hadn't been able to do anything about it. He'd been very busy . . . he wasn't sure what we wanted . . . after the big build-up, I must admit I felt a bit let down. 'But we could go into Newport on Monday and do something about it. In the meantime, aren't we happy as we are?' So we settled down to a few amorous cuddles and got through the weekend.

Monday morning found us in Newport and outside Boots. 'I'll wait outside.' I pushed my reluctant bridegroom through the door, and within a few minutes, he was out again, red-faced and awkward. 'Well, did you get it?' 'No, it was a lady assistant and I couldn't ask her.' So . . . in I went and out I came. 'Boots do not sell contraceptives,' she told me, haughtily. 'You'll have to go to Timothy Whites for that sort of thing.' So on we went and by this time I was getting really

Our wedding day, 1940.

fed up. Did Josie, the little junior office girl I had been talking to, have all this trouble? Timothy Whites were much more helpful after I had explained to a kindly assistant that I'd just married a soldier and we were worried. Did I want disposable or reusable? I wasn't sure. 'Both,' I said and the price shook me. Half a crown for a packet of three! Or one for two shillings. Love was going to be rationed at this rate.

We went on from Newport to the coast, and sat on the beach at Alum Bay, a cloudless blue sky above, and no other soul except ourselves. Suddenly, a loud rumbling noise startled us. 'Thunder!' Eric shook his head. 'I only wish it was thunder. It's gunfire from the beaches over there.' So we sat, sad in our happiness, thinking of the friends from our youth group who were among the many thousands waiting for help and rescue. 'Do you think they'll get home?' I shuddered to think of them, waiting in the sunshine, never in my wildest dreams imagining that it was as bad as we afterwards knew it was. We gathered some of the coloured sand, and then left the beach; it was somehow too sad to sit there enjoying ourselves.

At least, I'd solved our immediate problem . . . or had I? That night, we sat on the edge of the bed and tried to wrestle with the contents of the envelope! I can't help wondering though, as I write this some sixty years later, how do today's young folk know what to do? Unless they all go on the pill, who tells a schoolboy in love how to put on a condom? By the time he's finished wrestling with it, I should think the urge must have gone off! 'Listen dear,' I said at last, 'wouldn't it be better if you didn't unroll the thing first?' With all these problems, I was beginning to think sex was highly overrated if we had to be so calculating and so prosaic about it all. Where was the wonderful joining in perfect union, melting into each other, becoming one flesh like the wedding service said, if we had to burden ourselves with expensive bits of rubber that wouldn't stay in the right place. Maybe it would be better to take a chance and hang the consequences. If we had a baby, somehow we'd manage, other people did.

The days together were wonderful! The weather was perfect and we learned to know each other even more. I realised, too, that Eric's domineering mother, embittered as she was, had done her best to crush any enterprising spirit her sons might have shown and Eric had been completely under her thumb, with always the 'look what sacrifices I've made for you' theme uppermost in her mind whenever he wanted to do anything of his own free will. Before the week was up, I knew what a battle I had on my hands, but I was fiercely protective of my beloved, and I knew too that he had never known love of any kind until he met me, and I had plenty to give.

First, we had the war to get through, but after that, we were going to have the perfect love-filled home. So our wonderful week passed, and we arrived home to find Eric's registration papers awaiting him. He was due that very day and after a hasty cup of tea, he dashed off to register for military service, and now we knew we had only weeks of married life before he was called up.

For the first few weeks, all went well. Mother-in-law was reasonable, helpful even, suggesting I leave the washing up when I hurried to catch my train in the mornings. She praised my cooking, and retired to her own room in the evenings, leaving us alone. In spite of the grim war news and the evacuation of Dunkirk, we were wonderfully happy together, knowing that the happiness was to be short lived. Time solved the problems that we had in our first week of living together, for I made up my mind that in this respect, if in no other, Eric was going to have to play the leading role. It was hard going at first, as he just didn't seem to know what love was all about. He looked on me as some delicate piece of china to be admired from afar, and he was full of inhibitions and anxiety on my behalf. But he gradually thawed out and surprised himself as well as delighting me; and after I had a few chats with the girls at the office, we overcame the awkward fumblings with the wretched condoms and saved money by carefully washing and re-using them. At least, if we were taking chances, we were minimising them!

Things were getting grim at the factory. Whereas many clothing factories were raving busy with war work, most of our machines were not built to take heavy army clothing and it was not easy to get war work contracts. At last, our dear friendly boss and his father made the sad decision to close down much of the workroom and the staff were asked politely to look for other work. I was really sad to go, but my old friend Colin at the fabric manufacturer, Celanese, who had tried to have an affair with me long before I was married, told me he was going into the RAF and offered me his job. So I made the transfer from Holborn to Hanover Square and tried to settle down to dealing with masses of paperwork concerning thousands of yards and rolls of material instead of half a dozen pairs of knickers and pyjamas. Instead of buyers of luxury retail goods I was trying to soothe the irate buyers of huge quantities of mundane material suitable for making soldiers' uniforms and underwear. I wasn't nearly so happy, and work was interrupted every few hours by air raid warnings. Nothing came of them, but it was a break from the tedium of office routine and we accepted the trips to the below-ground shelter as part of wartime life.

Eric was now on very short time. There was not much in the way of printing ink wanted for magazines, but he was home much earlier than me and usually had the vegetables prepared and any unfinished household chores completed before I got back. He seemed very quiet, though, and there was often an atmosphere which made me think something was wrong. At length I mentioned it to my mother, who, living in the flat upstairs and having access to the garden, would surely know if anything was wrong. At first, she shrugged and said it was none of her business, but after I pestered her a few times she told me that the old lady was making Eric's life a misery when I was not around. She had been taunting him about doing the chores and preparing the vegetables.

'That's right,' she would say. 'Play housemaid while she's gallivanting about up the West End with those rich boyfriends from her office. Then she comes home and takes all your wages, earns more than you and never gives you a penny. I always knew you were a damn fool to take up with her in the first place. God help you.'

'Eric doesn't shout back at her, in fact he doesn't answer, but she does nag and nag so,' said my mum, and I nodded ruefully. 'That's not his way,' I said, 'but I'm glad you told me.' I didn't mention it to Eric, no point in letting him think my mother had been telling tales, but it did worry me. Not that I cared what she said about me, but it was the everlasting taunting that he had to endure when I was not there. Something had to be done.

But matters came to a head sooner than I anticipated. One evening, my mother called me upstairs as soon as I came home.

'She's got a new theme now,' she whispered. 'Keeps telling him that she'll do for him unless he gives her back her money. She says that every stick you own has been paid for with her hard-earned cash which he has stolen from her post office book and she's going to tell the minister that his favourite deacon is a thief!'

I knew then that matters were coming to a head, and that evening I told Eric I knew what she had been saying.

'It's the money I took from my post office book,' he explained. 'You remember, she hid the book thinking I'd never be able to get married while she had my money. Her money is in her own book, including the pay-out she got from her accident. Not a penny of the cash in my book belonged to her.'

That night, I was awakened by loud sobbing and moaning coming from her room. Eric jumped out of bed. 'Perhaps she's been taken ill, I'd better go and see.' He ran from the room and the sobbing ceased. Some minutes later, he returned, holding his hand to his cheek. 'I might have guessed,' he said. 'She was up to her old tricks.' 'What do you mean?' I could see angry red marks across his face.

'That's what she does and I fell for it as usual. She buries her face in the bedclothes and makes this moaning noise. Then, when I lean over her, she just lashes out at me.' 'You mean, she hit you?' I could scarcely believe it, but the evidence was all too clear.

'It's the first time she's done it since she's lived with us,' he said, climbing back into bed.

'And the last,' I muttered grimly.

Next morning, we sat down to breakfast together. 'I don't like the bruise on my husband's face,' I announced suddenly. 'Nor do I like these accusations.'

She sat calmly buttering her toast and made no answer, and I jumped to my feet, forgetting all the quiet speech I had mentally prepared.

'How dare you, how dare you!' I shouted. 'He is my husband, and you'll never get a chance to do that again. We've done our best, tried to give you a comfortable home and made you welcome. But no more. You are leaving here, today if possible.'

'I'd be glad to get away if I had somewhere to go,' she replied. 'You and him planned all this with your scheming parents, but he's had all my money and now you're stuck with me, whether you like it or not.'

Half an hour later, Eric and I were out together, reading all the notices in shop windows, and before long we had found a small one-bedroom flat, paid a week's rent and arranged for a removal van to come next day. All her furniture had been stored in our cellar, and my mum came and helped me put up curtains and clean the place. Next day, I went to work and came home to find peace . . . peace and a smiling husband. My mother grinned.

'Had to give the moving bloke an extra ten bob,' she said. 'They always charge extra for moving coal.' I went to the cellar. Yes, she had taken all my meagre coal ration, but I didn't care. We were free, free at last.

Eric wrote to his brother to tell him what had happened and next day they went together to see that she was settled in. When they came home, Norman shook his head. 'I knew it couldn't last,' he said. 'We have tried so many times. No one could live with her. I'm just surprised that Eric didn't walk out on her years ago. Anyway, thank you for trying.'

We happily turned her room into a dining room, and were very glad of it too, because my father had made a boarded shield for the window and it was the only ground-floor room which was not over the cellar, and therefore most suitable for a shelter, a fact that we appreciated very much in the months that followed.

My new-found joy in having Eric to myself without the watching eye of his mother was very short lived. The dreaded call-up papers arrived and he was to report on 5 September, to Woolwich of all places.

'Suppose you stay there for ages, you could get home every night,' I mused. Ever the optimist, I was planning for his homecoming that very weekend, little knowing what was in store.

On Saturday morning I went to the chapel to do the flowers, a task which I had recently undertaken, and then I called to see Janet and Auntie Lottie in Bethnal Green. They both seemed more than usually nervous, and when I left, the warning had gone, but we were getting used to these daytime raiders, even watching dogfights in the sky, but nothing much came of them as far as we were concerned. What did surprise me was to see a bus coming up from the dock area with shattered windows, and I wondered why it had not been taken out of service.

Back at the chapel, I found my dear friend, our minister, and he complimented me on the flowers I had arranged on his table. We were no longer using the church itself, there were so few folk around, and with so many huge windows it was not very safe from any stray bomb.

'Doubt whether I'll make it tomorrow,' he said. 'I think the waiting is really over. Our war starts today.' I looked at him in surprise, he was usually optimistic, 'I just hope you are wrong,' I answered. 'Eric has gone this week, gone to Woolwich.' 'Which is the last place anyone wants to be,' he said. 'They've started on the docks already. There are fires burning down there. I'm just off to open up the shelter. There will be a good many homeless before tonight is over.'

I gave him a hug and with a quick 'God bless', I hurried back to the station and the peace of Leytonstone. Somehow, the war didn't seem so near here but I knew it was a fool's hope to expect Eric home that day.

Dad called me into the garden early that evening. 'God almighty, look at that. The bloody devils.' The sky looking over towards the docks was a lurid red. No wonderful sunset, but fire, fire lighting up the sky before it was even dark. The warning had gone long since but we tended to ignore it until something started to happen, like heavy gunfire or droning planes. 'Don't know why we bother with the bloody blackout,' he muttered, 'they've got enough light of their own to see every target they want. We'll be lucky to see tomorrow's light, though, but don't tell your mother. Make sure we've got drinking water and torches in the cellar though.' I made a flask of tea as well, and had just taken it to the cellar when it seemed that all hell broke loose. It was barely dark yet, but we heard the planes droning overhead, the screech of falling bombs and the loud clatter of our gunfire. Mum hurried down the stairs, tea cosy firmly on her head and the cat in her arms, and Dad and I joined her in the cellar. One thing I was glad about, we didn't have Eric's mother to worry about. She had refused to come to the cellar even when Eric was at home, and during the previous short raids we had experienced there was always the anxiety of feeling mean leaving her alone. Goodness knows how she was coping, but at the moment that was not my problem.

I have often wondered since how we got through that first night of the Blitz. We tried to put a brave face on it and Dad and I played a few games of draughts, but it was very half-hearted. In the end, I rolled myself in a blanket and crept into a big zinc bath, a relic from the Bethnal Green days when we had no bathroom. I slept

Early in the morning of 21 September 1940 Bethnal Green received its first parachute mine, which caused extensive damage to Allen & Hanbury's factory and the surrounding area. (Tower Hamlets Local History Library and Archives)

too, just waking momentarily when the bangs were extra loud; and when there was a lull, Dad slipped up to my kitchen and made tea.

Morning found us amazed that we were still whole and unscathed. There were no broken windows either, but a quick look outside the front door showed damage in the next road. There was a nasty smell of smouldering too, and we wondered again how the rest of the family had fared. There was no possibility of going over to Bethnal Green, no buses or trains running, and so much broken glass and debris in the roads that I was scared to cycle.

We switched on the wireless, but knew that no way would we hear the truth, no one was going to let Hitler know how successful that night had been, but it didn't really dawn on me that this was only the beginning. It was almost as if we had had a heavy thunderstorm, or a gale, it was over and we had survived. Once more, poor deluded Doris. If anyone had told me what was to come, I'd have said we couldn't take it, but I've found through the years that we do take it, whatever it is.

It was a sad Sunday; the not knowing was the worst part. Eva and Jim called round. They didn't speak to me, but it was awkward for them, because Mum and Dad were down in my flat, but they had not spoken since the wedding hat fiasco, though how they could keep up such childish pettiness in the face of such trouble just amazed me. They didn't stay long, anxious to get back before the next raid, but Eva did say to Mum that Mr Brown was a real coward, sitting hunched up under the stairs which he considered the safest place. 'And he's got the thick tea cosy on his head,' she added; and I remembered my Dad on the day war was declared, giving our tea cosy to Mum. I think wonderful Mr Brown went down in my estimation from that day on!

Sunday night was similar to Saturday, but Dad made a decision. 'If we are going to be out of our beds every night like this, we'll make other arrangements.' We decided to use the dining room as one big bedroom. I didn't like the cellar anyway, so I was in agreement. Dad had refused to have an Anderson shelter messing up his garden and he would not hear of our going to a public shelter.

On Monday morning I tried to get to the office on time. What a joke. When I reached Hanover Square at 1.30, I was one of the first in, having climbed over masses of broken brickwork, shattered glass and miles of fire hoses. There was no post, and no work to be done. No phone line and no customers clamouring for fabric. No chance of a drink even, so we were not sorry to be told to go home again and to stay home for the week.

15

Miss Green

It was some time later that I heard one of the most amazing stories of faith, concerning one of the ladies from our church. Our minister, whom we all called PG, spent the night organising his shelter, as he had expected, and was going home in the early morning. As he made his way along Grove Road, he looked in horror at the devastation and noticed that one or two houses, roofless and tottering, still had their basements intact. He remembered Miss Green, who lived there with her elderly mother, and he made his way down the steps of the house where they lived. To his surprise, he was greeted at the door by Miss Green, hat and coat on and a look of excitement on her thin face.

'Oh, Pastor,' she cried, 'I'm so glad we had the chance to see you before we set off.' 'You are very wise to be going,' he answered. 'What arrangements have you made?' Her thin face lit up. 'That's just it, Pastor, we just don't know. We are leaving it to the Lord, just like Abraham in the Bible. You know, where it says, he went out, not knowing whither he went.'

'But you can't do that, Miss Green,' he cried. 'Come along to my shelter, until we can make some arrangements.' She shook her head. 'No, I've made my plan. Been taking money out of my account. You know, what I've saved for a rainy day, and you can't get a more rainy day than this, can you?' She picked up her packed case and hitched her handbag on to her shoulder. 'Come along, Mother.' She held out her hand, 'Goodbye Pastor, do take care.'

They stepped over the rubble and began walking along the road, refusing the offer of his help. 'But there isn't any transport,' he argued, and she smiled as though he was a wayward child. 'The Lord will provide,' she answered simply, and to his surprise, within a few minutes, a small army van drew up alongside, driven by one of his own young people in army uniform, who jumped out quickly. 'Hello there, where are you off to?' he asked and Miss Green grabbed his hand. 'Oh, I just knew the Lord would send someone,' she cried. 'We are just off to the station. Any station,' she added. 'Wherever you might be going.'

He scratched his head and looked at her in dismay. 'Well, believe it or not, I am trying to get to Paddington, but when I'll get there, I just don't know.'

'Paddington! Oh, Paddington's fine.' She handed him the heavy case and began to help her mother into the van.

The minister shook his head as they drove slowly away, and Harold, the young driver, told us later what an uncanny experience it had been. Every time he came to a blocked road and sat hesitating, whichever diversion he chose turned out to be the best one and eventually he reached Paddington. Once there, the two ladies got out and he had to get away to look for the colonel he was supposed to be meeting, amazed at the simple faith of his passengers. The two ladies went into the station, carefully avoiding broken glass and debris. There was no sign of an open booking office, and not many signs of life; only a few bewildered-looking folk like themselves, milling around in a dazed manner, but Miss Green and her mother walked purposefully forward on to the concourse, and saw a train standing at a platform.

'This must be for us,' announced Miss Green. 'There isn't another train here.' She settled her mother into a compartment and stood by the door until she actually saw a uniformed official. 'Where is this train going?' she called, and the porter shook his head. 'Should be going to Reading,' he replied. 'But don't ask me when, or if we'll ever get there.'

'Reading? Oh, that's fine.' She sat down beside her mother with a contented sigh, and some time later the train moved off, with just a few army personnel and bedraggled workmen aboard. Every five minutes or so they stopped, but the intrepid travellers took no notice until, after about two hours, they eventually stopped at a station.

'Twyford! Never heard of it, but it must be for us.' Miss Green alighted with her mother, and looked around delightedly. No sign of any damage, no smell of burning. No sign of war. 'Now, I'll just explain to the ticket man why we have no ticket,' she said, 'and I'm sure he will help us.'

This she did, and he just waved them through without asking for any money, though he was unable to help when she asked him if he knew of a guest house or small hotel they could go to. 'Any accommodation has been snapped up this last day or two,' he said. 'You might have been better to go direct to Reading.'

Miss Green smiled at him. He wasn't to know she was acting under divine guidance! 'We just have to wait a minute, Mother,' she said, and the old lady smiled and nodded happily, her faith in her daughter being as great as her daughter's faith in the Lord. At that moment, a car pulled up outside the station and they became aware that the driver was looking at them in the same expectant manner that they were looking at him. He got out of his car and before she could speak, he approached her diffidently, touching his hat as he did so.

'Are you from London?' he asked. 'Indeed we are, and waiting on the Lord to guide us to a place of rest,' she answered simply, and he held out a welcoming hand, his face lighting up with a smile.

'Then if you will permit me to take your case and to trust me enough to get into my car, I believe that the Lord has indeed sent me to meet you.'

They needed no second bidding and on the drive, he explained what had happened. He and his wife had been on holiday and, returning home at the weekend, they had found that all their friends and neighbours had taken in evacuees. He had been on the point of going to the WVS when his wife had stopped him. 'I think this room has been kept for someone special,' she said. 'Go down to the station and see if there is anyone there looking for a place to stay.' 'So that's what I did,' he finished, drawing up outside a pleasant bungalow. 'Milly, my good lady, will be so pleased I found you, and I know she is already preparing a meal for you.'

Milly was indeed pleased to see them. 'I'd much rather have the Lord's choice of visitors than the WVS's,' she laughed, escorting them to a beautiful double bedroom. So there began a long and lasting friendship and for one little family the war brought untold happiness. Even when it ended, Miss Green of great faith and her mother never came back to Bethnal Green, only to visit and tell what great things the Lord had done for them.

For most of us, the next few weeks brought nothing but sleepless nights and daily tales of horror and injured friends or relatives. My wonderful hopes of seeing Eric every few nights was but a dream, and then, when he did come, it was to tell me that he was off next day and had no idea where. Auntie Lottie and little Janet were bombed out of their flat, but they were not injured, and so they came to live with us for the duration, a far happier proposition than the cantankerous old dear we had had before. While Eric was away I lived with my family. It helped with the rations too, because one single ration book gave such a small portion of everything that meat and cheese were almost non-existent, and the points system was easier spread over several ration books.

Night times were really funny. We all slept together in my downstairs dining room, it being reckoned the safest. We just laid mattresses on the floor and slept in a row. Dad, Mum and me, Auntie Lottie and Gwen when she was home on leave. If Eric came in, then he slept between Mum and me, and Janet lay across our feet. When Eva and Jim had to leave their home temporarily because of an unexploded bomb, then they slept with us too! Dad said it was better that way, because if we went at least we would all go together!

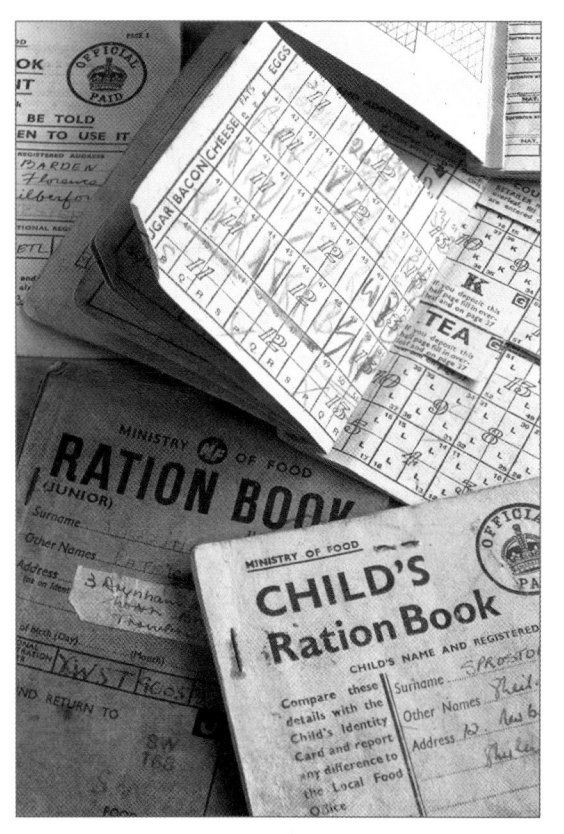

When I heard from Eric, he was stationed in Oldham, happily settled in a civvy billet and I felt almost envious. There were no raids, not even any warnings, and the lady with whom he was staying had four soldiers billeted on her. She had four sons who were all in the services and she certainly made other mothers' sons welcome. She and her

Ration books.

daughter were Salvationists, and Eric was delighted to find himself in such congenial surroundings with a Christian family. He was on a three-month course at a technical college and was free at weekends. He had been to the local Baptist chapel and thoroughly enjoyed it; and, he added in his letter, Mrs White had told him there was always room for me if things got too bad! What joys this conjured up in my mind!

Then, the very next week, came another of those amazing coincidences that so often awaited me round every corner. Our office, tired of the everlasting difficulties and problems caused by the Blitz, decided to relocate their headquarters to one of the branch offices. Most of the staff were going to Nottingham, and just a few to Manchester, which was the financial centre. I lost no time in asking to go to Manchester, skipping the fact that I had no experience in finance, apart from costing underwear, and had no idea what a calculating machine was, let alone how to use one! But the fact that I could arrange my own billet and was free to go at any time was in my favour, and the mere fact that I had at least done costing, swayed the managers, and I was given a post as accounts clerk in Manchester.

I could hardly wait to get home and tell them the news, and it didn't take me long to make arrangements.

So, for a few months, I was able to leave behind all the misery of London, and my beloved met me in Manchester and took me to meet his dear Mrs White. What a saint she was! She gave us a double room to ourselves, and this time I was determined that there was to be no wretched bit of rubber to spoil everything! So, if I started a baby, what of it? Babies were being born all the time, other people managed and survived. Besides, army pay now included allowances for children, and I certainly didn't intend that Eric should go overseas and leave me childless. Not if I could help it, anyway!

So we began a most happy period in our life together. The biggest worry we had, a joint one, was maths! Eric could not comprehend algebra! Night after night I tried to help him with simple equations, but somehow it all remained a complete mystery to him. And I struggled at the ornate St Anne's Square office in Manchester where they had been expecting a fully fledged accounts clerk, with all the intricate workings of a huge Sunstrand calculator at her fingertips. But I fudged my way through and my wacky sense of humour stood me in good stead.

I just could not stand the office manageress and I told the girls that I didn't like women bosses anyway. None of them liked her either, and when they realised that I was on their side, and not the snooty know-all from headquarters that they expected, they became very friendly and helped me no end. I remember once showing them a conjuring trick I knew with a plate, but unfortunately the plate I used was a bone china one belonging to madam herself, and the trick went wrong and the plate lay on the ground in a dozen pieces just as she flounced into the room.

'I'm so sorry, words cannot express how sorry I am to have had an accident with your best plate,' I murmured, 'I'll try my very best to replace it somehow.' She glared at me and I knew then that I would have no trouble from the girls.

It was a fantastic few months. Food rationing seemed to be no problem, probably because with all the four soldiers' ration books in addition to their own, the White family had enough and to spare. A further bonus was the fact that it was easy to get to Bolton, and Peggy, originally my senior and now a dear friend from Colstons, was married and living in Bolton. Eric and I were able to get across to visit several weekends and I thoroughly enjoyed seeing her and her little daughter. Oh, they all had babies except me!

Soon, Christmas 1941 was with us, the third Christmas of the war, and on the Saturday before the 25th, we went shopping in Manchester. The shops were still full of lovely things and we wandered around, looking at all the wonderful presents we would buy if only we had the money and the coupons. We seemed to have made so many friends in Oldham that never a weekend went by without an invitation. This evening, we were eating with friends, when suddenly the warning went, followed almost immediately by heavy gunfire, the very first I had heard since my arrival. We went out into the garden and looked across the hills to Manchester. All too familiar to me, the lurid glow lighting up the sky and the distant whine of falling bombs. We hurried back home to Mrs White and found her sitting anxiously by the fire. 'Oh, I was so worried about you all,' she heaved a sigh of relief. 'I'll be glad when the boys get in.' What a big-hearted woman she was, with all her own sons away, in much more danger, worrying herself over other mothers' sons.

We spent a sleepless night and although Oldham itself was not really damaged, Manchester was left in a similar mess to London after its first Blitz raid. On Monday morning, trying to make my way through the blitzed centre, I thought of all the lovely things we had seen in the shops on Saturday, all destroyed. If they had only known what was going to happen, they could have given them all away! I smiled at my own foolishness. Always, life would be different, if we only knew in advance!

Once again, I was hugging a secret to myself, because again I hoped I was pregnant. That always happened to girls who had sex without protection, always. I missed my own family at Christmas, but with four soldiers and Mrs White's daughter in the house, there was plenty of fun and Jerry, having made a statement on Manchester, renewed his attack on London between unexpected attacks on Bristol, Portsmouth, Plymouth and many other places. We never knew where the next attack would be, which I suppose was part of the strategy.

Immediately after Christmas, the joy of living for me was considerably dimmed, because Eric and the other soldiers departed, leaving me alone in Oldham – and to make matters worse, I found out I was not pregnant after all! That really shook me, when I thought of all the patient self-discipline of the last five years! Perhaps we need not have bothered to wait after all. Anyway, I was bitterly disappointed, especially as I was so many miles away from my beloved. I expect my work suffered, my heart wasn't in it any more and I passed a miserable week. Then I heard that Eric had a seven-day leave due and I went straight in to the boss to ask for a week's unpaid leave. This was not my friendly Mr Colston, though, and he just looked at me and shook his head.

'I'm afraid not,' he said, 'you'll get a holiday in due course, but definitely not at the moment!' I looked at him in disbelief. 'But I'm not asking for a holiday,' I pointed out, 'I'm just asking for an unpaid week off.'

To make matters worse, the office manageress was in there with him, and her look was definitely a smirk. I looked at her and saw red. 'There is a war on, you know,' I said angrily, 'and my first duty is to my soldier husband. He is going home, to our home, and I am going to be there to look after him.'

I turned to the door, and he called out, 'If you go, if you dare to go, you need not come back.'

'Oh, thank you, sir,' I replied, and as I went out I made my final shot. 'If you want my advice, you'll employ only withered spinsters like you already have, because all the married girls are going to put their men first.'

I flounced out of the office and packed everything from my desk. A hasty goodbye to my new-found friends and round to the post office to send a couple of telegrams. Then it was back to say a fond farewell to dear Mrs White and off on the train, back to my beloved.

Mum was pleased to see me, but shook her head at my impulsive behaviour. 'Throwing up a good job like that,' she said. 'You won't get a decent reference either. You haven't served your notice, you haven't even got your cards, how will you get another job?'

I shrugged. 'Mum, times are changing. It's easy to walk out of one job into another these days. Don't worry, I'm not,' and neither did I.

Eric came home next day, and we had a wonderful week together. We even gave up sleeping in the dining room with the family and slept in our own bed, only getting up when things got too noisy and close. Perhaps familiarity bred contempt, but we somehow managed to ignore the night-time raids, and since other parts of the country were taking such a heavy pasting, we had quite a few raid-free nights.

We went to visit my dear friend Gladys, who had married the week before us. She was living with her mother and grandmother in a block of flats in Hackney, having been bombed and injured in an earlier raid. She was pregnant and we were very anxious about the baby, but fortunately all was well. She made us laugh, because she had been pulled unconscious from the wreckage of her home, and only regained consciousness in the ambulance. Apparently, she opened her eyes, felt herself drifting along, and vaguely noticed a white-clad figure by her side. She remembered that her last thought had been, as things crashed around her, that she was being killed by a bomb and she now thought she was on the way to heaven. 'Is it a long journey?' she asked the figure by her side, convinced that it was an angel. 'No dear, hospital's only about ten minutes away now.'

'Do you know, Mousie, for a moment I was almost disappointed!' She was one of the only people who still called me by my school nickname.

'Hang on, don't forget Cyril. He's only stationed in Scotland!' laughed Eric, 'so let's have no more talk about heaven. We've lots of living to do here first.'

'Yes, a little house with a garden for the baby. And Eric and Cyril coming in every evening for tea, and happy evenings all together, after we've put the children to bed. . . .' Gladys sighed and looked around the stark fourth-floor flat. 'It's dreaming about the wonderful future that keeps us ploughing through the present.'

We agreed with her, little knowing what was to happen, especially to Gladys's dreams. On the following Monday, having said my goodbyes to Eric, I went up to Oxford Street, intending to call in at head office in Hanover Square to face the music, as Manchester had not sent on my employment cards. Passing Debenham & Freebody, which was shattered but still trading, I met Mr Colston coming out. I greeted my old boss enthusiastically, appreciating him all the more after dealing with the miserable old blighter in Manchester.

'Hello,' he smiled. 'What are you doing here? I thought you'd be running Celanese by now!' I grinned and told him what had happened. 'If I gave my girls the sack every time one of them took time off because of husband's leave, I'd have no good workers left,' he laughed. 'We have plenty of work now, why don't you come back and work for me?' Not for the first time in my life, I could have hugged him. 'I'd just love to,' I answered, 'see you tomorrow.' We shook hands and off I went, walking on air, without having asked about wages, or duties. Back. I was going back to Colstons, back to the place and the work I loved.

Eric was soon moved on from Woolwich, and I usually managed to spend a weekend with him, wherever he went. Leeds, York, Chester, Grimsby: all those places, which had only been names to me in the past, were now real places, and I, the little cockney kid who had been scared out of her wits being taken into a posh restaurant for a meal, was now calmly walking into hotels and guest houses and catching trains to distant places. At least the war was broadening my horizons, as it was for countless others.

We had one funny experience in York. I had met Eric on Saturday lunchtime, and we had just set out on a stroll by the river, when I noticed an elderly man in front of us on the towpath, pushing a pram. He was staggering along, definitely having had too much to drink; and once or twice he went perilously near the river edge, and I feared for the baby. We kept behind him, and when he staggered to a seat and stretched out at full length on it, I sat down fairly near him on the grassy bank and Eric sat down beside me. At first, we just chatted, but Eric was anxious to get on, there was so much of York he was eager to show me, but I refused to move. 'How can we leave the baby like that?' I asked.

Then I tore a piece of paper from my diary and wrote a note. 'The man in charge of this baby has obviously been drinking and is now asleep by the river. I am going to stay here until he wakes up and will see that he leaves the towpath safely.' Then I went to the pram and carefully tucked the note inside the baby's clothing. I resumed my watch on the grass in spite of Eric's sighs, and fortunately, before much longer, the old chap woke up, turned the pram round and made his way back to the road, all the better for his long doze and oblivious to the evidence he was taking with him! Sixty years on and I still wonder at the outcome!

16

Ups and Downs

Getting enough to eat was not so much of a problem to Mum as getting things that would please Dad. Always, she had put him and his likes first; only the best was good enough, and the best, even if her meagre pocket had stretched far enough, was not available.

One of his favourite dishes, and mine too, incidentally, was eels in a thick parsley sauce. Of course, cockneys are always supposed to thrive on jellied eels, but they are a poor substitute for the ones my mum cooked. Cut into short lengths, served with mashed potato and lashings of onion and parsley sauce in big soup plates, they were a meal like no other and I can still drool as I remember sucking the succulent flesh from the bones. What a culinary delight!

Alas, eels had all but vanished from the market, and when they were available they were mostly thin things that Mum would have turned up her nose at before the war.

On one momentous occasion, however, she was shopping in Roman Road when she saw a stall with lovely, live, fat eels. She joined the queue and prayed that they wouldn't all be gone before her turn. For once, her luck was in and there were still some squirming in the tray when her turn came to ask for her pound. Before the war, the stall keeper always chopped them, even asking what size we required, but those days were gone, and the live eels were thrust into a single sheet of newspaper. Mum usually kept spare paper in her shopping bag, but she had not been expecting to get this treat.

'Can't you wrap 'em a bit better, Fred?' she pleaded, but he shrugged his shoulders. 'Don't yer know there's a. . . .' 'Yes, I know all right,' she interrupted, stuffing the wet and wriggling mass into her bag. She hurried away, wondering how much longer she would be able to afford such luxuries. Two shillings for a pound, and only one sheet of paper! Still, Dad would be pleased. Then she stopped. Something wet on her foot. She looked down, to see one of her precious eels wriggling away in the gutter. Mum was after it like a shot, but in telling us about it afterwards, she reckoned it was one of the hardest tasks she'd ever had, to catch and hold the slippery treasure. As she retrieved it and tried to put it away, its companion tried to make its escape, but Mum was resourceful and finished up by removing her scarf and tying the eels firmly inside. I reckon she chopped them up with a vengeance when she eventually got them home!

Mum would always try to make things look appetising and when we once had a tin of pink salmon, she mashed it up and added some cochineal drops to make it red! She used the same method when someone gave her a couple of sticks of green rhubarb and I'm sure she eyed the wild pigeons hopefully, recalling pigeon pie of old!

We were just into the spring when Eric came home on an unexpected leave, with the news that I had been dreading. This was to be his embarkation leave, so he had asked for his rail pass to be made out to Torquay. 'We'll have one holiday before I go,' he said, 'and really enjoy ourselves.'

We did have a good time too, even though it was impossible to get down on the beach anywhere. I was disappointed that the longed-for baby had not started, I just couldn't believe that it could be so difficult. But I hoped that being away and free from the worry of air raid warnings and family sleeping around us, things would work out. On our return home, however, we found a telegram had been delivered, and my mother, not knowing our address in Torquay, had opened it, and left it for us to read, two days later! It was to recall Eric from leave!

Next morning, he returned to Woolwich, and it was some days before I heard from him. His explanation for not returning immediately had been accepted, but the company had moved on. So he and another private in the same position were sent on to Leeds, only to find that the company was not there. They were kept for the night and then sent on to Oswestry where no one had ever heard of them. From there they were sent to Chester, and after that it seemed they went round the country.

Eventually, being supposedly an instrument mechanic, he was housed, as a temporary measure, in a small, newly finished private house in Luton. It was a small estate of new houses, where the building had been halted by the outbreak of war, and the army had taken it over. He was put to work in a civilian engineering workshop together with a few other soldiers and as many civilian employees. And there he stayed! Months later, we received a postcard from one of his friends who had gone while he was at Torquay; he was in the Middle East and being kept busy. As for Eric, the army must have forgotten him, although he received his pay and had to keep to army regulations, but he was able to come home on a weekend pass nearly every weekend, and as Luton was only a short journey from home, he came home even when he didn't have a pass! The only difference was that he avoided the railway and the redcaps, taking several different buses to get home.

Gladys's baby was born in May, on the night of one of the heaviest raids we had had for some time. The government had by now insisted that civilians help the ARP by belonging to fire-watching groups. Office workers had a rota for night-time watching for incendiary bombs, and people at home had to take their turn throughout the night. We were in groups of two, and as there were insufficient tin hats to go round, we were given our two-hour shifts and at the end of the two hours, we had to go and deliver the tin hats to the next people on our list. I really hated it when I was on duty from midnight until two a.m. Even if there was no raid, we were supposed to be up and ready to do firefighting and when the shift was up, I had to take the two tin hats to the next people, who lived in the next road. How I hated that eerie walk in the dark, especially when there was no moon.

One very windy night, I was coming back to my house, when I became aware of someone behind me. At least, I was convinced that someone was following, until I plucked up my courage and stopped, turned round and shone my dim torch, and it was only a bunch of leaves. But I was scared for a minute or two. Auntie Lottie shared my fire-watching duties with me, and we soon came to an arrangement. Instead of getting up two nights a week, we decided that only one of us would, unless there was a raid, which was not very often. But even so, it was difficult to get back to sleep again. Pregnancy was one of the things that excused you the fire-watching duties, and even that didn't come my way!

On this particular night in May, I was on for the ten-twelve watch, which was not too bad; it meant that I could get a decent night's sleep. Soon after nine, I decided to wash my hair. We never had such luxuries as hair dryers, and my thick mop took a long time to dry, so as I was going to be up until midnight anyway, it seemed a good time. It was dripping wet when the warning went, and we hadn't had a raid for weeks! Noise followed, a bomb whined nearby, followed by an explosion, and I knew I had to get out into the street. I pushed my wet hair into the tin hat and went outside, just as another bomb whined. A warden pushed me down on to the ground, and after the din, came a shrill piercing voice. 'Doris, you'll catch your death of cold, out there with that hair all wet.' Even the warden laughed. 'As long as I don't catch my death any other way,' I muttered. There was quite a lot of nearby damage that night, but no really heavy big bombs and no lives were lost in our neighbourhood, although in the city and West End it was very severe.

Poor Gladys, labouring away in hospital, said she wished one of the bombs had fallen on her, but that was a very short-lived wish, and she was thrilled with her little daughter. Cyril was now in the Middle East and there was no chance for him to see his baby. It was unusual for babies to be born in London hospitals at that time but I think it was probably because the hospital had been keeping her under their care since she had been injured in the earlier raids.

I just couldn't wait to go and see her, envious as well as thrilled for her. She called the baby Daphne, and I looked at the dear little soul and prayed that she would not come to any harm in this awful war. Poor little Daphne, life was certainly no bed of roses for her, just as it never was for her mother.

Eric and I seemed to have reached a perfect understanding and our utter faith in each other made my mother shake her head in disbelief. Sometimes, when he came home for a weekend, he would bring a friend with him, one whose home was too far away for a short trip, and on one occasion when I was expecting him I answered the doorbell to find one of these friends and not my dear husband! 'Eric's pass has been cancelled,' he explained, 'but he told me to come in any case. I hope it's all right.' I made him welcome and we had a good weekend together using Eric's bike and going to Epping Forest, but the girls at the office on Monday could not believe it. On another occasion, he brought an ATS girl home for the weekend because he felt sorry for her as her husband had been reported missing and she was upset.

As for me, I had developed a lasting friendship with our minister. PG, as he was known, was not having a very happy time. His wife and children were away and he was trying to keep the church going and run the homeless shelter, besides taking a turn at the warden post situated at the church. Sometimes we would cycle instead of

*Queen Elizabeth visiting St Peter's Avenue, Bethnal Green, 17 June 1943.
(Tower Hamlets Local History Library and Archives)*

catching the train to Bethnal Green, and after the service we would go back together through Victoria Park and on through Hackney, but if the sun was shining, we would often stop in the park for a while and sit talking. Often, he would phone me at lunchtime in the office, and we had long discussions on every subject imaginable. I could tell him things that I never confided to anyone else; only he knew the depth of my love for Eric, which sometimes surprised even myself!

Occasionally he came to tea on Sunday, but mostly he would go to the Browns, or to Eva and Jim, but I usually managed to meet him there. I found him a stimulating companion and he really meant a lot to me.

One Sunday morning, I arrived at the church at the same time as he did and as I greeted him, I noticed his glasses were badly smeared. 'Oh dear,' I said, 'how are you going to preach a good sermon with glasses you can't see out of!' I carefully cleaned them with a hankie and put them back in place. 'Nice to be looked after,' he smiled, and we went into the church.

I never gave the matter another thought, it was so trivial, but a fortnight later, I arrived at church to find PG's wife standing just inside the door.

'Hello,' I greeted her, 'I didn't know you were home. Are you staying, or are you just on a visit?'

'I'm home to stay,' she replied, 'and in future I shall clean dear's glasses myself!' It was such an unexpected reply, and her manner was so cold, that I was completely taken aback. Then I felt angry. Who on earth could have told her . . . and who among all our 'Christian' friends could have been so small minded? And what else had she been told? Perhaps someone had seen us cycling together in the park, or worse still, sitting together on a park bench. Stupid fools. If only they had been able to see in my diary or if his wife had been able to see it, she'd have known she had nothing to fear from me.

Funnily enough, Eric had been home the previous week and my diary entry that weekend makes it plain where my love and loyalty lay:

> As often before, I felt that we left earth, that our naked souls met in some wondrous heaven, and then, when they had learnt some new thing about each other, and had kissed with a deep and lasting love, back they came, our two souls, slipped back into the contented bodies of their owners – and we drifted into dreamland, the dear dark head on my breast and a warm firm hand around me. What joy – what unutterable joy – and hardly can I conceive the joy of peacetime. Would this have been an everyday experience, or is it the infrequency that adds to our delight? When peace does come again, how dearly will we appreciate it? How will we strive to preserve it? Yet even now, we squabble among ourselves, at the office, with family folk, with our friends.

Yes, I had had a really lovely weekend, and somehow, I felt convinced that this time something had happened. And when my regular date had passed without anything happening, I felt really sure that our longed-for baby was on its way.

There were no pregnancy kits in those days, and even the doctor didn't want to know until the second month had passed, but I did not need anyone to tell me that I was pregnant at last.

I walked on air for a week or so, but I only told my close friends at the office and I didn't write to Eric with the news. One reason, I wanted to tell him face to face; and I didn't want to build his hopes up until I had it confirmed. But I began to make plans. White wool – you just could not buy white wool, and unlike today, when I have seen one of my great-grandchildren dressed for her first Christmas in black velvet, babies wore white. Then I remembered some ancient white knitting. I had planned to make Eric a white pullover years ago, but knitting had never been my strong point, and it had never been finished. So I carefully unpicked it, a fact which my mother found a bit intriguing.

Then, alas for dreams, I woke one night in real pain, and by the morning, I knew there was no baby. I was lying miserably in bed, when my mother came in with my morning cup of tea, her face grim. 'Singapore has fallen,' she said, putting the cup on the table. 'Things are getting worse and worse.'

'Singapore isn't the only thing that's fallen,' I cried bitterly, 'I've miscarried.'

Lovely Mum that she was, she took over at once, insisting that I saw the doctor and telling Auntie Lottie to phone the office and say that I had flu. It was a fortnight before I felt well enough to go back to work and the girls were commiserating with me when the boss walked in.

'Glad to see you back, Doris,' he said. 'I've just come back myself, I've had the same thing.'

I don't know how the girls managed to keep from hooting with laughter, but the poor man had no idea what he'd said, and they didn't know my mother had said I'd had flu.

Eric's mother had settled down reasonably well in her little flat and seemed to enjoy being independent. Eric had bought her a canary, and it gave her a lot of pleasure, singing and singing at the open window. Opposite her house was a small open space, a bomb site from one of the earliest raids; there was a barrage balloon there and the WAAF girls were most friendly. They would chat to her when she went shopping; and it seemed to me that she was becoming almost human! We always made a point of calling whenever Eric was home, but always together. Never again was she going to get her hands on my beloved!

One day I had a surprise visit from one of Mrs White's sons from Oldham, and I was glad to be able to put him up for a few days. I felt I was repaying Mrs White for her kindness to us. He was going overseas and had embarkation leave, but there had been some delay and he had a few days' freedom before going. We had a good time together and even managed to get to a London show, but sadly, that was the last time I ever saw him, and the last time his mother saw him too.

I had one delightful week in Bolton. Eric was on a course in Bury, and a friend from pre-war days had married and was living in Bolton. Eric had been to see her, and she invited me up for a week. Mr Colston was not like the miserable Manchester boss and willingly allowed me the time off, so that we were able to enjoy a wonderful week together. Of course, Eric was busy every day, but free in the evenings and found it easy to get an all-night pass. There were no raids to worry about, and Peggy had the most charming little daughter. We had worked together for years before the war and had great fun recalling the episodes of the past. To think that our biggest worry at one time had been whether there was enough lock-knit in stock to make the four dozen pairs of peach knickers that we had rashly promised to Harrods by a certain date!

'We just didn't know what was coming,' laughed Peggy, and we sat thinking. All this was beyond our imagination. To think that we used to look up in the sky to see the aeroplane write 'Oxo' or some other short message. 'It's not what they write now,' I said, 'it's what they throw down.'

We had more or less given up the Sunday school at our church. The children seemed to have lost all sense of discipline after they returned from their evacuation and besides, there were no longer any teachers around for them. No longer did we have half a dozen keen young men to deal with the boys, and the boys were not eager to listen to the old ladies who were available. I wondered if the old days would ever come back, but knew in my heart that they had gone for ever.

Besides having lost most of my girls to evacuation, two had died with TB and then one of my very best friends, a lovely young girl of 19, had also died. She had been engaged to Ernest, one of the group of six who had been planning to go to the Isle of Wight with us, and Ernest, having been called up early in the conflict, was absolutely shattered to lose his sweetheart.

He came to see me when he had leave, and I tried to comfort him. Hand in hand, we went for a long walk in the forest, but I found it difficult to know how I, who had so much to look forward to, could console him, when he had nothing. He and Rene had made such plans, as had all of our little 'gang'. I hardly liked to tell him how happy Eric and I were, but surprisingly by the end of his leave he thanked me and said how much more resigned he felt, even if not any happier. Resignation is a poor substitute for happiness, but I expect it's better than resentment, and I sincerely hoped that the day would come when he would find another partner to love.

I had let the months drift by since my miscarriage, but now, with autumn coming along, I felt it was time to try again. We talked it over in the office, all the young soldiers' wives were fond of giving each other advice, and we commiserated with each other when our plans went wrong, but in the end I devised a foolproof plan.

Eric was back at Luton, where we had made many friends who issued open invitations for me to go and stay whenever I liked, and Eric found it so easy to get an all-night pass – and even if he didn't, he knew how to get back to his billet before breakfast – so I waited until he had a ten-day leave due, bought a season ticket from St Pancras to Luton, and for the fortnight before his leave, I travelled up to Luton every evening after leaving the office. My boss shook his head at me. 'Can't imagine why you are doing that, Doris,' he said. 'With the trains the way they are, it must be nearly bedtime by the time you've got there and had your dinner!' Once again, the dear man had made the girls laugh and he didn't know why! But Eric's friends cooperated willingly and we had some very happy times together until the day when the longed-for leave came around.

During the next ten days there were no raids at all; we went up to town and saw several shows and films. I think *Rebecca* made the most impression! Anyway, I wonder I didn't wear my poor husband to a shadow, but he thrived on all the loving. He had had so little in his single life, no loving of any kind, that to be the whole object of another's love was nearly beyond his comprehension!

I was sorry indeed when he went back to Luton, but this time I was convinced that all would be well and that I was pregnant, and as Christmas drew near, I was really sure. The fourth Christmas of war came and it looked very bleak. The war situation was brighter: we were actually making headway in North Africa and for a change we were doing the chasing, but it was hard to be optimistic.

Dad was very ill; he had a growth somewhere in his head and as Christmas approached he went into hospital. Mum actually got a jar of mincemeat and you would have thought it was solid gold. It was reposing on the sideboard when I came in one evening, and then there was the discussion regarding the fat to make the mince pies, all much more important to Mum than Rommel and the Eighth Army: we solved the problem with liquid paraffin from the chemist. It really made good pastry though it was best not to tell the family, especially Dad, what we had used. Lots of folk used the stuff and it didn't taste funny, at least not very much, but I supposed people associated it with the paraffin we used for fires and suchlike. We had a few apples too, a bit wrinkled in the skin, and Janet polished them over and over. Auntie Lottie brought home from the wholesale chemist where she worked a tin of Ovaltine substitute, which was not saleable as it had got damp, but she managed to dig out pieces and we mixed it with powdered milk and made a special drink. But our heart was not in it all, with Dad in hospital, Eric away and Gwen not home either. Not even the mince pies could really fill us with the Christmas spirit.

It was in the afternoon of Christmas Eve that Dad walked in, accompanied by Gwen. She had got unexpected leave and called to see Dad in hospital. He was there, just waiting for the results of tests, so he decided he'd rather wait at home and walked out. Mum put her coat on, picked up her purse and bag, and with a muttered 'Shan't be long' she went out. When she came home, there was a look of absolute triumph on her face as she unwrapped a newspaper parcel. And there was a rabbit! Very skinny, but a whole rabbit! She'd mortgaged our next week's ration, but when she told the butcher how her husband had come from hospital and her daughter from the ATS, he had reached under the counter and produced the rabbit. 'No corned beef for Christmas,' she laughed.

The crowning touch came a couple of hours later. Eric walked in, with cigarettes for Dad and a whole bar of chocolate, together with a 48-hour pass! From doom and gloom to carolling gladness. We really enjoyed that Christmas of 1942. Looking back, it must have been the leanest Christmas I have ever spent, but oh, it was a happy one.

Sadly, our dear friend PG announced his resignation from our church the following weekend, and I knew I should miss him sorely. But he was really ill; he had been knocked off his bike in the blackout and so badly injured that his face was almost unrecognisable. His jaw was fractured and he had countless other injuries because the driver had not stopped, maybe he didn't know he had hit anyone, and another car had hit him as he lay in the road. He had made a slow recovery, but he was never really fit after the accident and was compelled to give up his rest centre warden work. That meant he needed a church that could support him, and Victoria Park certainly could not do that.

When I told Eric, he wondered if the time had come for us to leave too, especially now that I was definitely pregnant and would soon have to give up the bike rides. It was quite a journey to go to church every week, and we had sometimes gone to a small one nearby, in Leyton, where we had met some very friendly people. We had only really kept on going to Bethnal Green to support PG; even so, it was going to be a terrible wrench. It was there I had learnt what life could mean, there I had first learnt another way of life and there I had met God. Not just the God that everyone knew, but the real God of love who shaped my life and gave it purpose.

It was at the new church that I met Hilda, who was to become one of my dearest friends. Her husband was in the RAF and stationed in this country, so she saw him on regular leaves. She too was hoping that she might have a baby, but no luck so far. It was really strange that before the war we all thought that only one sexual experience would result in pregnancy, yet we seemed to keep meeting girls whose hopes got dashed time and again.

We did not get so many raids these days, but there was one which has remained in my mind over the years. It was on a Saturday, around teatime, when the warning went. Mum was worried, because we were expecting Gwen home that weekend, and she was always glad to have us all safely under her roof when there was a raid on. We heard a bomb fall quite near, and as soon as things quietened down Mum went outside and spoke to a warden. To our dismay, the bomb had fallen on Leytonstone station just as the train had left. There was a tunnel under the platform, where passengers who wanted to go on the other side went through. The bomb hit the platform, straight through to the tunnel, and those unfortunate folk who had got off the train and crossed to the other side were killed. Mum came in, white-faced and stricken. 'Do you reckon Gwen was on that train?' she cried, but we could not console her because we didn't know. We sat and looked at each other, silent and scared stiff with anxiety. It was nearly two hours later, when we heard a key in the door and Gwen appeared. 'I missed the blooming train,' she commented, 'and then there was a notice saying that there were no further trains to Leytonstone. So I had to get the bus and it took ages.'

Mum flung her arms around her and burst into tears. 'Thank God you missed it,' she cried, 'or you'd have been dead now.'

When I went into the factory on Monday I heard a grim sequel to the story. There was a very popular girl, one of our sample hands, who was a member of a nearby church. Apparently, she had fallen in love with one of the church officers, a married man with a family. There was a lot of talk and she and her lover decided to go away together. But then, her conscience got the better of her and she went to see her minister, who persuaded her to give up the man, however much it hurt her to do so. She was on her way home after breaking with him when that bomb fell, and she was killed. As her minister wrote afterwards, she did the right thing and had made her peace with God. Of course, we know that God is a forgiving God, but how much better to go into His presence with a clear conscience.

The episode made a deep impression on the girls who worked with her and it made some of them hesitate before they did what they knew to be wrong.

I was now happily sure of my pregnancy and applied for my cod liver oil and orange juice, one of which I hated and one I loved. No need to enlarge on which was which, but I took both as prescribed.

Then there arose another problem. Where was the baby to be born? No London hospital was taking maternity cases, except for emergencies, and my mother certainly didn't want me to have the baby at home. So it was a case of evacuation. Fortunately we were not expected to leave until a month before the due date, so it was some time before I would have to go away. I worked until the end of April, so I had May and June in which to enjoy being a lady of leisure. I had gathered quite a few scraps of silk and satin over the previous months, and enjoyed making little garments. Not that I was very good with a needle and even more hopeless with knitting needles, but I struggled on, helped a bit by Auntie Lottie, who was worse than me at following a knitting pattern. She tried to knit a baby vest, but when it was finished I had to point out that she had neglected to make any armholes!

Poor baby, a good thing it had Gwen and Mum to make good our mistakes. One of the first things I bought was an enamel potty! They were in short supply, and in those days, babies were trained from birth to perform in the correct place. Not that they did, but it was the done thing to try and persuade them. My father heard of someone with a real coach-built pram for sale and Eric's brother's wife offered me her baby's cot, as they were not having any more children.

And so time moved on until I had to leave London for the birth of our first child.

17

My Daughter is Born

A few weeks before the great event was due, I received my marching orders. If travelling by train to the venue, I was to show my pink form at the railway station! But I had to rendezvous at Hackney hospital, so no need to show my pink form. We had almost begun to accept the war as a way of life now. No longer did we expect the war to be over by Christmas, not any Christmas, and my diary records the stark fact that we were getting hardened to suffering:

Our army has achieved glorious victory in North Africa and not an axis uniform remains but is a prisoner in our hands. Our RAF is wonderful, bombing and bombing 24 hours a day, and we say 'Good work' knowing that thousands of everyday folk like ourselves are dying by our bombs.

Gladys called to see me with little Daphne but, unusually for her, was a bit depressed. 'It's such a big responsibility to be a parent alone,' she said, 'I'm always afraid I won't be successful. Oh, I wish Cyril was here.' I tried to comfort her, reminding her that Eric had promised Cyril that we would always be there for her, until he came home, but that only made her all the more upset. Easy for me to talk, with Eric always popping home for odd weekends as well as getting regular leaves. She was not sure where her husband was, only somewhere in the Middle East, and his letters were so irregular and said so little.

Ernest, the friend whose girlfriend had died of TB, had been home again and taken me to the pictures, and my mother's face had told me what she thought about that! We had a very happy few hours together before he went away again. He seemed to drift in and out of my life and I once wrote in my diary that I had three stars on my horizon, PG, Ernest and Gladys, but they were the stars surrounding my sun, my special beloved.

At last, the great day came and on Friday 9 July, I set out for Derbyshire, or somewhere like that. It was all very vague and we were not given any forwarding address. We were taken to St Pancras station, about fifty of us, and the train took us to Loughborough. By the time we reached there I had heard enough horror stories about evacuation to make my hair stand on end, but I tried to shut my ears and my mind to the tales about the ill-treatment of adult evacuees, and made up my mind that I would take it all with a pinch of salt until I found otherwise. The WVS met us at the station and we were taken to a church hall where we were asked if we were willing and able to pay for our keep. It was a sort of means test and one of the party had warned us, 'Just say you are a private's wife and offer to pay half of what they suggest, whatever it is.' So when my turn came and I was asked where and how I lived, what rent and other outgoings I had, and could I afford 14 shillings a week, I just muttered, 'Seven and six'. The man in charge said, 'Thank you, bring it in when you come to the ante-natal clinic,' and that was that.

Women seemed to be drifting in now and the names of the evacuees were called out and away they went, with their respective landladies, while I just sat and sat.

I found myself thinking of the slaves of old waiting to be sold, and beginning to wonder what would happen if no one claimed me. At last, I was the only one left, and the WVS lady sighed. 'Come on, dear,' she said, 'I'll take you there. She was told to pick you up at three o'clock.' Poor start this, but maybe there was some reason. We went on a very short car journey and stopped outside a neat little terraced house. She helped me with my case and knocked. No answer. 'Oh well,' she said brightly, 'probably still shopping and forgotten the time. I've such a lot on, I'll just leave you. Have a good stay. Goodbye for now,' and she was in her car and away before I could utter a word of protest!

Never in my life, before or since, have I felt so helpless and desolate. Standing on the pavement with my heavy case, aching and weary with the long journey, it was hard to keep the tears from rolling down my cheeks. Where was she, this woman who was supposed to be there for me for the next four weeks? After about ten minutes, a woman came out from a house opposite.

'You're in for a long wait, dear,' she said kindly, then altered her tone. 'Spiteful, cunning bitch, that's what she is. Needs a few bombs around her, 'cos she doesn't know what it's like. You'd best come in with me, because I reckon she'll stay out until she thinks everyone has gone home. Come on, dear.' She picked up my case and took my arm. Crossing the little road, I wished with all my heart that this was where I could stay, but I knew that was wishful thinking when she said, 'I'm from Hull myself, so I know all about raids. We all lost everything, my mum and dad and my cousins, and we've all been packed into this one little house, but we are so grateful to be alive that nothing else matters. You won't find any sympathy here, though; they are all mad about having pregnant women billeted on them. Kids would be easier.' She busied herself as she talked and handed me a cup of tea and a biscuit.

'You can stay here until she comes home, she'll be back before six thirty, that's when her lord and master gets in; and a right old devil he is.' My spirits sank even lower. What on earth had I let myself in for? We sat and talked and she told me about the bombing in Hull. 'Grimsby has had a few too,' she added. 'I would like to see a few fall here,' she laughed, 'as long as only the locals suffered.'

Suddenly, she jumped to her feet. 'Here she comes. God, she's going to be so mad, thinking she's dodged them. Come on, let's spoil her plan,' and she picked up my case and steered me across the road, with a grin on her pleasant face.

'Here you are, Mrs Smith,' she said, 'I've been looking after your evacuee. Thought she looked a bit tired. Been travelling all day.'

A look of absolute horror came over Mrs Smith's face. 'But it's all arranged. I'm not having anyone. Me health won't stand it.'

'Well, you'll have to take her in tonight anyway, and settle up with them tomorrow. Afraid I'll have to go now. Goodbye dear, hope you get on all right,' she added as she went back across the road, leaving me standing with my welcoming host.

'You'd better come in,' she muttered, making no attempt to help me with the heavy case, 'but I don't know what Dad will say, I really don't.' She looked me up and down and sighed. 'I'll show you up to the bedroom, but don't unpack, because he won't let you stay, he really won't.'

I lugged the case up the narrow staircase and felt almost joyful. Oh, how I hoped he would not let me stay. That was something we both agreed on anyway! The bedroom was clean and neat, and there was a bathroom next door, but no toilet that I could see which could be awkward during the night. She only stayed a minute or so, then went out, leaving me alone, wondering what on earth to do.

A few minutes later I heard footsteps. I looked out of the window and saw a heavily built, stocky man, not unlike my father, coming up the garden path. I think it was this likeness to my father which made me feel I knew how to deal with him. Probably a bully boy, like Dad in the Bethnal Green days, before time and poor health had mellowed him.

I listened to murmured voices for a few minutes, then a roar. 'You stupid fool! Let her get her foot in the door! After all the trouble I went to, to get you that paper. Can't you do anything right?'

'It wasn't my fault. I did exactly as you said, I stayed out all afternoon. It was that busybody across the road.' Mrs Smith was now raising her voice. 'I've told her she's not staying, not to unpack, but we can't do anything until tomorrow.'

'Saturday tomorrow, office won't be open. You've got yourself landed all weekend now, stupid fool.' I stood in the bedroom, wondering whether to make an entrance or wait until the storm subsided, not sure what to do next. I said a little prayer for help, for surely I needed help now. 'Please, God,' I whispered, 'please help me.' Then, amazingly, my eye fell on a book on the window-ledge. Just an ordinary story book, but as I opened it, I saw that it was a Sunday school prize, awarded to Martin Smith, and the label was headed Baptist church, so I looked around and found two other books, each awarded from the same local Baptist church. So, they had Baptist church connections and maybe this was my clue.

I went down the stairs, steep, carpeted stairs they were, with a door at the bottom, which made them very dark. I walked into the small sitting room, where the Smiths sat, one each side of the table.

'Good evening,' I addressed the bully boy. 'I'm afraid I've been dumped on you, but there's nothing I can do about it. If I have to stay, I promise not to give you any trouble. . . .' He interrupted my little speech. 'That's what you think. The last one had fleas in her head and she smelt. Made Mother feel sick.'

'And the one before that made the bed wet, ruined the mattress when her waters broke in the night,' added Mrs Smith.

I was pretty ignorant myself about these waters. I only knew what I'd read, and whether there were drops or floods I had no idea. 'I assure you I'll take adequate precautions,' I said calmly, 'and as for my head, I'm sure it's quite free of lice. But I'm perfectly willing to undergo an inspection at the health clinic if you wish.' At that moment, the front door opened and a young girl in her teens walked in. 'Well, Bet, we've got another of them, owing to your mother's stupidity,' the father greeted his daughter, and she gave me a half-hearted smile and a nod.

'Tea will be in twenty minutes,' Mother informed me gloomily, so I excused myself and went upstairs, glad that I had brought my own toiletries, including towels, with me. Bet came up behind me, so I turned to her and played my trump card.

'I noticed that your folk have attended the Baptist church,' I said. 'Do you think you could tell me how to get there sometime? I wouldn't like to miss going on Sunday, like I always do at home.' She turned and looked at me. 'OK. I usually go myself, so you can tag along with me if you like. Just so that you know the way.' She turned round and ran down the stairs and I heard her talking to her dad.

Tea was an almost silent meal, but halfway through Dad cleared his throat and made a sudden announcement. 'Mother and I have talked it over, and decided you can stay, just as long as you behave yourself.' Then followed a long list of dos and don'ts which were mostly about times. I gathered that I was not allowed to stay indoors unless it was raining, but if they were all out, then I was definitely not allowed in, except of course at night. If they were out for the evening I had to go to my room before they left. I was expected to help Mother, which of course I had intended to do; and there were numerous petty rules about not leaving my belongings around. It amused me, because I saw only too clearly that they had connections with the Baptist church, and even if they didn't attend themselves, it appeared that Bet did, and they didn't want to get a bad name there.

On the Saturday I helped with a few chores, and being informed that there was no lunch on Saturday, I went into the town, and a very unwelcoming place it seemed to me. I went into a small café and met several of the girls I had travelled up with and apart from one, no one seemed to be happy in their billet. We all envied the girl who was staying in a cottage with a dear little old granny, who treated her like a granddaughter and made a fuss of her. 'Even wanted to give me breakfast in bed,' she laughed happily. One or two were to be given bed and breakfast only and had to be out from nine a.m. until six at night. So I considered myself lucky.

But I had to admit that they had a point, these everyday ordinary folk, whose small town had been invaded by so many women in the very last stages of pregnancy. I soon learnt that besides the tales that the evacuees told, there were stories about some of the visitors: women who didn't bother to help, who used foul language, or even failed to call the ambulance in time and had their babies in their billets. The local children called out, 'here come the big bass drummers' if several went by together, and the neighbouring schoolboys referred to Loughborough as pimple town. I felt angry myself once when, coming out of Woolworths, an elderly man bumped into me and cursed, knocking me into the road with his elbow. 'Keep out of my way, blasted woman,' he bawled, and I yelled back, 'To think that my husband is fighting for the likes of you,' which was not strictly true, since he was sitting comfortably in his billet in Luton.

Fortunately, the weather was dry and warm, and it was no great hardship to stay out, although I was glad to sit in the little park and rest my legs. Almost every day, one or other of our number would be missing, gone to the land of the blessed, as we called the maternity homes. There were two, and we had both telephone numbers, to call alternatively, daytime or night. Apparently, the night-time place was by far the best, though how we knew that I could not imagine, since none of them came back after the babies were born. In the centre of the little park was a tower, with bells which sometimes played tunes. It was called a carillon and was worth listening to. Except for one Saturday afternoon, when I was feeling particularly weary, and those bells began to play the well-known piece from *Messiah*: 'Come unto me, all ye that labour and are heavy laden!' Did the musician play that on purpose? Was it his idea of fun, or was it to comfort?

Wearily, I dragged myself home, if it could be called home, and Mr Smith called to me before I could get upstairs. 'Want you a minute, Mrs Bailey.'

Something was wrong; what had I done now?

'Would you mind lifting the seat when you go to the lavatory? Your suspenders are scratching the polish. It isn't Bet, or Mother, they know better, and it's only since you came.'

I felt like yelling, 'Heavens, it's only a blooming outside lav in the yard!' but I meekly said 'Sorry' and hoped that was the end of the conversation, but no, he had been brooding over something, because he continued, 'How much longer do you intend to stay? Only I start my holidays next week and I don't want you hanging around.'

'I don't intend to stay any longer than I have to,' I replied, 'and if it was up to me, I'd be gone tomorrow. I'm visiting the clinic tomorrow and maybe they can give me an idea. Are you going away on holiday?' Maybe they were and if so perhaps the maternity home would take me in.

'No, I'm not,' he replied, 'but you'll have to get up and out early and not come back until evening. It's my holiday, after all.'

'I'll see what I can do,' I answered shortly and went from the room, up those flipping narrow stairs with thick carpet and a linen cover over the carpet to protect it, and brown paper at the top and the bottom to protect the protection! A house full of spit and polish and no love it was, and I choked back the tears. Only that morning Mrs Smith had informed me that she hoped I wouldn't start the baby in the daytime, because she didn't know how to use a telephone, and the previous day she had hoped I wouldn't start at night and disturb their rest. Not even at the church had I found any love. No one ever spoke to me. After Bet had taken me that first Sunday, she had gone off with her own young friends and I sat alone. It was all so different from my own beloved Victoria Park or even the church at Luton, where Eric had been made so welcome, or the church at Oldham, where we had made so many friends. Yet it must have been evident that I was one of the evacuees. Maybe that was why they didn't speak to me.

I went to bed early, and was one of the first at the ante-natal clinic next morning. To my dismay, in answer to my anxious query 'How much longer?' the doctor shook his head and patted me. 'Come and see me in a fortnight. That baby is firmly tucked under your ribs, so don't be impatient.'

The nurse looked sympathetically as my eyes filled with tears. 'Got one of those billets have you dear?' and when I nodded she looked angrily out of the window. 'God, I'd pray for a bomb or two on this place if it wasn't for all you poor mums stuck here. Even if I had to stay here myself.' When I reached home, Mrs Smith was waiting anxiously. 'Well, what did they say?' 'Told me to be patient, it will come when it's ready,' and I did not point out that my due date was still twelve days away. Now, if ever, I was going to pray for a miracle. 'Please God. I just can't stay here next week. They don't want me, it's hard enough now. Please let this baby come now.' I didn't often get down on my knees and pray like I did then, but it was so important and I knew, I just knew God could do it. I got up and decided to go out for a coffee, and as I went out of the door I slipped on the brown paper and slid, almost gracefully, on my bottom straight down the stairs, ending up with a bump at the door.

'What on earth are you doing?' came a querulous voice as I scrambled to my feet rubbing my posterior. 'Hurrying my baby maybe,' I said jokingly, and she looked at me enquiringly. 'Are you all right?' she asked, and I knew she wouldn't have asked if bully boy had been at home. 'Yes thanks,' I replied. 'My own stupid fault.'

That evening, I went to my room early. Faith without works is dead had long been one of my favourite texts. If you believe God is going to answer prayer, then you had to show you had faith, so I proceeded to pack my case carefully. When everything was in, I made sure I had fourpence ready on the dressing table, ready for the phone call; and then I got ready for bed. I went to sleep too, and was suddenly awakened by a sudden terrific pain. Golly, it was like no other, and if this was only the beginning, what on earth would the end be like? I felt fine when I sat up, and I began to wonder if I had imagined it. But no, twenty minutes later came another, and when another hit me with equal force, I got up and began to dress. There was a knock on my door, and Bet stood there. 'Are you all right?' she asked.

'I think it's started,' I replied, and she grabbed the fourpence from the dressing table.

'Don't worry, I'll go and phone now,' she said and was out of the house within one minute. Mrs Smith put her head cautiously out of her bedroom door and when she saw I was up and dressed, she shut it again quickly – scared, or afraid I might drop the baby on her carpet. Whatever, she didn't want to get involved and I never saw her again. Bet stayed with me for a few minutes until the ambulance came. I was glad the night shift had taken over and that I was bound for Whatton House, a beautiful estate owned by Lord Crawshaw. I had heard from the other girls that it was lovely there, and I was looking forward to my stay, though not exactly to the next few hours. I walked, almost awestruck, into a beautiful hall where a smiling nurse came and took my case and guided me up an imposing wide oak staircase. It was this staircase that impressed me most of all. 'When I come down these stairs again, I shall be a mum,' I told myself, thrilled at the very thought.

Lord Crawshaw. He invited all the babies born at Whatton during the war to Sunday tea in June 1997.

After a brief examination, the nurse gave a sigh. 'You've got a long way to go yet,' she said, 'lucky if you make it before tomorrow.'

'Oh, I don't mind,' I exclaimed, 'as long as you don't send me back.'

'Another one of those!' she retorted angrily. 'I suppose she couldn't wait to get you here. You'd think they'd be only too glad to help the Londoners, but they are not. I wouldn't be sorry to see a few bombs dropped here, as long as you girls were out of it.' 'That's funny,' I said, 'you're the second nurse who's said that to me.'

'That's how we all feel,' she answered. 'They don't know when they are well off. But the Crawshaw family are wonderful. They do all they can to help. Even give us their garden produce to help feed you all. Pity there aren't more like them. Come on, let's give you a good dose of castor oil and put you to bed.'

The next few hours were not very pleasant, but I tried to remember a wise old saying I had heard. An optimistic old man once told his pastor that he lived through all the troublesome areas of his life relying on one text from the Bible. 'And it came to pass.'

'Yes?' prompted the minister, 'which one of the many verses that start like that?'

'Any of them,' came the reply. 'And it came to pass, and pass it does.'

And so I found it, and at five o'clock that afternoon my dear little daughter was born and changed my life for ever.

What a different world it was then, from the confinements of today! We were not allowed to set one foot out of bed, not even for a bath or to go to the loo, for eight days, and then we were only lifted out of bed for five minutes while the bed was changed. On the ninth day we actually had a bath, and on the tenth we were allowed to help bath the baby and shown how to change a nappy. On our last afternoon, we were allowed to go into town on the bus on our own. It was a strange feeling, walking round without carrying all before us, and of the six girls accompanying me not one felt like visiting their hostess of the previous month!

On the thirteenth morning, we were transported to the station, carrying our precious bundles of joy, and with what a thrill I met Eric and Mum at St Pancras. She was Mum's first grandchild, my lovely little Angela, and she was indeed a joy to us all. It seemed I had no problems at all with her; she rarely cried and would lie contentedly in her pram for hours. Janet adored her, and would creep quietly down the stairs every morning to be allowed to nurse her first great-grandchild. As for

Ever helpful, Angela helps with the tea-making at her birthplace.

Eric, I knew I had given him his heart's desire and we both thanked God that he was still in Luton and able to get home on leave; and sneak home without leave every other weekend. Apparently, one of the soldiers there had 'found' a book of passes, and they were handed around, signed by 'Captain Newman'. 'We all thought Newman was a good choice,' Eric explained, 'if anyone gets stopped and a redcap phones our camp, he might ask "have you got a Newman there?", and as we are always getting new men, we might get away with it!' It was just a silly joke really, but things were so lax at Luton and as Eric avoided the railway stations, there was never any problem.

Once more, he had been on a course at Bury, and there came a letter from Peggy inviting me up to stay with her, but with Angela so young I thought it unwise to make the journey – and that's the very first time that I had had to put Eric second to the baby! As I sat writing to decline the invitation, I wondered whether Eric would realise it too, because a visit to Peggy would mean hours spent with my beloved.

18

Flying Bombs

Yet another Christmas came round, the fifth Christmas of this never-ending war, and we tried to make the most of it. Janet bought balls of string which were not rationed, or even difficult to obtain, and crocheted shopping bags for us all. When these bags were boiled in the weekly wash, they came out soft and white, and incredible as it seems, I still have mine in use sixty years later! Old woollen jumpers were unpicked and reknitted and a good thick winter skirt could be made from an army blanket, which for a time was unrationed. So we made presents for each other and enjoyed our Christmas.

About this time Eva became suddenly much more friendly, even nursing the baby at times, and then I realised that at last she was actually pregnant herself. There were no more snide remarks about me being a broody bitch and before long she was asking my advice about various matters.

Eric and I settled into our new church life, although it could never be Victoria Park to me, but I made friends there and found too the same God of love and comfort. Hilda, my special friend, was now expecting twins, which was very exciting. The compulsory evacuation of expectant mothers had ended, and both Eva and Hilda had opted for births in London.

Then, just at Easter, came the news that Cyril had been killed at Anzio. Gladys was devastated; she had been nervous about bringing up Daphne. Somehow she seemed lacking in confidence and had talked so much about how Cyril would know what was best. She had had such a short time with him, just a few weeks and then a couple of short leaves before he went overseas. Only a few weeks before his death, I had had a long letter from him, written at sea, talking in such joyful terms of the happy times we were all going to have together. Now he was gone from us and I knew not how to comfort Gladys. I had so much, still my beloved husband was stationed at Luton and the only times he moved from there were to be sent on courses. I don't think he learnt much there either. They were all instrument mechanical courses and he came back each time to the same job and the same pay. It didn't worry me that the army seemed intent on wasting money, I only thanked God that he was still around. He did have one spell in Grimsby, spending much of the time out on a fort in the Humber, but we laughingly said that was as far overseas as he went.

There were rumours floating around now, the longed-for second front would be happening soon, and as everybody knew, the war could not end until this had taken place. So when we heard, on 6 June, that we had actually landed, there was great rejoicing, as well as apprehension.

Of course, we had the Americans to help us, and this was the beginning of the end . . . or perhaps just the end of the beginning! Once again we whispered the words, 'over by Christmas', because our troops were well prepared this time and there had been plenty of time for planning. And now, things were happening at last. And Eva was eight months pregnant, which at the time seemed to us far more important!

We didn't have long to wait for something to happen. The army had gained a strong foothold in France, all the news was good, except for the anxious families who only knew their sons were over there, but before the second front was more than a week old we had a strange air raid. Strange, that the warning went before midnight, and although nothing seemed to be happening, every now and then was an unusual noise, more like a small plane in trouble. Once, Dad looked out in the garden and came in with a smile of satisfaction.

'It's all OK, I think. I've just seen the bugger go over on fire. Never heard any gunfire though, but he's been hit all right.' A moment later, we heard an explosion, some distance away. 'He's come down somewhere,' stated Dad. 'Hope he didn't hit anything.'

It was morning before the All Clear sounded, and we had hardly cleared breakfast before another warning sounded. We switched on the news, but beyond telling us

The first V1 flying bomb fell on a railway bridge in Grove Road on 13 June 1944. (Tower Hamlets Local History Library and Archives)

what we knew, that there had been enemy activity during the night, it was all very vague. It was not until evening that we realised that these were not normal raids. Auntie Lottie came home from work in Bethnal Green to tell us that a plane, light blazing from it, had fallen on the railway arch in Grove Road; and to this very day there is still a plaque by the arch recording the fact that the first flying bomb fell there.

Terrified of them at first, fearful of the unknown, we soon accepted them as a fact of the war, and they had several nicknames. The favourite one among East Londoners was 'doodlebug'.

One afternoon, I called to visit Eric's mother, who, since the birth of her grandchild, had become almost friendly. Angela was asleep in her pram, so I left her outside the house while I went in to take some shopping, but hearing the everlasting warning, I left and hurried for home. It was only about ten minutes' walk, but I heard the ominous sound of the thing overhead, and then, horror of horror, it cut out! It was all right as long as you could hear it buzzing, but once it stopped, then you knew your chances were pretty slim. I felt my legs tremble, but I pushed the pram like mad, as though I knew which way to run, and then I heard it explode, some way from me. I didn't look back, but continued my wild dash for home, and I had just got in when another one fell. I was shaken, but thanked God that we had not been injured, and then Auntie Lottie came in from work.

'Oh Dods,' she said. 'That thing fell in Vernon Road!' Vernon Road, where Eric's mother lived! Leaving the baby in my mother's care, I dashed back the way I had come, impeded now by ambulances, fire engines and ARP vans. I reached Vernon Road and stood gazing at what had been the barrage balloon site and was now a mass of chaos. And opposite the site, the rickety walls of partly demolished houses, in one of which my mother-in-law had been sitting drinking a cup of tea. And my baby, in her pram, had been sleeping outside until five minutes before it fell! I made enquiries, endlessly worrying police and wardens, until I ascertained an elderly lady had been taken from the wreck and was now on her way to Whipps Cross. I sent a telegram to Eric, who was temporarily in Buntingford, and then I tried to get news from the hospital. At first the hospital said there was no one of that name there, told me to 'try the mortuary' and I felt like screaming down the phone, it was so callous a voice, but I expect they had been inundated with enquiries.

Eric got home later that night and we went to the hospital, where we found his mother was alive, but badly injured. She had numerous broken bones; and we learnt afterwards that she had been coming down the stairs when the front door, with its big glass panel, had blown in on top of her before the ceiling caved in. Sadly, all five of the WAAF girls manning the balloon site had been killed.

Although Mrs Bailey was barely conscious, she was whispering about Joey. 'He'll be so frightened,' she cried. Joey was the little canary we had given her for Christmas, and next morning, I went back to the bomb site with Eric. At first the wardens were adamant, no way could we go there, but Eric was firm and told them that he had promised his mum that he would rescue her pet. 'At your own risk then,' shrugged the warden, and so we made our way up the broken debris-laden staircase, and there, on the kitchen table, stood the cage, with Joey still chirruping away amid the plaster and glass. We took the cage and made our way back home, where Joey settled down as happily as ever.

Eric's mum never came home again, and when Angela was old enough to talk she always referred to her as 'Grandma in bed'.

The next week, Eva's little son was born, and Jim came home from the hospital after seeing his wife to find that his house had been damaged. Not hopelessly, but until it was made safe he was unable to go back. It was funny really, because my father took him out to 'wet the baby's head' and Jim, not used to drinking, came back slightly the worse for wear. We all laughed, because he sat at my dining table, propping his head up with both hands, sighing with happiness and annoyance.

'Amazing,' he kept saying. 'A baby and a bomb at the same time.' He repeated this so many times that we were helpless with laughter.

Eva had several problems with her premature baby and for a week or so his little life was balanced between life and death, but he made it safely and Mum and I managed to get the house straight and clean before they were able to bring him home.

After a month of the flying bombs, another of Mrs White's sons came to see me. He was stationed in London and, realising how difficult things were, he got in touch with his mother and she, dear soul, wrote and invited me to go to Oldham for a long rest with my baby.

The government were once again urging people to evacuate, so I didn't have to pay my fare but went as an evacuee, which meant I could get help with the extra expense of living away from home.

What a welcome awaited me! I met friends, even one of the girls from the Manchester office, and once again I was able to take Angela to the park without dreading hearing the flying bomb engine cut out. Ever since my close encounter with one, I had been nervous to be out with my baby.

One afternoon I made my way to Bolton, to see my friend Peggy. She had lost her little

Mrs White with one of her sons, and Eric in uniform.

2-year-old suddenly, and was very tearful. But she was expecting another baby and I offered to go and look after her when the time came, so after spending two happy months with Mrs White, I went with Angela to stay in Bolton, when Peggy's baby was almost due. What fun we had! Then, amazingly, I had a letter from Gladys, forwarded from Leytonstone, and learnt that she had been evacuated to a little village near Bury! We lost no time in getting in touch with her, and she came across to see us, bringing Daphne. Once again, I thanked God for His goodness to me, as I listened to these two dear friends of mine, one having lost a dear husband and the other a precious baby.

The flying bomb menace was not so bad now in London, as our RAF flyers had found the best way to tackle them, and met them as they came in over the coast. Since they had no pilot on board, they were unable to respond to attack, and the RAF boys were able to shoot them down. Further, our army was fast overrunning the sites from which they had been launched, and it seemed as though we had once again triumphed over the danger that Hitler had devised for us. But not before thousands had perished, and countless others lost their homes. Gradually, though, even the blackout was partially lifted, and very dim lighting allowed. The evacuees streamed home again, and we dared to hope that the end of this very dark tunnel was in sight. Nevertheless, I stayed on in Bolton as I had promised Peggy and the day came when her second little daughter was born.

19

VE Day and Peace

Eric was again in Bury, and my home was always where my beloved was, so although things looked brighter now I had no incentive to return to London. We had one wonderful weekend when we went out together and had the opportunity to talk and decided that the time was ripe to think about a brother or sister for Angela. Of course, this would be the last Christmas of the war. But would it? The sixth one! It was halfway through December when Eric came in with the news that he was going back to Woolwich, so once more I packed my bags and made the journey home. Mum was delighted to welcome me, but she seemed a little bit wary.

'Hope you've not made a mistake,' she said, 'but I think there's another new weapon coming over.'

'No Mum, the war is nearly over,' I laughed. 'France and Belgium are liberated, things are going well and no way can Jerry send trouble over from the coast. Let's think about Christmas next week.'

She shook her head, and a few nights later, I was awakened by a terrific explosion. 'What the hell!' exclaimed Dad. 'Why the devil hasn't the warning gone?' We looked at each other, and listened to the silence around us. No planes, no gunfire, just a grim silence.

'I told you so,' Mum whispered. 'One of the women in the fish queue told me last week about it. Rockets, that's what they are. Fired from Germany, planned to fall on London. Anywhere. Just to kill. I expect they'll send over thousands, you'll see.'

Thank God they did not come in their thousands, but these V2s, as they were called, were the utmost in terror weapons. There was no warning, they just dropped from the sky, and there was no time pattern either, except that I felt safer to go shopping soon after one had fallen, since they were fairly infrequent.

We enjoyed our Christmas and it was uneventful. Hilda now had her twins, a boy and a girl, and her husband was still in England, so she was able to go and visit her relations in Devon, near to where he was stationed. I was already fairly certain that my second baby was on the way, which rather surprised me, after all the effort it had taken to get pregnant previously.

Again, my mother shook her head at me. So many times she had to do that, where I was concerned! But she was only thinking of my welfare, bless her. 'Not the best time to bring another baby into this mess,' she sighed. 'I only hope you know what you're doing.'

'Mum, this baby will be one of the first peace babies to be born, and if it's a little girl, we will call her Dawn.' I was most emphatic about it, and she smiled. 'As long as I'm not left holding the baby.' She tried to make light of it, but I knew she had never forgotten Rosie's death, all those years ago. For this reason she rarely offered to babysit for me; she was always afraid of sudden death striking while she was in charge.

'Everything will be fine, Mum.' I tried to cheer her up, but she shrugged her shoulders and went upstairs.

It was eight-thirty on the following Saturday morning. I had taken Angela from her cot and sat her on her little potty in front of the bedroom gas fire. A bitterly cold January morning it was, and I dressed hurriedly. Then it happened. A deafening noise, and glass shattered. The curtains streamed in towards us and I grabbed Angela in my arms. There was a rumbling noise somewhere, and looking out of the room, I saw that half the dining room ceiling had fallen down. Angela looked up cheerfully from the shelter of my arms. 'Bang,' she said. I called up to Mum, but she was already halfway down the stairs. 'All right?' I nodded. 'What about Janet?' 'She's all right, she was still asleep, with her head under the covers. There was some plaster down in her room, but she's not hurt.'

Some poor folk were, though, and many were dead. The V2 had fallen very near, on the houses in the road leading to the school. If it had not been a Saturday, there would have been hundreds of children in that road and the death toll would have been higher. But my friendly butcher had been killed in his shop, and the nearby Methodist church minister and his family had been wiped out, apart from one little girl. We were all deeply shocked, and the sight of the huge pile of rubble where families had been living their happy everyday lives left their neighbours grieving. It was so very near, and we had been spared.

It took us a long time to clear up, and we had to get used to living with bare rafters, but we had a roof over our heads, and we had our lives and limbs intact. The curtains were tattered, but that was a minor detail. Angela seemed untroubled by it all; it did not seem to have worried her. I supposed that she was too young, and yet she told me only recently that she remembered it all. She even knew which ceiling came down, so it must have made an impression, although she was only eighteen months old at the time.

That V2 certainly made us a bit nervous about going out, but since no one knew where or when, or had any warning, there was just nothing we could do, so it was best to adopt a philosophical attitude of 'whatever will be will be', and carry on as normal.

Mum kept asking me if I planned to go away with this coming baby, but I shook my head and gave her a definite no. Loughborough again! I was going to take my chance with Hitler's new weapon, or anything else he threw at us, but I was staying in London.

Fortunately, our troops overran the launching sites before long and the last and most deadly weapon was halted. Now we could clearly see the end in sight, at least in Europe. As for the Far East, we did not seem to be making much headway, but it

A Bethnal Green street party, one of the many held in the East End to celebrate the end of the war, 1945. (Tower Hamlets Local History Library and Archives)

was more remote, except for the families of those poor soldiers and airmen involved. We heard sad tales about the harsh treatment meted out to the prisoners, but the optimistic few thought that Japan would give up as soon as Hitler did.

Nowadays, we were likely to hear good news when we switched on the wireless and by the beginning of May we knew that the German army in Italy had surrendered, that Mussolini was dead and that the Russians were in Berlin. Then we had the wonderful news that Hitler too was dead and the war was all but over. The last siren had sounded and the blackout ended, and on Tuesday 8 May, the war in Europe officially ended.

How gladly we celebrated VE Day! Eric was able to get home for the day, and in the evening we went to church, to give God thanks for all His wondrous mercies to us. Oh, our gratitude was going to be such that we could never complain again about anything, about shortages, or black market, or unmended windows and cracked ceilings. When we had husbands to live at home, would we, the young wives of the war, ever grumble at them? In the first flush of peace, it was truly going to be peace on earth.

But it was an entirely different world from that which had ended in September 1939. To me, one of the most striking things was the attitude of workers towards their employers. It was going to be a world of equality, where the humble would be able to climb. I thought of my mother's expression, class is class, and knew that it would no longer apply. Anybody could be somebody.

All these things went through my mind in those first heady days of peace. Of course, there was still the war in the Far East, but it seemed unlikely that we would be bombed, or that our way of life would be upset again, but it was still there, and the war was not yet really over.

On a hot Saturday in early August, I went into hospital and again, Eric was able to sneak home from Luton. Unlike today's dads, there was no suggestion of him staying with me, though I don't think he would have done, even given the opportunity, but he did sit with me until nine o'clock, and at 1 a.m. our dear little son was born.

On Sunday morning, I sat up in bed and read the grim news of Hiroshima; a terrible news item that overshadowed even our joy. How could it be right, to rejoice over such dreadful killing and maiming? Yet, if it ended the conflict, how many lives would be saved? You needed the wisdom of Solomon to say whether it was right or wrong.

That afternoon, before Eric went back to Luton, he produced a telegram form in which he informed himself of the baby's birth, and requested Mum to take it to the post office on Monday to send to Luton. She did so, and he was given a 48-hour compassionate leave to visit me and see the baby!

He admitted that it was a bit difficult to pretend that he was receiving news, when the officer informed him that he had a son! On 14 August, I came home from hospital, and the very next day came the end of the war. The real end!

What did we all expect? That it would suddenly be different? That food would appear by magic? That clothes and goodies would appear in the shops? If we did, then we were in for a bitter disappointment. If anything, things were tighter than ever, and if we expected our husbands to all come marching home, then even that wasn't quite what we expected.

The demobilisation, like the call-up, was gradual, and I found myself most impatiently waiting for the great day to come. Throughout the latter part of the year, it was a real struggle to keep myself from getting despondent. Trevor was a really difficult baby; he cried so much that the clinic sent me to Great Ormond Street Hospital to have him thoroughly checked over, but they could find nothing wrong.

'It's just that you have a real crosspatch baby, I'm afraid,' said the kindly doctor. 'You'll just have to hope he grows out of it.' It was extra hard, since I had had such an easy time with Angela, who had lived up to her angel name. Yes, I write in the past tense, because with the coming of her little brother, she became so jealous that she led me a dance indeed. She developed tantrums whenever she could not get her own way, she wanted attention whenever I was busy with the baby, and her favourite word was 'now! now! now!' To make matters worse, incredibly, Eric was moved at last from Luton, from his cosy little home from home with all his friends, and was stationed in Salisbury, with its harsh military regime, and his leave was only when he was officially given leave!

So the first months of peace were hardly the joyous ones I'd dreamed about for so long, but they passed, as everything does, and my road was nowhere near as hard as that of some of my friends. Gladys was very brave and had gone back to work, having been offered a job in Cyril's office, and her mother was caring for Daphne. Once again, Eric was fortunate enough to get Christmas leave, and we spent a very happy if lean Christmas. Gwen was demobbed quickly, and found herself a nice post as a switchboard operator. No more overlocking knickers for threeha'pence a pair. She thrived on her new life and really enjoyed going to work. Her only complaint was that all men were rotters, and some more rotten than others! So I don't think that her wartime experience of men was a very happy one!

At last came the new year, the start of a new era, and on 25 January, at 10 p.m., came my beloved. Into the house, carrying his demob suit in a cardboard box, civvy ration book in his pocket, and all his stored up love and affection for us, his very own family.

From that day, we had another fifty-one years of life together, fifty-one years of deep happiness that none of the minor trials of life could ever destroy. He was, and always will be, my beloved Eric and I thank God, with all my heart, for giving him to me for so long a time.